THINKING ON THE WEB

THINKING ON THE WEB

Berners-Lee, Gödel, and Turing

H. PETER ALESSO and CRAIG F. SMITH

WILEY-
INTERSCIENCE

A JOHN WILEY & SONS, INC., PUBLICATION

Published by John Wiley & Sons, Inc., Hoboken, New Jersey
Published simultaneously in Canada.

For general information on our other products and services or for technical support, please contact our Customer Care Department within the United States at (800) 762-2974, outside the United States at (317) 572-3993 or fax (317) 572-4002.

Wiley also publishes its books in a variety of electronic formats. Some content that appears in print may not be available in electronic formats. For more information about Wiley products, visit our web site at www.wiley.com.

Library of Congress Cataloging-in-Publication Data:

Alesso, H. P.
    Thinking on the Web : Berners-Lee, Gödel, and Turing / by H. Peter Alesso, Craig F. Smith.
      p. cm.
    "A Wiley-Interscience publication."
    Includes bibliographical references and index.
    ISBN-13: 978-0-471-76814-2
    ISBN-10: 0-471-76814-6
    1. World Wide Web. 2. Artificial intelligence. 3. Semantic Web. I. Smith, C. F.
    (Craig Forsythe), 1950- II. Title.

    TK5105.888.A3755 2006
    004.67′8–dc22

                                        2006041614

Printed in the United States of America

10 9 8 7 6 5 4 3 2 1

To: Chris and Kathy

CONTENTS

FOREWORD

The modern world is becoming networked at an amazing rate. At the core of this process of change is the revolutionary impact of information technology on society through the World Wide Web (WWW). What is next in the development of the WWW, an intelligent WWW? The authors of this enlightening book provide a forward-looking approach to the development of an intelligent "semantic" web, based on the classic works of Gödel, Turing, and Berners-Lee.

Gödel's insights are essential in understanding the limits of logic applications through the discovery of decidability limits. Turing's work defines the basis of machine intelligence. The fresh new look at Berners-Lee sets up the path for WWW evolution toward a new intelligent environment of the semantic web.

The synergy of the ideas of Gödel, Turing, and Berners-Lee illustrate the emergence of a coherent philosophy of machine intelligence and AI, which provides a focus for the well-written text of this book. This approach allows the authors to give insightful answers to critical questions concerning the capability of the Web to provide for machine intelligence and complex problem solving.

The creative use of interludes between the chapters as a parallel set of dialogs allows the authors to delve into some of the most important philosophical issues underlying the exciting advance toward a new ideal, a semantic web. This writing device not only provides insight, but is a delightfully enjoyable complementary approach to the technology discussions of the text.

Overall, this book provides synergistic analysis and critical thinking that is highly relevant to the ongoing societal revolution in information technology. It offers a unique melding of big ideas with a style and approach that makes it a delightful reading experience.

PROFESSOR ALEX BORDETSKY

Department of Information Science
Naval Postgraduate School
Monterey, California

PREFACE

Tim Berners-Lee, Kurt Gödel, and Alan Turing are the pivotal pioneers who have opened the door to the Information Revolution. Through their contributions, we are witnessing the remarkable refashioning of the Information Age, which began with the introduction of the computer in the 1950s, into the Information Revolution as the World Wide Web evolves into a resource with intelligent features and capabilities.

The contributions of Gödel (what is decidable?), Turing (what is machine intelligence?), and Berners-Lee (what is solvable on the Web?) are central to just how much "intelligence" can be projected onto the Web.

Web intelligence is an issue of philosophy as much as application. It has been suggested that the next generation of Web architecture, the Semantic Web, creates an Artificial Intelligence (AI) application that will make Web content meaningful to computers, thereby unleashing a revolution of new abilities. More realistically, however, the Semantic Web may add semantics to the Web along with some limited AI capabilities to produce a more useful Web. Creating the Semantic Web with just the right balance between greater logic expressive power and achievable computer reasoning complexity is still being questioned and analyzed. An overly structured layering of many languages to deliver logic and machine processing would probably over-design the future Web architecture leading to a top-down command structure and weak adoption in the development community. The goal of this book is to present and explore many of the challenging issues in achieving the appropriate balance of powerful reasoning with reasonable complexity on the Web.

BACKGROUND

The Greek philosopher Aristotle considered intelligence to be the main distinguishing feature of humans when he described man as a "rational animal." He also established many precedents in the study of logic and began the process of codifying syllogisms, a process later extended by the mathematician Leibnitz. In addition to his work in developing the mathematics of calculus, Leibnitz initiated an effort to represent human logic and reasoning as a series of mechanical and symbolic tasks. He was followed by logicians, such as by George Boole, who developed Boolean logic, paving the way for the use of mechanical rules to carry out logical deductions.

While it is still not possible to resolve controversial differences of opinion over the nature of human intelligence, it is possible to recognize certain attributes that most would agree reflect the concept. These include such attributes as: the ability to learn; the ability to assimilate information; the ability to organize and process data; and the ability to apply knowledge to solve complex problems. By extension then, many of these real intelligence attributes can be traced into the various areas of research in the field of artificial intelligence. Artificial Intelligence addresses the basic questions of what it means for a machine to have intelligence.

WHAT IS DECIDABLE?

In the 1930s, the mathematical logician, Kurt Gödel, established that, in certain important mathematical domains, there are problems that cannot be solved or propositions that cannot be proved, or disproved, and are therefore undecidable. Whether a certain statement of first-order logic is provable as a theorem is one example; and whether a polynomial equation in several variables has integer solutions is another. While humans solve problems in these domains all the time, it is not certain that arbitrary problems in these domains can always be solved. This is relevant for artificial intelligence, since it is important to establish the boundaries for a problem's solution.

One critical area explored in this book involves the implications of Gödel's discovery for the World Wide Web.

WHAT IS MACHINE INTELLIGENCE?

In 1947, shortly after the end of World War II, English mathematician Alan Turing first started to seriously explore intelligent machines. By 1956, John McCarthy of MIT contributed the term "Artificial Intelligence." By the late 1950s, there were many researchers in AI most basing their work on programming computers. Eventually, AI became more than a branch of science: It expanded far beyond mathematics and computer science into fields such as philosophy, psychology, and biology.

However, in Turing's seminal work, more than 50 years ago, he determined that a computer can be called intelligent if it could deceive a human into believing that it was human. His test—called the Turing Test—consists of a person asking a series of questions of both a human subject and a machine. The questioning is done via a keyboard so that the questioner has no direct interaction with the subjects, human or machine. A machine with true intelligence will pass the Turing Test by providing responses that are sufficiently human-like that the questioner cannot determine which responder is human and which is not. A scaled down version of the Turing Test, known as the Loebner Prize, requires that machines "converse" with testers only on a limited topic in order to demonstrate their intelligence.

As participants of the Information Age, we could ask: "Is the World Wide Web intelligent?" For the most part, the Web can be considered to be a massive information system with interconnected databases and remote applications providing various services. While these services are becoming more and more user oriented, the concept of smart applications and services on the Web is still in its infancy, and today we could not refer to the Web as intelligent.

In this book, however, we will examine how the Web may be pushing the boundaries of intelligence and Turing's Test. We will consider how the Semantic Web's goal of machine processing using powerful reasoning with reasonable computational complexity relates to the concept of machine intelligence.

WHAT IS SOLVABLE ON THE WEB?

In the late 1980s, AOL, CompuServe, and Microsoft were investing fortunes in proprietary networks that offered mostly duplicated and limited amounts of information to the public for a fee. It was Tim Berners-Lee who designed a cheap, efficient, and simple way for free universal access to great stores of information. As a result, today's Web is essentially hypertext for human consumption. The next generation Web, however, may need to extend these capabilities to automatic machine processing.

As the inventor of the World Wide Web, Tim Berners-Lee is also the originator of the proposed next generation Web architecture: the Semantic Web. Currently, his World Wide Web Consortium (W3C) team works to develop, extend, and standardize the Web's markup languages and tools. The objective of the Semantic Web architecture is to provide a knowledge representation of linked data in order to allow machine processing on a global scale. To provide this, the W3C has developed a new generation of open markup languages that are now poised to unleash the power, flexibility and, above all, logic of the next generation of the Web.

While search engines that index Hypertext Markup Language (HTML) pages find many answers to searches and cover a huge part of the Web, they also return many irrelevant results. There is no notion of "correctness" to such searches. And the growth of the Web has resulted in a combinatorial explosion of possibilities that is becoming quite intractable.

By contrast, logic (inference) engines could apply reasoning power to solve problems on the Web. However, while these engines have been able to restrict their output to provably correct solutions, they suffer from computation complexity limitations as they go through the mass of connected data across the Web. The issue of what is solvable on the Web is directly related to reaching a balance of powerful expressive reasoning with reasonable computational complexity.

The objective of the Semantic Web is therefore to provide the best framework for adding logic, inference, and rule systems to the Web. A combination of mathematical and AI issues complicates this task. The logic must be powerful enough to describe complex properties of objects, but not so powerful that agents can be tricked when asked to consider a paradox.

If an engine of the future combines a reasoning engine with a search engine, it may actually be able to produce useful results. It will be able to reach out to indexes that contain very complete lists of all occurrences of a given term, and then use logic to weed out all but those that can be of use in solving the given problem.

Two important technologies for developing the Semantic Web are already in place: eXtensible Markup Language (XML) and the Resource Description Framework (RDF). eXtensible Markup Language lets anyone create their own tags. Scripts or programs can make use of these tags in sophisticated ways, but the scriptwriter has to know how the page writer uses each tag. In short, XML allows users to add arbitrary structure to their documents, but says nothing about what the structure means. Resource Description Framework was developed to extend XML. The goal of RDF is to make work easier for autonomous agents and automated services by supplying a rudimentary semantic capability.

The next steps up the Language Pyramid of the Web include the Web Ontology Language (OWL) and a rule systems markup capability.

The Semantic Web will develop software agents that can interpret information and perform a service automatically. Differences in terminology between businesses will be resolved using standard abstract domain models, and data will be exchanged using translation services. Software agents will be empowered to auction, negotiate, and draft contracts automatically.

Achieving powerful reasoning with reasonable complexity is the ultimate goal for the Semantic Web because it will lead to machine processing and services automation on a global scale. The challenge is finding the best layering of ontology, logic, and rule markup languages for the Semantic Web that will offer solutions to the most useful Web information processing. Essentially, Berners-Lee is designing the Semantic Web to find what is solvable on the Web.

THIS BOOK

Important mathematical and practical limitations present serious challenges for development of the Semantic Web. These limitations touch some of the most difficult problems in mathematics and logic, such as machine intelligence, undecidability, paradox, recursion, and computational complexity. Throughout the book we struggle with both abstract and practical questions in order to delineate both the opportunities and challenges.

In addition, we present Web Ontology and Logic: the solution of the W3C to deliver machine processing and services automation on a global scale through Semantic Web architecture built upon layers of open markup languages.

Finally, we highlight some of the philosophical issues that underpin the Information Revolution with a threaded series of vignettes between the chapters.

Our goal with this book is to offer a stimulating as well as practical view of "Thinking" on the Web.

ACKNOWLEDGMENTS

We are grateful to the online discussion forums, papers, research, and suggestions of the DAML Services Coalition (also known as the OWL-S Coalition) as a whole: Anupriya Ankolenkar, Mark Burstein, Grit Decker, Jerry Hobbs, Ora Lassila, David Martin, Drew McDermott, Sheila McIlraith, Srini Narayanan, Massimo Paolucci, Bijan Parsia, Terry Payne, Marta Sabou, Monika Solanki, Tran Cao Son, Naveen Srinvasan, Katia Sycara, and Honglei Zeng. They generously shared their ideas and work with regard to OWL-S Semantic Web Services.

Thanks to the World Wide Web Consortium www.w3.org/, which provides not only recommendations and specifications, but references, discussion groups, documentation, and software tools for public review. In particular, Chapters 5, 6, and 9 were drawn in part from the published material of www.w3.org.

We are indebted to several organizations for the special permission granted to include material from previous works including: "Print Gallery" by M. C. Escher, The M. C. Escher Company-Holland (www.mcescher.com), "The Escher and the Droste Effect" by Hendrik Lenstra and Bart de Smit (escherdroste.math.leidenuniv.nl/), various figures and tables from the authors' previous work with publishers Addison-Wesley and A. P. Peters, Inc., and the "spot" example from the work of X. Wang (charlestoncore.musc.edu/ont/example/).

We would like to acknowledge *The Cambridge Quintet* by J. L. Casti as the inspiration for many of the debate concepts included in the interludes presented between the chapters of this book. We would also like to acknowledge *Semantic Web Primer* by G. Antoniou and F. van Harmeten as the inspiration for several logic examples presented. We thank G. Naudts (www.agfa.com/w3c/2002/02/thesis/An_inference_engine_for_RDF.html) as the inspiration for the RDF inference engine example presented in Chapter 8. We acknowledge the many contributors to forums and public discussion groups including: public-sws-ig@w3.org, www-ws@w3c.org, and seweb-list@www1-c703.uibk.ac. It is not possible to identify individual authors of each particular thread of various inspiring ideas, however, the contributions have added to the overall public knowledge and understanding of many important issues relevant to machine intelligence.

In addition, we would like to acknowledge the outstanding guidance and assistance of George J. Telecki, Associate Publisher at Wiley-Interscience and his staff, including Rachel Witmer and Kellsee Chu, in the preparation of this work.

WHO THIS BOOK IS FOR

The primary audience for this book is the general tech-savvy public, as well as computer science students and professional Web developers looking for insight into the next generation Web architecture and technologies.

This book offers a balanced perspective for developing machine-processible complex logic on the Web. It creates a vision of how solvable problems can be logically addressed on the Web to produce a modest semblance of machine intelligence. The unique advantage of this book is that it addresses these sophisticated artificial intelligence (AI) concepts for the Web, but presents the material at a level appropriate for a computer literate audience, as well as the computer science student. The intent is to offer insight to the merely curious, as well as the professional.

In addition, the audience for this book includes the general tech-savvy public, software developers, Web designers and Web developers who are new to application programming and looking to evaluate the direction of AI technology applications; software architects interested in advanced semantic architecture, as well as how AI and Web services relate to each other; and computer scientists, mathematical logicians, educators and students who wish to gain experience with Web logics and semantic technology.

THE ORGANIZATION OF THIS BOOK

This book is organized into two parts: Part I, "What is Web Intelligence" and Part II, "Web Ontology and Logic."

We begin Part I (What is Web Intelligence) with a presentation of the development of the Information Revolution and how the Web contributes to human productivity (Chapter 1). Then in Chapters 2–4, we weave the contributions of Gödel (what is decidable?), Turing (what is machine intelligence?), and Berners-Lee (what is solvable on the Web?) into a coherent mosaic of intelligent Web capabilities.

In addition, we highlight the more controversial philosophical issues through the use of interludes: a threaded series of vignettes presented between chapters. The point and counterpoint debate on many of the most controversial topics in artificial intelligence (AI) attempts to lay bare the essential issues. But, before we can achieve anything approaching AI or "thinking" on the Web, the next generation Web architecture must be able to support the basic elements of logic and automation.

In Part II, we present Web Ontology and Logic: The solution of the W3C to deliver Semantic Web architecture built upon layers of open markup languages. The Semantic Web will support machine-processing capabilities that will automate Web applications and services. Berners-Lee has suggested that Web technologies would benefit from integration of the Semantic Web's meaningful content with Web Services' business logic.

For the Semantic Web to provide intelligent features and capabilities, it will have to trade-off the expressive power of new logic languages against the computational complexity of processing large semantic networks. The layered language approach of the W3C seeks to implement a balanced approach toward building the Semantic Web.

Agents on the Semantic Web will perform tasks by seeking information from Web resources while communicating with other Web agents. Agents are simply pieces of software that work autonomously and proactively. In most cases, agents will simply collect and organize information by utilizing metadata, ontologies, and logic.

Part II (Web Ontology and Logic) begins with Chapter 5. This chapter opens with our presentation of Semantic Web markup languages by introducing Resource Description Framework (RDF). Chapter 6 describes the Web Ontology Language (OWL). In Chapter 7, Ontology Engineering is introduced, while in Chapter 8 Logic, Inference and Rule Systems are discussed. Chapter 9 presents the current state of development for the Semantic Web Rule Language (SWRL).

Achieving powerful reasoning with reasonable complexity is the ultimate goal. The challenge is finding the best layering of ontology, logic, and rule markup languages for the Semantic Web that will offer solutions to the most useful Web applications. These include accomplishing important tasks automatically on the Web, such as search, query, and information acquisition for collaborative Web applications and services. In Chapter 10, the Semantic Web applications are presented in general. Chapter 11 details Semantic Web Services. Chapter 12, offers the latest in Semantic Search Technology. Chapter 13 discussed Semantic Patterns and Adoptive Software that may play an important role in automation on the Web. Chapter 14 summarizes the state of Semantic Tools. Finally, Chapter 15 summarizes the challenges and opportunities for the Semantic Web and Zeno's paradox.

ASSOCIATED RESOURCES

The Semantic Web Organization has developer software resources at http://www.SemanticWeb.org and the World Wide Consortium can be found at http://www.w3.org/Consortium/Activities. In addition, the DAML Services Coalition is available at http://www.daml.org/services/. MITs AI Laboratory hosts the OXYGEN Project and is available at http://oxygen.lcs.mit.edu/. An associated Web site for this book is available at http://www.web-iq.com to provide reference material, errata, and discussion forums.

PART I

WHAT IS WEB INTELLIGENCE?

Today, the world is experiencing the excitement of an historic change. We find ourselves in the midst of an information revolution, the result of rapid advances in technology built in great part upon the shoulders of three pivotal pioneers: Kurt Gödel, Alan Turing, and Tim Berners-Lee. Through their contributions, we are witnessing the remarkable refashioning of the Information Age, which began in the 1950s, into the Information Revolution as the World Wide Web evolves into a resource with intelligent capabilities.

The contributions of Gödel (what is decidable?), Turing (what is machine intelligence?), and Berners-Lee (what is solvable on the Web?) are important milestones toward just how much "intelligence" can be projected onto the Web.

While the capabilities and scope of today's World Wide Web are impressive, its continuing evolution into a resource with intelligent features and capabilities presents many challenges. The traditional approach of building information systems has consisted of custom-made, costly database applications. However, this is changing. Information services are beginning to use generic components and open global standards to offer widely accessible graphical presentations with easier interaction. As a result, benefits are accruing to transactions over the Web including such areas as: e-commerce, banking, manufacturing, and education.

At the heart of the Information Revolution is the transformation of the world toward a knowledge economy with a knowledge society. Helping to forge this transformation is the World Wide Web Consortium (W3C), which is working to deliver global machine processing built upon layers of open markup languages.

The key question is: "How far can we go in enhancing the expressive ability of the Web while still offering tractable solutions?"

In Part I (what is Web Intelligence), we begin with a discussion of the development of the Information Age and how the Web contributes information services that benefit human productivity. Then, the contributions of Gödel in Chapter 2, Turing in Chapter 3, and Berners-Lee in Chapter 4, are introduced and woven into a portrait of potential intelligent Web capabilities.

Both abstract and practical questions of intelligence, logic, and solvability are explored in order to delineate the opportunities and challenges facing the development of Web capabilities. In addition, we highlight some of the philosophical issues that underpin the Information Revolution with a threaded series of vignettes or interludes that are presented in between the chapters.

1

EMPOWERING THE INFORMATION AGE

OVERVIEW

It is widely accepted that the technology of today's Information Age has had a major impact on global communications and commerce, and that it will continue to support major improvements in human productivity. However, while the World Wide Web is making significant contributions to this progress, there remain many challenges to its further development into a resource with intelligent features.

For the Information Age to achieve its full potential in improving human productivity, at least two key new advances must still be achieved: (*1*) ubiquitous access to transaction applications of all types; and (*2*) intelligent software applications enabling automated transactions.

For example, Web Services require human processing to be implemented. In addition, Web Services rely on the interoperation of two competing proprietary server frameworks to successfully communicate complex business logic. The solution of the W3C to both of these problems is to deliver automatic machine processing globally through a Web architecture utilizing layers of open markup languages.

This chapter begins by highlighting what is meant by the concepts of "thinking" and "intelligent applications" on the Web. Then, the development of the Information Age and the emergence of the Web as an empowering force for global change is presented. We discuss the forces behind the Information Revolution that are transforming the world's economic and social systems, and producing

Thinking on the Web: Berners-Lee, Gödel, and Turing, by H. Peter Alesso and Craig F. Smith
Copyright © 2006 John Wiley & Sons, Inc.

the demand for intelligent features on the Web. Next are presented the limitations of today's Web and the need for intelligent automatic capabilities through the development of the Semantic Web.

In addition, some of the philosophical issues that underpin the information revolution are highlighted, by providing the first of a threaded series of vignettes in Interlude #1 entitled "Thinking about Thinking," following this chapter.

THINKING AND INTELLIGENT WEB APPLICATIONS

When the philosopher René Descartes proclaimed his famous observation "Cogito, ergo sum," he demonstrated the power of thought at the most basic level by deriving an important fact (i.e., the reality of his own existence) from the act of thinking and self-awareness.

Today, the term "thinking" is frequently loosely defined and ambiguously applied. For that reason, it is important to provide a brief preview of what we mean by the term in the context of intelligent applications on the World Wide Web.

In general, thinking can be a complex process that uses concepts, their interrelationships, and inference or deduction, to produce new knowledge. However, thinking is often used to describe such disparate acts as memory recall, arithmetic calculations, creating stories, decision making, puzzle solving, and so on.

Some aspects of the concept of thinking can be inferred by recognizing that an individual can be identified as intelligent if they have accurate memory recall, the ability to apply valid and correct logic, and the capability to expand their knowledge through learning and deduction. Ultimately, self-awareness and consciousness are important if not central aspects of human intelligence, but these characteristics prove much more difficult to analyze or emulate than other, more direct indicators of intelligence.

The term "intelligence" can be applied to nonhuman entities as we do in the field of Artificial Intelligence (AI). But frequently we mean something somewhat different than in the case of human intelligence. For example, while one might be quite impressed with the intelligence of a child prodigy who can perform difficult arithmetic calculations quickly and accurately, a computer that could perform the same calculations faster and with greater accuracy would not be considered to be particularly intelligent. An individual who has rapid memory recall and who has accumulated sufficient amounts of information to consistently win games such as Scrabble, or Trivial Pursuit, might also be considered to be very intelligent; while a computer storing much greater quantities of accessible factual information would not.

It is recognized that human thinking involves complicated interactions within the biological components of the brain, and that the process of learning is also an important element of human intelligence. Increasingly, software applications perform tasks that are sufficiently complex and human-like that the term intelligent may be appropriate. Whereas AI can be seen as the science of machines that behave intelligently (or simulate intelligent behavior), the concept of intelligent applications entails the efforts to take advantage of AI technologies to enhance applications and make them act in more intelligent ways.

This brings us to the question of Web intelligence or intelligent software applications on the Web. The World Wide Web can be described as an interconnected network of networks, but that does not go quite far enough. The present day Web consists not only of the interconnected networks, servers, and clients, but also the multimedia hypertext representation of vast quantities of information distributed over an immense global collection of electronic devices. With software services being provided over the Web, one can readily see an analogy to the human (or machine) thinking process where information is stored, accessed, transferred, and processed by electronic patterns in electrical devices and their interconnections.

However, the current Web consists primarily of static data representations that are designed for direct human access and use. Search engines are one Web technology designed to automatically process information from large numbers of Web sites to deliver useful processed information, but the search methods used today have rudimentary capabilities. The key to moving to the next level is the improvement of the ability of software applications to communicate directly with one another, and the representation of information in ways that are far more usable by software applications.

An important framework for creating such meaningful abilities can be provided by the proposed next generation of Web architecture: the Semantic Web.

Leading the Way

The Greek philosopher Aristotle considered intelligence to be the main distinguishing feature of humans when he described humans as "rational animals." He also established many precedents in the study of logic and began the process of codifying syllogisms, a process later extended by other mathematicians. Logicians then developed logic with mechanical rules to carry out deductions.

The nature of human intelligence is still controversial, but it is possible to recognize certain attributes that most would agree reflect the concept. These attributes include: the ability to learn, the ability to assimilate information, the ability to organize and process data, and the ability to apply knowledge to solve complex problems. Many of these real intelligence attributes can be traced into the field of artificial intelligence. Artificial intelligence addresses the basic questions of what it means for a machine to have intelligence.

There have been many contributors to the concepts of thinking, logic, and intelligence, but in this book the focus will be on three pioneers who had a profound affect in shaping the Information Revolution: Gödel, Turing, and Berners-Lee.

In the 1930s, the logician, Kurt Gödel, established that, in certain important mathematical domains, there are problems that cannot be solved or propositions that cannot be proved, or disproved, and are therefore undecidable. This is relevant to the field of artificial intelligence because of the limits and boundaries that can be inferred from Gödel's insights. We will revisit Gödel and his contributions to the Information Revolution in Chapter 2.

In 1947, mathematician Alan Turing first started to seriously explore the concept of intelligent machines. He determined that a computing machine can be called intelligent if it could deceive a human into believing that it was human. His test—called the Turing Test—consists of a person asking a series of questions to both a human subject and a machine. The questioning is done via a keyboard so that the questioner has no direct interaction with the subjects; human or machine. A machine with true intelligence will pass the Turing Test by providing responses that are sufficiently human-like that the questioner cannot determine which responder is human and which is not. We will investigate Turing and his contributions to the Information Revolution in Chapter 3.

The inventor of the World Wide Web, Tim Berners-Lee, is also the originator of the proposed next generation Web architecture, the Semantic Web. The objective of the Semantic Web architecture is to provide a knowledge representation of linked data in order to allow machine processing on a global scale. Chapter 4 presents Berners-Lee and his contributions to the Information Revolution. But before the detailed discoveries of these pioneers are examined, let us find out how the Information Age began and progressed until it became evident that an intelligent Web was a necessary requirement for the fulfillment of the Information Revolution.

THE INFORMATION AGE

We are accustomed to living in a world that is rapidly changing. This is true in all aspects of our society and culture, but is especially true in the field of information technology. Most are aware of the rapid advances in computer and information technology as exemplified in "Moore's law," the observation made in 1965 by Gordon Moore, co-founder of Intel, that the number of components on integrated circuits had doubled every 18 months.

As a result, it is common to observe such rapid change and comment simply that "things change." But, even accepting the reality of rapid change, when can we assess that the change has actually improved human productivity? And what types of change can produce transformation on a global scale?

To gain an historical perspective of global change, take a brief look back. Over the millennia, mankind has experienced two global revolutionary changes: the Agricultural Revolution and the Industrial Revolution. Each produced over a 100-fold factor of improvement in the access to basic human resources and subsequently freed individuals to pursue higher level cultural and social goals. In addition, over the past half century, many have been pondering the possibility that the technological inventions of the Information Age may in fact be of such scope as to represent a third revolutionary change: the Information Revolution.

Should the rapidly changing world of the Information Age be considered a global revolutionary change on the scale of these earlier revolutions? In order to address this issue we must compare it with the changes associated with the Agricultural Revolution, which began around 8000 B.C. and continued through around 1700 A.D., and the Industrial Revolution, which began around 1700 and is still continuing to spread across the underdeveloped world even today.

Ten thousand years ago, humans lived in migratory groups and with the aid of flexible, rapidly evolving cultures, these loosely organized groups of "hunter–gatherers" were able to adapt to virtually all the climate zones and environmental niches on the planet, from the Arctic to temperate zones to the tropics. They fed themselves by hunting, herding, fishing, and foraging. The essence of hunting and gathering economies was to exploit many resources lightly rather than to depend heavily on only a few. Small, mobile human populations subsisted on whatever resources were available within their territory. In such small, continuously moving communities, there was little opportunity for economic or other kinds of specialization to develop. What one person knew and believed, the entire group tended to know and believe. Life was communal; cultural and technical knowledge and skills were widely diffused.

However, a major and dramatic turning point in human social development occurred when humans discovered the utility of agriculture. Agriculture resulted in living permanently in one place. Living in one spot permanently means exploiting a relatively small amount of land very intensively and over a long period of time.

To survive, agriculturalists had to collect all their food for the year at one or two harvest times, rather than gathering year round. Nothing, therefore, could be allowed to interrupt the harvest. This is due to a very narrow window of opportunity for planting and cultivating. Under this kind of pressure, agricultural communities became more time-conscious. Agriculturalists also had to store the produce of their fields for the rest of the year, protect it from moisture, vermin, and thieves, and learn to distribute supplies so the community could survive and still have seed for next year's planting. These conditions created a new kind of life style.

While a hunter–gather acquired resources from 100 acres to produce an adequate food supply, a single farmer needed only 1 acre of land to produce the equivalent amount of food. It was this 100-fold improvement in land management that fueled the agricultural revolution. It not only enabled far more efficient food production, but also provided food resources well above the needs of subsistence, resulting in a new era built on trade.

The Agricultural Revolution crept slowly across villages and regions, introducing land cultivation and a new way of life. During the long millennia that this revolution progressed, the world population was divided into two competitive categories: primitive and civilized. The primitive tribes continued in the mode of hunting–gathering while the civilized communities worked the land. The civilized communities produced foodstuffs for their own use with a surplus to allow for trade.

Because farmers consumed what they produced directly and traded their surplus locally, there was a close relationship between production and consumption. However, as trade developed the Agricultural Revolution encouraged the construction of the roads that facilitated the exchange of specialized produce on an expanding scale until it eventually become global.

This evolutionary transition to an agricultural basis for society was still incomplete when, by the end of the seventeenth century, the Industrial Revolution unleashed a new global revolutionary force. Societies, up until this period, had used human and animal muscle to provide the energy necessary to run the economy. As late as the French revolution, millions of horses and oxen provided the physical force that supported the European economy.

Where a single farmer and his horse had worked a farm, during the Industrial Revolution, workers were able to use a single steam engine that produced 100 times the horsepower. Consequently, the Industrial Revolution placed a 100-fold increase of mechanical power into the hands of the laborer. It resulted in the falling cost of labor and this fueled the economic growth of the period. The new industrialization process moved rapidly over Europe and across the other continents. It utilized flowing water, wood, coal, oil, and gas to generate energy that in turn produced an abundance of food and material goods.

In contrast to the agricultural cycle of planting and harvesting, the industrial society followed the continuous linear timing of machines to build inventory and maintain stored goods. This enabled consumers to be far removed from the producer. The industrialization process, therefore, broke down the close relationship between local production and consumption. The result was a stockpiling of resources at strategic locations along the distribution path. Again this revolutionary change also stimulated the intellectual growth of the society in order to meet the skill requirements for the workers.

The Industrial Revolution was defined by the application of power-driven machinery to manufacturing. It was not until 1873 that a dynamo capable of prolonged operation was developed. Through the nineteenth century the use of electric power was limited by small productive capacity, short transmission lines, and high cost. The coming of the railroads greatly facilitated the industrialization process and the building of transcontinental railroads mimicked the early growth of roads during the beginning of the Agricultural Revolution.

The Industrial Revolution became characterized by six basic characteristics: Standardization: mass production of identical parts. Concentration: work and energy maintained locally. Centralization: authoritative leadership. Specialization: division of labor. Synchronization: work at the pace of machines. Maximization: strategic planning.

One important development was the construction of the railroads that facilitated the exchange of raw materials into finished products on a global scale.

The 1950s—the decade that introduced the computer—began the latest historic turning point, the Information Age. However, it did not approach its full potential toward reducing information transaction costs until the computer was networked for global communications beginning in the 1990s with the growth of the Internet.

Today, the Information Age is establishing a new set of rules to replace those of the Industrial Revolution. For example, "standardization of parts" is being replaced by parts "designed and manufactured to custom specifications." And "concentration of workers" is being replaced by flexible work forces including "telecommuters." And most importantly, "concentration of stockpiles" is being replaced by "just-in-time" inventory and reductions in planning uncertainty.

As a result, production and consumption are continuing to move further apart. For many years, the falling cost of information has shifted power from the hands of the producers into the hands of the consumer. Even so, the cost of information has generally changed very slowly. The evolution of information distribution from writing to the printing press took thousands of years. However, once moveable type was developed, the transition rapidly accelerated. When significant drops in the cost of information occurred, as a result of the printing press, only certain types of organizations survived. From the ancient empires to the world's industrial giants, leaders have recognized that information is power. Controlling information means keeping power.

In fact, it was the high cost of information that made early civilizations most vulnerable. If a temple was sacked, it meant the loss of all available knowledge: from when to plant crops to how to construct buildings. Information was expensive to collect and maintain, and as empires rose and fell, the cost of information remained high. Empires in China, India, and Europe all used large, expensive bureaucracies to control information collection and dissemination.

The Roman Empire set the pace of communications by constructing 53,000 miles of roads, thereby eliminating the traditional dependence on water transportation. The Empire lasted for centuries and spread its administration across Europe, West Asia, and North Africa. Couriers traveled over Roman roads to the furthest reaches of the Empire. Rome also moved the management of knowledge from the temples to libraries for civil administration and learning. But for access to information resources, one still had to go to the libraries, which meant that information had limited distribution.

The invention of the printing press enabled common people to gain access to scientific knowledge and political ideas. By the sixteenth century, information moved into the hands of the people and out of the strict control of the state. In a similar dramatic change, the invention of the telegraph produced the possibility for instant widespread dissemination of information, thereby liberating economic markets. So while there has been continuous improvement in information flow for centuries, it is also clear that only within recent years has the pace accelerated as a result of the computer and the Internet.

Today, there is a competitive collision of industrial-based organizations and information-based systems. Information-based technology systems are the catalysts for the rapid change that has led to the dissemination of information throughout the workplace and home. The world's leading nations are experiencing a shift to knowledge-based economies requiring knowledge workers. These knowledge workers must be highly educated and possess significant technology skills. As a result, technology is facilitating globalization of the world economy and requiring a more highly educated society.

While it is still to be determined if the Information Age will actually become a revolution comparable in scope to the Agricultural and Industrial Revolutions, it remains a strong candidate. Indeed, service workers today complete knowledge transactions many times faster through intelligent software using photons over IP switching, in comparison to clerks using electrons over circuit switching technology just a few decades ago.

By the mid-twentieth century, the explosion of available information required greater information management and can be said to have initiated the Information Age. As computer technology offered reduced information costs, it did more than allow people to receive information. Individuals could buy, sell, and even create their own information. Cheap, plentiful, easily accessible information became as powerful an economic dynamic as land and energy.

The falling cost of information followed Moore's law, which said that the price performance of microprocessors doubled every 18 months. Starting in the 1950s, mainframe computers cost $10 million/MIPS (Million Instructions Processed per Second). By 1996, the comparable cost for the readily available PC was at $1/MIPS.

While the computer has been contributing to information productivity since the 1950s and has experienced the cost reduction due to Moore's law, the resulting global economic productivity gains were slow to be realized. Until the late 1990s, networks were rigid and closed, and time to implement changes in the telecommunication industry was measured in decades. Since then, the Web has become the "grim reaper" of information inefficiency. For the first time, ordinary people had real power over information production and dissemination. As the cost of information dropped, the microprocessor in effect gave ordinary people control over information about consumer products.

What makes the Web such a catalyst for change is its ability to take advantage of the marginal cost of information both for business-to-consumer (B2C) and business-to-business (B2B). While traditional company clerks once used electrons over the phone system circuit switching technology, today's service workers can now process multiple orders acquired through automatic services through intelligent software using photons over IP packet switching. Thus, the Web is the least expensive of all communication media and is a natural marketplace.

Today, the service worker is beginning to see the productivity gains in rapidly communicating knowledge transactions. A service worker can now complete knowledge transactions 100 times faster using intelligent software and ubiquitous computing in comparison to a clerk using written records. As a result, the Information Revolution places a 100-fold increase in transaction speed into the hands of the service worker. Therefore, the Information Revolution may be based on the falling cost of information-based transactions, which in turn fuels economic growth.

A defining feature of each revolution has been the requirement for more knowledgeable and more highly skilled workers. The Information Age clearly signals that this will be a major priority for its continued growth. We can expect the Web to play a central role in the development of the Information Revolution because it offers a powerful communication media that is itself becoming ever more useful through intelligent applications.

Over the past 50 years, the Internet/Web has grown into the global Information Superhighway. Just as roads connected the traders of the Agricultural Revolution and railroads connected the producers and consumers of the Industrial Revolution, the Web is now connecting everybody to everybody in the Information Revolution.

THE WORLD WIDE WEB

How is the World Wide Web managing knowledge and empowering the Information Revolution? Does rapid change and improved information productivity require more intelligent Web capabilities? What technologies offer the best opportunities for sustained powerful change? Let us explore these questions by briefly evaluating the development and limitations of today's Web technology.

The history of the Web extends back more than 40 years. Looking back, we can find early signs of network architecture in the 1960s. The RAND Corporation began research sponsored by the U.S. Air Force to determine how to develop robust, distributed communication networks for military command and control that could survive and function in the event of a nuclear attack.

This initial study led to the development of the Advanced Research Programs Agency Network (ARPANET) an agency of the U. S. Department of Defense. In addition to robustness, it promoted the sharing of supercomputers among scientific researchers in the United States. ARPANET originally consisted of four nodes in the western U.S. (the University of California at Los Angeles, SRI of Stanford, California, the University of California at Santa Barbara, and the University of Utah) connected in a system that was to become the precursor to the Internet.

The ARPANET was a success right from the very beginning. Over those first few years, the network developed and expanded as new sites (nodes) were added, and as new capabilities and features were introduced, such as software and protocols to facilitate email and file transfers. Although the ARPANET was originally designed to allow scientists to share data and access remote computers, email quickly became the most popular application. The ARPANET became a high-speed digital postoffice as people used it to collaborate on research projects. It was a distributed system of "many-to-many" connections.

Transmission Control Protocol/Internet Protocol (TCP/IP), a suite of network communications protocols used to connect hosts on the Internet was developed to connect separate networks into a "network of networks" (e.g., the Internet). These protocols specified the framework for a few basic services that everyone would need (file transfer, electronic mail, and remote logon) across a very large number of client and server systems. Several computers linked in a local network can use TCP/IP (along with other protocols) within the local network just as they can use the protocols to provide services throughout the Internet. The IP component provides routing from the local to the enterprise network, then to regional networks, and finally to the global Internet. Socket is the name for the package of subroutines that provide access to TCP/IP.

The mid-1980s marked a boom in the personal computer and superminicomputer industries. The combination of inexpensive desktop machines and powerful, network-ready servers allowed many companies to join the Internet for the first time.

Corporations began to use the Internet to communicate with each other and with their customers. By 1990, the ARPANET was decommissioned, leaving only the vast network-of-networks called the Internet with over 300,000 hosts.

The stage was set for the final step to move beyond the Internet, as three major events and forces converged, accelerating the development of information technology. These three events were the introduction of the World Wide Web, the widespread availability of the graphical browser, and the unleashing of commercialization.

In startling contrast, AOL, CompuServe, and Microsoft were investing fortunes in proprietary networks that offered mostly duplicated and limited amounts of information to the public, but for a fee. Tim Berners-Lee on the other hand was designing a cheap, efficient, and simple way for universal access to great stores of information for free.

In 1991, Berners-Lee, working at European Particle Physics Laboratory of the European Organization for Nuclear Research, Conseil Européen pour la Recherche Nucléaire, (CERN) in Switzerland, introduced the concept of the World Wide Web.

The Web combined words, pictures, and sounds on Internet pages and programmers saw the potential for publishing information in a way that could be as easy as using a word processor, but with the richness of multimedia.

Berners-Lee and his collaborators laid the groundwork for the open standards of the Web. Their efforts included the Hypertext Transfer Protocol (HTTP) linking Web documents, the Hypertext Markup Language (HTML) for formatting Web documents, and the Universal Resource Locator (URL) system for addressing Web documents.

Today, we reach the Web through commercial browsers, such as, Internet Explorer or Netscape Navigator. These browsers are powerful applications that read the markup languages of the Web, display their contents and collect data.

The primary language for formatting Web pages is HTML. With HTML the author describes what a page should look like, what types of fonts to use, what color the text should be, where paragraph marks come, and many more aspects of the document. All HTML documents are created by using tags. Tags have beginning and ending identifiers to communicate to the browser the beginning and ending text formatted by the tag in question.

In 1993, Marc Andreesen and a group of student programmers at NCSA (the National Center for Supercomputing Applications located on the campus of University of Illinois at Urbana Champaign) developed a graphical browser for the World Wide Web called Mosaic, which he later reinvented commercially as Netscape Navigator. The graphical browser greatly stimulated Web development.

Soon studies of Web traffic began to show signs that all Web sites were not "equidistant." That is, some sites were acting as hubs and garnishing a dominant share of the "through" traffic. In addition, some Web sites acted as prominent sources of primary content, and became authorities on the topic, while other sites, resembled high-quality guides acted as focused hub, directing users to recommended sites. By 1994, the W3C was founded under the leadership of Tim Berners-Lee to develop standards for the Web.

LIMITATIONS OF TODAY'S WEB

Over the past several decades, the Web has changed from a distributed, high-reliability, open system, to a Web dominated by portals, such as Yahoo, Google, AOL, and MSN, which control much of the traffic. While the W3C developed open Web standards, vendors have been customizing their applications for efficient business logic processing through their proprietary servers and applications.

By the year 2000, the introduction of Web Services led to a dichotomy of Microsoft's Windows (.NET) and Sun's Java (J2EE) frameworks within the server community infrastructure. As a result, the Web moved strongly toward becoming a decentralized network with highly critical hubs. The eXensible Markup Language (XML) was developed as a markup language based on the principles and rules of Standard Generalized Markup Language (SGML) and uses tags that are not predefined. This gives XML great flexibility, and extensibility. The XML remains the interoperable bridge for exchanging data between J2EE and .NET, and as a result XML is an essential support for both Web Services' frameworks.

Nevertheless, the problem with performing intelligent tasks, such as automated Web Services, is that they first require human assistance, and second that they must rely on the interoperation and inefficient exchange of the two competing proprietary server frameworks to successfully communicate complex business logic.

The Web is still based on HTML, which describes how information is to be displayed and laid out on a Web page for humans to read. In effect, the Web has developed as a medium for display of information directly to humans; there has been no real emphasis on establishing the capability for machine understanding and processing of web-based information. HTML is not capable of being directly exploited by information retrieval techniques; hence processing of Web information is largely restricted to manual keywords searches.

Because the World Wide Web has its origin in the idea of hypertext, the Web is focused on textual data enriched by illustrative insertions of audiovisual materials. The status quo paradigm of the Web is centered on the client–server interaction, which is a fundamentally asymmetric relationship between providers inserting content onto the Web hypertext (the server) and users who essentially read texts or provide answers to questions by filling out forms (the clients).

Today, the development complex networks of meaningful content remains difficult. Web browsers are restricted to accessing existing information in a standard form. In addition, some of today's basic Web limitations include search, database support, interoperable applications, intelligent business logic, automation, security, and trust. As a result, the Information Revolution awaits the next break-through to fully open the information flow.

THE NEXT GENERATION WEB

A new Web architecture called the Semantic Web offers users the ability to work on shared knowledge by constructing new meaningful representations on the Web. Semantic Web research has developed from the traditions of AI and ontology languages and offers automated processing through machine-understandable metadata.

Semantic Web agents could utilize metadata, ontologies, and logic to carry out its tasks. Agents are pieces of software that work autonomously and proactively on the Web to perform certain tasks. In most cases, agents will simply collect and organize information. Agents on the Semantic Web will receive some tasks to perform and seek information from Web resources, while communicating with other Web agents, in order to fulfill its task. The roadmap for building the Semantic Web is discussed in detail in Chapter 4.

WHY INTELLIGENT UBIQUITOUS DEVICES
IMPROVE PRODUCTIVITY

For the Information Revolution to succeed, two key elements are necessary: (1) ubiquitous access to transaction applications of all types and (2) intelligent software applications producing automated transactions. The results could be orders of magnitude improvement in all decision and financial transactions creating significant improvements in human productivity.

Ubiquitous access can be achieved through the World Wide Web just as soon as small wireless devices become globally distributed: thereby extending the reach of the desktop personal computer to the persons themselves. Intelligent software applications can become available just as soon as the Semantic Web offers intelligent automatic applications.

By applying the power of Moore's law, wireless chip technology will allow cellular carriers to build networks for less and promote all of the four basic attributes of the Information Revolution: decentralization, reduced middle management, automatic knowledgeable customer service, and vertical and horizontal organization.

As computers have evolved over the past several decades, they have become smaller (main frames to handheld devices) and mobile (wired to wireless). The numbers of computing machines ranges from consumer items (in the trillions), home appliances (10s of billion), handheld devices (100 million), computers (10s of million), and the Web (1).

Within the next decade, the most prevalent computers may actually be small mobile wireless devices that combine the capabilities of cell phones, personal digital assistants (PDAs), pocket-sized PCs, and tablets. Their small size, relatively low cost, and wide availability from many manufacturers will ensure that many people will have one, or more. The computing environment of small mobile wireless devices will be very different from today's predominant desktop computing environment.

How much faster will intelligent applications over wireless Web devices improve productivity? No one knows. But accessible intelligent Web features offer a significantly enhanced contribution to an Information Revolution.

Roughly one-half of today's world economy involves some related office work. This includes buying and selling transactions, banking applications, insurance, government, and education forms, and business-to-business transactions. The required information processing is currently being done mostly by specialized humans and secondarily by machines. For the most part, information technology has been a tool to improve the productivity of the human work force. Even in that role, the Web is only beginning to scratch the surface of office work and commercial transactions.

Banking, which typically involves straightforward, standardized transactions, could be one of the first major areas for widespread small device wireless access. The ubiquitous mobile phone is the new contender in financial services and it carries with it the potential for much broader access. Unlike earlier experiments with smart cards and PC banking services, mobile devices look like a natural channel for consumer financial services. Mobile operators have built networks and technology capable of cheap, reliable, and secure, person-to-merchant and person-to-person payments. Wireless telecommunication can augment the payment system.

Small mobile devices using the Web will offer consumers as well as businesses access to products and services anytime, anywhere, and by shifting even more power from producers to consumers, the falling cost of information provides a powerful feedback loop for the economic production cycle. The introduction of millions of small devices at the fingertips of consumers no matter where they are will require more Web Services. Web Services will enable information transactions of every kind and automation of these activities will certainly mean a fundamental empowerment of the Information Age to meet its true potential.

It is this need for ubiquitous connection to global computational resources that is signaling the arrival of the Information Revolution connecting everybody to everybody. All we are waiting for now is the intelligent, automatic applications to make transactions occur at the speed of light.

CONCLUSION

This chapter presented the development of the Information Age and the emergence of the Web as an empowering force for global change. From this chapter, we may conclude that: The Web empowers individuals on a global scale, but that the evolution of the Web requires the development of more intelligent features. The Semantic Web could play a vital role in transforming the Information Age into the Information Revolution as intelligent automatic applications speed up transactions. But, important limitations present challenges to developing Semantic Web architecture. These limitations touch some of the most difficult problems in mathematics and logic, such as machine intelligence, paradox, recursion, undecidability, and computational complexity.

In the next chapters, we will continue to consider the contributions of Kurt Gödel (what is decidable?), Alan Turing (what is machine intelligence?), and Tim Berners-Lee (what is solvable on the Web?) and attempt to weave them into a coherent portrait of AI on the Web. The result will provide insight into the progress of the World Wide Web to empower the Information Revolution by introducing "thinking" on the Web.

EXERCISES

1-1. Plot the trend of Moore's law from 1970 to today. Then project processor performance for the year 2020 based on Moore's law.

1-2. Estimate the growth of small devices and desktop computers in the next 5 years. Plot the ratio of small devises to desktop computers.

1-3. List the possible uses for small devices that may develop within the next 5 years.

1-4. Explain how HTML limits the manipulation of information.

1-5. Consider how logic paradoxes could prevent finding solutions on the Semantic Web.

Some of the interesting philosophical issues involved with Web intelligence will be highlighted through the use of a threaded series of vignettes or interludes presented between chapters. The following is the first interlude entitled "Thinking about Thinking."

Figure 1-1. Print Gallery. Used with permission from M. C. Escher's "Print Gallery" © 2005, The M. C. Escher Company-Holland, All rights reserved www.mcescher.com.

INTERLUDE #1: THINKING ABOUT THINKING

John picked up the two double Latte Grandes and walked over to the corner table near the fireplace where Mary was setting up the chess game. She took a pawn of each color and concealed them in her hands before offering two fists to John.

Putting the cups down, he tapped Mary's left hand and was pleased to see the white piece as he took his chair.

John said "Playing chess always reminds me of the game between IBMs Deep Blue Supercomputer and the reigning World Chess Champion at the time, Garry Kasparov." He glanced at the board, "d4, I think," as he moved his pawn.

Mary said, "Me too." Mary smiled to herself as she moved her own queen's pawn forward to d5. She knew that John had strong feelings about the limits of true Artificial Intelligence and she hoped to gain an advantage by baiting him. "That was the first time a computer won a complete match against the world's best human player. It took almost 50 years of research in the field, but a computer finally was thinking like a human."

John bristled slightly, but then realized that Mary was just poking a little fun. Taking his next move, c4, he said "You can guess my position on that subject. The basic approach of Deep Blue was to decide on a chess move by assessing all possible moves and responses. It could identify up to a depth of about 14 moves and value-rank the resulting game positions using an algorithm developed in advance by a team of grand masters. Deep Blue did not think in any real sense. It was merely computational brute force."

Mary reached over and took John's pawn, accepting the gambit. "You must admit," she replied, "although Kasparov's 'thought' processes were without a doubt something very different than Deep Blue's, their performances were very similar. After all, it was a team of grand masters that designed Deep Blue's decision-making ability to think like them."

John played his usual Nc3, continuing the main line of the Queen's Pawn Gambit. "You've made my point," he exclaimed, "Deep Blue did not make its own decisions before it moved. All it did was accurately execute, the very sophisticated judgments that had been preprogrammed by the human experts."

"Let's look at it from another angle," Mary said as she moved Nf6. "Much like a computer, Kasparov's brain used its billions of neurons to carry out hundreds of tiny operations per second, none of which, in isolation, demonstrates intelligence. In totality, though, we call his play 'brilliant'. Kasparov was processing information very much like a computer does. Over the years, he had memorized and pre-analyzed thousands of positions and strategies."

"I disagree," said John quickly moving e3. "Deep Blue's behavior was merely logic algebra—expertly and quickly calculated, I admit. However, logic established the rules between positional relationships and sets of value-data. A fundamental set of instructions allowed operations including sequencing, branching, and recursion within an accepted hierarchy."

Mary grimaced and held up her hands, "No lectures please." Moving to e6 she added, "A perfectly reasonable alternative explanation to logic methods is to use heuristics methods, which observe and mimic the human brain. In particular, pattern recognition seems intimately related to a sequence of unique images connected by special relationships. Heuristic methods seem as effective in producing AI as logic methods. The success of Deep Blue in chess programming is important because it employed both logic and heuristic AI methods."

"Now who's lecturing," responded John, taking Mary's pawn with his bishop. "In my opinion, human grandmasters do not examine 200,000,000 move sequences per second."

Without hesitation Mary moved c5 and said, "How do we know? Just because human grandmasters are not aware of searching such a number of positions doesn't prove it. Individuals are generally unaware of what actually does go on in their minds. Patterns in the position suggest what lines of play to look at, and the pattern recognition processes in the human mind seem to be invisible to the mind."

John said, "You mean like your playing the same Queen's Gambit Accepted line over and over again?" as he castled.

Ignoring him, Mary moved a6 and said, "Suppose most of the chess player's skill actually comes from an ability to compare the current position against images of thousands of positions already studied. We would call selecting the best position (or image) insightful. Still, if the unconscious human version yields intelligent results, and the explicit algorithmic Deep Blue version yields essentially the same results, then why can't I call Deep Blue intelligent too?"

John said, "I'm sorry, but for me you've overstated your case by calling Deep Blue intelligent," moving Qe2. He continued, "Would you like to reconsider your position?"

Mary moved Nc3 and said, "Of course not, I still have plenty of options to think about alone this line."

2

GÖDEL: WHAT IS DECIDABLE?

OVERVIEW

In Chapter 1, we suggested that small wireless devices connected to an intelligent Web could produce ubiquitous computing and empower the Information Revolution. In the future, Semantic Web architecture is designed to add some intelligence to the Web through machine processing capabilities. For the Semantic Web to succeed, the expressive power of the logic added to its markup languages must be balanced against the resulting computational complexity. Therefore, it is important to evaluate both the expressive characteristics of logic languages, as well as their inherit limitations. In fact, some options for Web logic include solutions that may not be solvable through rational argument. In particular, the work of Kurt Gödel identified the concept of undecidability where the truth or falsity of some statements may not be determined.

This chapter reviews some of the basic principles of logic and related them to the suitability for Web applications. First, the basic concepts of logic are reviewed, and the various characteristics and limitations of logic analysis are discussed. The First-Order Logic (FOL) and its subsets, such as Descriptive Logic and Horn Logic, which offer attractive characteristics for Web applications, are introduced next. These logic frameworks set the parameters for how expressive Web markup languages can become.

Second, we investigate how logic conflicts and limitations in computer programming and Artificial Intelligence (AI) have been handled in closed environments to date. We consider how errors in logic contribute to significant 'bugs' that lead to crashed computer programs.

Third, we review how Web architecture is used to partition the delivery of business logic from the user interface. The Web architecture keeps the logic restricted to executable code residing on the server and delivers user-interface presentations residing within the markup languages traveling over the Web. The Semantic Web changes this partitioned arrangement. Finally, the implications of using logic in markup languages on the Semantic Web are discussed.

PHILOSOPHICAL AND MATHEMATICAL LOGIC

Aristotle described humans as a "rational animal" and established the study of logic beginning with the process of codifying syllogisms. A syllogism is a kind of argument in which there are three propositions, two of them premises, one a conclusion.

Aristotle was the first to create a logic system that allowed predicates and subjects to be represented by letters or symbols. His logic form allowed one to substitute for subjects and predicates with letters (variables).

For example: If A is predicated of all B, and B is predicated of all C, then A is predicated of all C. By predicated, Aristotle means B belongs to A, or all B's are A's. For example, we can substitute subjects and predicates into this syllogism to get: If all humans (B's) are mortal (A), and all Greeks (C's) are humans (B's), then all Greeks (C's) are mortal (A). Today, Aristotle's system is seen as mostly of historical value.

Subsequently, other philosophers and mathematicians, such as Leibniz, developed methods to represent logic and reasoning as a series of mechanical and symbolic tasks. They were followed by logicians who developed mechanical rules to carry out logical deductions.

In logic, as in grammar, a subject is what we make an assertion about, and a predicate is what we assert about the subject. Today, logic is considered to be the primary reasoning mechanism for solving problems. Logic allows us to set up systems and criteria for distinguishing acceptable arguments from unacceptable arguments. The structure of arguments is based upon formal relations between the newly produced assertions and the previous ones. Through argument we can then express inferences. Inferences are the processes where new assertions may be produced from existing ones.

When relationships are independent of the assertions themselves, we call them "formal." Through these processes, logic provides a mechanism for the extension of knowledge. As a result, logic provides prescriptions for reasoning by machines, as well as, by people.

Traditionally, logic has been studied as a branch of philosophy. However, since the mid-1800s logic has been commonly studied as a branch of mathematics and more recently as a branch of computer science. The scope of logic can therefore be extended to include reasoning using probability and causality. In addition, logic includes the study of structures of fallacious arguments and paradoxes.

By logic then, we mean the study and application of the principles of reasoning, and the relationships between statements, concepts, or propositions. Logic incorporates both the methods of reasoning and the validity of the results. In common language, we refer to logic in several ways; logic can be considered as a framework or system of reasoning, a particular mode or process of reasoning, or the guiding principles of a field or discipline. We also use the term "logical" to describe a reasoned approach to solve a problem or get to a decision, as opposed to the alternative "emotional" approaches to react or respond to a situation.

As logic has developed, its scope has splintered into many distinctive branches. These distinctions serve to formalize different forms of logic as a science. The distinctions between the various branches of logic lead to their limitations and expressive capabilities, which are central issues to designing the Semantic Web languages. The following sections identify some of the more important distinctions.

Deductive and Inductive Reasoning

Originally, logic consisted only of deductive reasoning that was concerned with a premise and a resultant deduction. However, it is important to note that inductive reasoning—the study of deriving a reliable generalization from observations—has also been included in the study of logic. Correspondingly, we must distinguish between deductive validity and inductive validity.

The notion of deductive validity can be rigorously stated for systems of formal logic in terms of the well-understood notions of semantics. An inference is deductively valid if and only if there is no possible situation in which all the premises are true and the conclusion false. Inductive validity on the other hand requires us to define a reliable generalization of some set of observations. The task of providing this definition may be approached in various ways, some of which use mathematical models of probability.

Paradox

A paradox is an apparently true statement that seems to lead to a contradiction or to a situation that defies intuition. Typically, either the statements in question do not really imply the contradiction; or the puzzling result is not really a contradiction; or the premises themselves are not all really true (or, cannot all be true together). The recognition of ambiguities, equivocations, and unstated assumptions underlying known paradoxes has often led to significant advances in science, philosophy, and mathematics.

Formal and Informal Logic

Formal logic (sometimes called symbolic logic) attempts to capture the nature of logical truth and inference in formal systems. This consists of a formal language, a set of rules of derivation (often called rules of inference), and sometimes a set of axioms. The formal language consists of a set of discrete symbols, a syntax (i.e., the rules for the construction of a statement), and a semantics (i.e., the relationship between symbols or groups of symbols and their meanings). Expressions in formal logic are often called "formulas."

The rules of derivation and potential axioms then operate with the language to specify a set of theorems, which are formulas that are either basic axioms or true statements that are derivable using the axioms and rules of derivation. In the case of formal logic systems, the theorems are often interpretable as expressing logical truths (called tautologies).

Formal logic encompasses a wide variety of logic systems. For example, propositional and predicate logic are kinds of formal logic, as ARE temporal, modal, and Hoare logic, and the calculus of constructions. Higher order logics are logical systems based on a hierarchy of types. For example, Hoare logic is a formal system developed by the British computer scientist C. A. R. Hoare. The purpose of such a system is to provide a set of logical rules by which to reason about the correctness of computer programs with the rigor of mathematical logic. The central feature of Hoare logic is the Hoare triple. A triple describes how the execution of a piece of code changes the state of the computation.

A Hoare triple is of the form:

$$\{P\} \ C \ \{Q\}$$

where P and Q are assertions and C is a command.

P is called the precondition and Q is the postcondition. Assertions are formulas in predicate logic. An interpretation of such a triple is: "Whenever P holds for the state before the execution of C, then Q will hold afterward."

Alternatively, informal logic is the study of logic that is used in natural language arguments. Informal logic is complicated by the fact that it may be very hard to extract the formal logical structure embedded in an argument. Informal logic is also more difficult because the semantics of natural language assertions is much more complicated than the semantics of formal logical systems.

Mathematical Logic

Mathematical logic really refers to two distinct areas of research: the first is the application of the techniques of formal logic to mathematics and mathematical reasoning, and the second, is the application of mathematical techniques to the representation and analysis of formal logic.

The boldest attempt to apply logic to mathematics was pioneered by philosopher–logician Bertrand Russell. His idea was that mathematical theories were logical tautologies, and his program was to show this by means of a reduction of mathematics to logic. The various attempts to carry this out met with a series of failures, such as Russell's Paradox, and the defeat of Hilbert's Program by Gödel's incompleteness theorems, which will be described shortly.

Russell's paradox represents either of two interrelated logical contradictions. The first is a contradiction arising in the logic of sets or classes. Some sets can be members of themselves, while others cannot. The set of all sets is itself a set, and so it seems to be a member of itself. The null or empty set, however, must not be a member of itself. However, suppose that we can form a set of all sets that, like the null set, are not included in themselves. The paradox arises from asking the question of whether this set is a member of itself. It is, if and only if, it is not!

The second form is a contradiction involving properties. Some properties seem to apply to themselves, while others do not. The property of being a property is itself a property, while the property of being a table is not, itself, a table.

Hilbert's Program was developed in the early 1920s, by German mathematician David Hilbert. It called for a formalization of all of mathematics in axiomatic form, together with a proof that this axiomatization of mathematics is consistent. The consistency proof itself was to be carried out using only what Hilbert called "finitary" methods. The special epistemological character of this type of reasoning yielded the required justification of classical mathematics. It was also a great influence on Kurt Gödel, whose work on the incompleteness theorems was motivated by Hilbert's Program. In spite of the fact that Gödel's work is generally taken to prove that Hilbert's Program cannot be carried out, Hilbert's Program has nevertheless continued to be influential in the philosophy of mathematics, and work on Revitalized Hilbert Programs has been central to the development of proof theory.

Both the statement of Hilbert's Program and its refutation by Gödel depended on their work establishing the second area of mathematical logic, the application of mathematics to logic in the form of proof theory. Despite the negative nature of Gödel's incompleteness theorems, a result in model theory can be understood as showing how close logics came to being true: Every rigorously defined mathematical theory can be exactly captured by a First-Order Logical (FOL) theory. Thus it is apparent that the two areas of mathematical logic are complementary.

Logic is extensively applied in the fields of artificial intelligence and computer science. These fields provide a rich source of problems in formal logic. In the 1950s and 1960s, researchers predicted that when human knowledge could be expressed using logic with mathematical notation, it would be possible to create a machine that reasons, or produces artificial intelligence. This turned out to be more difficult than expected because of the complexity of human reasoning.

In logic programming, a program consists of a set of axioms and rules. In symbolic and mathematical logic, proofs by humans can be computer assisted. Using automated theorem proving, machines can find and check proofs, as well as work with proofs too lengthy to be written out by hand. However, the computation complexity of carrying out automated theorem proving is a serious limitation. It is a limitation that will be discussed in subsequent chapters, which significantly impacts the Semantic Web.

Decidability

In the 1930s, the mathematical logician, Kurt Gödel shook the world of mathematics when he established that, in certain important mathematical domains, there are problems that cannot be solved or propositions that cannot be proved, or disproved, and are therefore undecidable. Whether a certain statement of first-order logic is provable as a theorem is one example; and whether a polynomial equation in several variables has integer solutions is another. While humans solve problems in these domains all the time, it is not certain that arbitrary problems in these domains can always be solved. This is relevant for artificial intelligence since it is important to establish the boundaries for a problem's solution.

KURT GÖDEL

Kurt Gödel (shown Fig. 2-1) was born April 28, 1906 in Brünn, Austria–Hungary (now Brno, the Czech Republic). He had rheumatic fever when he was 6 years old and his health became a chronic concern over his lifetime. Kurt entered the University of Vienna in 1923 where he was influenced by the lectures of Wilhelm Furtwängler. Furtwängler was an outstanding mathematician and teacher, but in addition he was paralyzed from the neck down, and this forced him to lecture from a wheel chair with an assistant to write on the board. This made a big impression on Gödel who was very conscious of his own health.

As an undergraduate, Gödel studied Russell's book *Introduction to Mathematical Philosophy*. He completed his doctoral dissertation under Hans Hahn in 1929. His thesis proved the completeness of the first-order functional calculus. He subsequently became a member of the faculty of the University of Vienna, where he belonged to the school of logical positivism until 1938.

Figure 2-1. Photo of Kurt Gödel.

Gödel is best known for his 1931 proof of the "Incompleteness Theorems." He proved fundamental results about axiomatic systems showing that in any axiomatic mathematical system there are propositions that cannot be proved or disproved within the axioms of the system. In particular, the consistency of the axioms cannot be proved.

This ended 100 years of attempts to establish axioms and axiom-based logic systems that would put the whole of mathematics on this basis. One major attempt had been by Bertrand Russell with *Principia Mathematica* (1910–1913). Another was Hilbert's formalism, which was dealt a severe blow by Gödel's results. The theorem did not destroy the fundamental idea of formalism, but it did demonstrate that any system would have to be more comprehensive than that envisaged by Hilbert. One consequence of Gödel's results implied that a computer can never be programmed to answer all mathematical questions.

In 1935, Gödel proved important results on the consistency of the axiom of choice with the other axioms of set theory. He visited Göttingen in the summer of 1938, lecturing there on his set theory research and returned to Vienna to marry Adele Porkert in 1938.

After settling in the United States, Gödel again produced work of the greatest importance. His paper "Consistency of the axiom of choice and of the generalized continuum-hypothesis with the axioms of set theory" (1940) is a classic of modern mathematics. In this, he proved that if an axiomatic system of set theory of the type proposed by Russell and Whitehead in *Principia Mathematica* is consistent, then it will remain so when the axiom of choice and the generalized continuum hypothesis are added to the system. This did not prove that these axioms were independent of the other axioms of set theory, but when this was finally established by Cohen in 1963, he used the ideas of Gödel. Gödel held a chair at Princeton from 1953 until his death in 1978.

Propositional Logic

Propositional logic (or calculus) is a branch of symbolic logic dealing with propositions as units and with the combinations and connectives that relate them. It can be defined as the branch of symbolic logic that deals with the relationships formed between propositions by connectives, such as compounds and connectives, shown below:

Symbols	Statement	Connectives
$p \vee q$	"either p is true, or q is true, or both"	Disjunction
$p \cdot q$	"both p and q are true"	Conjunction
$p \supset q$	"if p is true, then q is true"	Implication
$p \equiv q$	"p and q are either both true or both false"	Equivalence

A "truth table" is a complete list of the possible truth values of a statement. We use "T" to mean "true," and "F" to mean "false" (or "1" and "0," respectively).

For example, p is either true or false. So its truth table has just 2 rows:

p
T
F

But the compound, p ∨ q, has 2 components, each of which can be true or false. So there are four possible combinations of truth values. The disjunction of p with q will be true as a compound whenever p is true, or q is true, or both:

p	q	p ∨ q
T	T	T
T	F	T
F	T	T
F	F	F

Truth tables are adequate to test validity, tautology, contradiction, contingency, consistency, and equivalence. This is important because truth tables are a mechanical application of the rules.

Propositional calculus is a formal system for deduction whose atomic formulas are propositional variables. In propositional calculus, the language consists of propositional variables (or placeholders) and sentential operators (or connectives). A well-formed formula is any atomic formula or a formula built up from sentential operators.

First-Order Logic

First-order logic, also known as first-order predicate calculus, is a systematic approach to logic based on the formulation of quantifiable statements, such as "there exists an x such that ..." or "for any x, it is the case that ..." An FOL theory is a logical system that can be derived from a set of axioms as an extension of First Order Arithmetic (FOA).

First-order logic is distinguished from higher order logic in that the values "x" in the FOL statements are individual values and not properties. Even with this restriction, FOL is capable of formalizing all of set theory and most of mathematics. Its restriction to quantification of individual properties makes it difficult to use for the purposes of topology, but it is the classical logical theory underlying mathematics.

The branch of mathematics called Model Theory is primarily concerned with connections between first-order properties and first-order structures. First-order languages are by their nature very restrictive and as a result many questions cannot be discussed using them. On the other hand, FOLs have precise grammars.

Predicate calculus is quantificational and based on atomic formulas that are propositional functions and modal logic. In Predicate calculus, as in grammar, a subject is what we make an assertion about, and a predicate is what we assert about the subject.

Automated Inference for FOL

Automated inference using FOL is harder than using Propositional Logic because variables can take on potentially an infinite number of possible values from their domain. Hence, there are potentially an infinite number of ways to apply the Universal-Elimination rule of inference.

Godel's Completeness Theorem says that FOL is only semidecidable. That is, if a sentence is true given a set of axioms, there is a procedure that will determine this. However, if the sentence is false, then there is no guarantee that a procedure will ever determine this. In other words, the procedure may never halt in this case. As a result, the Truth Table method of inference is not complete for FOL because the truth table size may be infinite.

Natural deduction is complete for FOL, but is not practical for automated inference because the "branching factor" in the search process is too large. This is the result of the necessity to try every inference rule in every possible way using the set of known sentences.

Let us consider the rule of inference known as Modus Ponens (MP). Modus Ponens is a rule of inference pertaining to the IF/THEN operator. Modus Ponens states that if the antecedent of a conditional is true, then the consequent must also be true:

(MP) Given the statements p and *if p then q*, infer q.

The Generalized Modus Ponens (GMP) is not complete for FOL. However, GMP is complete for Knowledge Bases (KBs) containing only Horn clauses.

Another very important logic that will be discussed in detail in Chapter 8, is Horn logic. A Horn clause is a sentence of the form:

$$(Ax)(P1(x) \wedge P2(x) \wedge \ldots \wedge Pn(x)) \Rightarrow Q(x)$$

where there are 0 or more Pi's, and the Pi's and Q are positive (i.e., unnegated) literals.

Horn clauses represent a subset of the set of sentences representable in FOL. For example: P(a) v Q(a) is a sentence in FOL, but is not a Horn clause.

Natural deduction using GMP is complete for KBs containing only Horn clauses. Proofs start with the given axioms/premises in KB, deriving new sentences using GMP until the goal/query sentence is derived. This defines a forward chaining inference procedure because it moves "forward" from the KB to the goal.

For example: KB = All cats like fish, cats eat everything they like, and Molly is a cat. In FOL then,

$$KB = (Ax)\ cat(x) \Rightarrow likes(x, Fish) \tag{1}$$

$$(Ax)(Ay)\ (cat(x) \wedge likes(x, y)) \Rightarrow eats(x, y) \tag{2}$$

$$cat(Molly) \tag{3}$$

Query: Does Molly eat fish?

Proof:

Use GMP with (1) and (3) to derive: (4) likes(Molly, Fish)

Use GMP with (3), (4) and (2) to derive: eats(Molly, Fish)

Conclusion: Yes, Molly eats fish.

Description Logic

Description Logics (DLs) allow specifying a terminological hierarchy using a restricted set of first-order formulas. The DLs have nice computational properties (they are often decidable and tractable), but the inference services are restricted to classification and subsumption. That means, given formulas describing classes, the classifier associated with certain description logic will place them inside a hierarchy. Given an instance description, the classifier will determine the most specific classes to which the instance belongs.

From a modeling point of view, DLs correspond to Predicate Logic statements with three variables suggesting that modeling is syntactically bound.

Descriptive Logic is one possibility for Inference Engines for the Semantic Web. Another possibility is based on Horn Logic, which is another subset of First-Order Predicate logic (see Fig. 2-2).

In addition, DL and rule systems (e.g., Horn Logic) are somewhat orthogonal, which means that they overlap, but one does not subsume the other. In other words, there are capabilities in Horn logic that are complementary to those available for DL.

Both DL and Horn Logic are critical branches of logic that highlight essential limitations and expressive powers that are central issues to designing the Semantic Web languages. They will be discussed further in Chapter 8.

Using Full First-Order Logic (FFOL) for specifying axioms requires a full-fledged automated theorem prover. However, FOL is semidecidable and doing inferencing becomes computationally untractable for large amounts of data and axioms.

This means that in an environment like the Web, FFOL programs will not scale to handle huge amounts of knowledge. Besides, full first theorem proving would mean maintaining consistency throughout the Web, which is impossible.

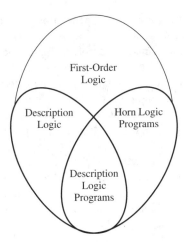

Figure 2-2. This diagram shows the relationship of DL and Horn Logic as subsets of FOL.

Relating Logic Fragments

In Figure 2-2, the outer ellipse represents FOL-based formalisms. The Horn rules are a subset as is the DL fragment of FOL. First-order logics includes expressiveness beyond the overlap, notably: positive disjunctions; existentials; and entailment of nonground and nonatomic conclusions.

Horn FOL is another fragment of FOL. Horn Logic Program (LP) is a slight weakening of Horn FOL. "Weakening" here means that the conclusions from a given set of Horn premises that are entailed according to the Horn LP formalism are a subset of the conclusions entailed (from that same set of premises) according to the Horn FOL formalism. However, the set of ground atomic conclusions is the same in the Horn LP as in the Horn FOL. For most practical purposes (e.g., relational database query answering), Horn LP is thus essentially similar in its power to the Horn FOL. Horn LP is a fragment of both FOL and nonmonotonic LP. This discussion may seem esoteric, but it is precisely these types of issues that will decide both the design of the Semantic Web, as well as its likelihood to succeed.

Higher Order Logic

Higher Order Logics (HOLs) provide greater expressive power than FOL, but they are even more difficult computationally. For example, in HOLs, one can have true statements that are not provable (see discussion of Gödel's Incompleteness Theorem). There are two aspects of this issue: higher order syntax and higher order semantics. If a higher order semantics is not needed (and this is often the case), a second-order logic can often be translated into a FOL.

In first-order semantics, variables can only range over domains of individuals or over the names of predicates and functions, but not over sets as such. In higher order syntax, variables are allowed to appear in places where normally predicate or function symbols appear.

Predicate calculus is the primary example of logic where syntax and semantics are both first order. There are logics that have higher order syntax, but first order semantics. Under a higher order semantics, an equation between predicate (or function) symbols is true, if and only if logics with a higher order semantics and higher order syntax are statements expressing trust about other statements.

To state it another way, higher order logic is distinguished from FOL in several ways. The first is the scope of quantifiers; in FOL, it is forbidden to quantify over predicates. The second way in which higher order logic differs from FOL is in the constructions that are allowed in the underlying type theory. A higher order predicate is a predicate that takes one or more other predicates as arguments. In general, a higher order predicate of order n takes one or more $(n - 1)$th-order predicates as arguments (where $n > 1$).

Recursion Theory

Recursion is the process a procedure goes through when one of the steps of the procedure involves rerunning a complete set of identical steps. In mathematics and computer science, recursion is a particular way of specifying a class of objects with the help of a reference to other objects of the class: A recursive definition defines objects in terms of the already defined objects of the class. A recursive process is one in which objects are defined in terms of other objects of the same type. By using a recurrence relation, an entire class of objects can be built up from a few initial values and a small number of rules.

The Fibonacci numbers (i.e., the infinite sequence of numbers starting 0, 1, 1, 2, 3, 5, 8, 13, ..., where the next number in the sequence is defined as the sum of the previous two numbers) is a commonly known recursive set.

The following is a recursive definition of person's ancestors: One's parents are one's ancestors (base case). The parents of any ancestor are also ancestors of the person under consideration (recursion step).

Therefore, your ancestors include your parents, and your parents' parents (grandparents), and your grandparents' parents, and everyone else you get by successively adding ancestors.

It is convenient to think that a recursive definition defines objects in terms of a "previously defined" member of the class. While recursive definitions are useful and widespread in mathematics, care must be taken to avoid self-recursion, in which an object is defined in terms of itself, leading to an infinite nesting (see Fig. 1-1: "The Print Gallery" by M. C. Escher is a visual illustration of self-recursion). (Figs. 2-4, 3-2, 4-2, 5-7, 6-4, 7-3, 8-5 are a progression of images that illustrate recursion).

KNOWLEDGE REPRESENTATION

Let us define what we mean by the fundamental terms "data," "information," "knowledge," and "understanding." An item of data is a fundamental element of an application. Data can be represented by populations and labels. Data is raw; it exists and has no significance beyond its existence. It can exist in any form, usable or not. It does not have meaning by itself.

Information on the other hand is an explicit association between items of data. Associations represent a function relating one set of things to another set of things. Information can be considered to be data that has been given meaning by way of relational connections. This "meaning" can be useful, but does not have to be. A relational database creates information from the data stored within it.

Knowledge can be considered to be an appropriate collection of information, such that it is useful. Knowledge-based systems contain knowledge as well as information and data. A rule is an explicit functional association from a set of information things to a specific information thing. As a result, a rule is knowledge.

Information can be constructed from data and knowledge from information to finally produce understanding from knowledge. Understanding lies at the highest level. Understanding is an interpolative and probabilistic process that is cognitive and analytical. It is the process by which one can take existing knowledge and synthesize new knowledge. One who has understanding can pursue useful actions because they can synthesize new knowledge or information from what is previously known (and understood). Understanding can build upon currently held information, knowledge, and understanding itself.

Artificial Intelligence systems possess understanding in the sense that they are able to synthesize new knowledge from previously stored information and knowledge. An important element of AI is the principle that intelligent behavior can be achieved through processing of symbolic structures representing increments of knowledge. This has produced knowledge-representation languages that allow the representation and manipulation of knowledge to deduce new facts from the existing knowledge. The knowledge-representation language must have a well-defined syntax and semantics system while supporting inference.

Three techniques have been popular to express knowledge representation and inference: (1) logic-based approaches, (2) rule-based systems, and (3) frames and semantic networks.

Logic-based approaches use logical formulas to represent complex relationships. They require a well-defined syntax, semantics, and proof theory. The formal power of a logical theorem proof can be applied to knowledge to derive new knowledge. Logic is used as the formalism for programming languages and databases. It can also be used as a formalism to implement knowledge methodology. Any formalism that admits a declarative semantics and can be interpreted both as a programming language and a database language is a knowledge language. However, the approach is inflexible and requires great precision in stating the logical relationships. In some cases, common sense inferences and conclusions cannot be derived, and the approach may be inefficient, especially when dealing with issues that result in large combinations of objects or concepts.

Rule-based approaches are more flexible and allow the representation of knowledge using sets of IF-THEN or other conditional rules. This approach is more procedural and less formal in its logic. As a result, reasoning can be controlled through a forward or backward chaining interpreter.

Frames and semantic networks capture declarative information about related objects and concepts where there is a clear class hierarchy and where the principle of inheritance can be used to infer the characteristics of members of a subclass. The two forms of reasoning in this technique are matching (i.e., identification of objects having common properties), and property inheritance in which properties are inferred for a subclass. Frames and semantic networks are limited to representation and inference of relatively simple systems.

In each of these approaches, the knowledge-representation component (i.e., problem-specific rules and facts) is separate from the problem-solving and inference procedures.

For the Semantic Web to function, computers must have access to structured collections of information and sets of inference rules that they can use to conduct automated reasoning. AI researchers have studied such systems and produced today's Knowledge–Representation (KR). This system is currently in a state comparable to that of hypertext before the advent of the Web. Knowledge–representation contains the seeds of important applications, but to fully realize its potential, it must be linked into a comprehensive global system.

COMPUTATIONAL LOGIC

Programming a computer involves creating a sequence of logical instructions that the computer will use to perform a wide variety of tasks. While it is possible to create programs directly in machine language, it is uncommon for programmers to work at this level because of the abstract nature of the instructions. It is better to write programs in a simple text file using a high-level programming language that can later be compiled into executable code.

The "logic model" for programming is a basic element that communicates the logic behind a program. A logic model can be a graphic representation of a program illustrating the logical relationships between program elements and the flow of calculation, data manipulation, or decisions as the program executes its steps.

Logic models typically use diagrams, flow sheets, or some other type of visual schematic to convey relationships between programmatic inputs, processes, and outcomes. Logic models attempt to show the links in a chain of reasoning about relationships to the desired goal. The desired goal is usually shown as the last link in the model.

A logic program may consist of a set of axioms and a goal statement. The logic form can be a set of "IF-THEN" statements. The rules of inference are applied to determine whether the axioms are sufficient to ensure the truth of the goal statement. The execution of a logic program corresponds to the construction of a proof of the goal statement from the axioms.

In the logic programming model, the programmer is responsible for specifying the basic logical relationships and does not specify the manner in which the inference rules are applied. Thus

$$Logic + Control = Algorithms$$

The operational semantics of logic programs correspond to logical inference. The declarative semantics of logic programs are derived from the term model. The denotation of semantics in logic programs are defined in terms of a function that assigns meaning to the program. There is a close relation between the axiomatic semantics of imperative programs and logic programs.

The control portion of the equation is provided by an inference engine whose role is to derive theorems based on the set of axioms provided by the programmer. The inference engine uses the operations of resolution and unification to construct proofs. Faulty logic models occur when the essential problem has not been clearly stated or defined.

Program developers work carefully to construct logic models to avoid logic conflicts, recursive loops, and paradoxes within their computer programs. As a result, programming logic should lead to executable code without paradox or conflict, if it is flawlessly produced. Nevertheless, we know that "bugs" or programming errors do occur, some of which are directly or indirectly a result of logic conflicts.

As programs have grown in size from thousands of line of code to millions of lines, the problems of bugs and logic conflicts have also grown. Today, programs, such as operating systems, can have >25 million lines of codes and are considered to have hundreds of thousands of bugs, most of which are seldom encountered during routine program usage.

Confining logic issues to beta testing on local servers allows programmers reasonable control of conflict resolution. Now, consider applying many lines of application code logic to the Semantic Web were it may access many information nodes. The magnitude of the potential conflicts could be somewhat daunting.

ARTIFICIAL INTELLIGENCE

John McCarthy of MIT contributed the term AI and by the late 1950s, there were many researchers in AI working on programming computers. Eventually, AI expanded into such fields as philosophy, psychology and biology.

Artificial Intelligence is sometimes described in two ways: strong AI and weak AI. Strong AI asserts that computers can be made to think on a level equal to humans. Weak AI simply holds that some "thinking-like" features can be added to computers to make them more useful tools. Examples of Weak AI abound: expert systems, drive-by-wire cars, smart browsers, and speech recognition software. These weak AI components may, when combined, begin to approach the expectations of strong AI.

Artificial Intelligence includes the study of computers that can perform cognitive tasks including: understanding natural language statements, recognizing visual patterns or scenes, diagnosing diseases or illnesses, solving mathematical problems, performing financial analyses, learning new procedures for problem solving, and playing complex games, like chess. A more detailed discussion on AI on the Web and what is meant by machine intelligence will be provided in Chapter 3.

WEB ARCHITECTURE AND BUSINESS LOGIC

So far, we have explored the basic elements, characteristics, and limitations of logic and suggested that errors in logic contribute to many significant bugs that lead to crashed computer programs. Next, we review how Web architecture is used to partition the delivery of business logic from the user interface. The Web architecture keeps the logic restricted to executable code residing on the server and delivering user interface presentations residing within the markup languages traveling along the Internet. This simple arrangement of segregating the complexity of logic to the executable programs residing on servers has minimized processing difficulties over the Web itself.

Today, markup languages are not equipped with logic connectives. So all complex logic and detailed calculations must be carried out by specially compiled programs residing on Web servers where they are accessed by server page frameworks. The result is highly efficient application programs on the server that must communicate very inefficiently with other proprietary applications using XML in simple ASCII text. In addition, there is difficulty in interoperable programming that greatly inhibits automation of Web Services.

Browsers, such as Internet Explorer and Netscape Navigator, view Web pages written in HyperText Markup Language (HTML). The HTML program can be written to a simple text file that is recognized by the browser and can call embedded script programming. In addition, HTML can include compiler directives that call server pages with access to proprietary compiled programming. As a result, simple-text HTML is empowered with important capabilities to call complex business logic programming residing on servers both in the frameworks of Microsoft's .NET and Sun's J2EE. These frameworks support Web Services and form a vital part of today's Web.

When a request comes into the Web server, the Web server simply passes the request to the program best able to handle it. The Web server does not provide any functionality beyond simply providing an environment in which the server-side program can execute and pass back the generated responses. The server-side program provides functions as transaction processing, database connectivity, and messaging.

Business logic is concerned with logic about: how we model real-world business objects, such as accounts, loans, travel; how these objects are stored; how these objects interact with each other, for example, a bank account must have an owner and a bank holder's portfolio is the sum of his accounts; and who can access and update these objects.

As an example, consider an online store that provides real-time pricing and availability information. The site will provide a form for you to choose a product. When you submit your query, the site performs a lookup and returns the results embedded within an HTML page. The site may implement this functionality in numerous ways.

The Web server delegates the response generation to a script; however, the business logic for the pricing lookup is included from an application server. With that change, instead of the script knowing how to look up the data and formulate a response, the script can simply call the application server's lookup service. The script can then use the service's result when the script generates its HTML response.

The application server serves the business logic for looking up a product's pricing information. That functionality does not say anything about display or how the client must use the information. Instead, the client and application server send data back and forth. When a client calls the application server's lookup service, the service simply looks up the information and returns it to the client.

By separating the pricing logic from the HTML response-generating code, the pricing logic becomes reusable between applications. A second client, such as a cash register, could also call the same service as a clerk checking out a customer.

Recently, eXtensible Markup Language (XML) Web Services use an XML payload to a Web server. The Web server can then process the data and respond much as application servers have in the past.

The XML has become the standard for data transfer of all types of applications and provides a data model that is supported by most data-handling tools and vendors. Structuring data as XML allows hierarchical, graph-based representations of the data to be presented to tools, which opens up a host of possibilities.

The task of creating and deploying Web Services automatically requires interoperable standards. The most advanced vision for the next generation of Web Services is the development of Web Services over Semantic Web Architecture.

THE SEMANTIC WEB

Now let us consider using logic within markup languages on the Semantic Web. This means empowering the Web's expressive capability, but at the expense of reducing Web performance.

The current Web is built on HTML and XML, which describes how information is to be displayed and laid out on a Web page for humans to read. In addition, HTML is not capable of being directly exploited by information retrieval techniques. The XML may have enabled the exchange of data across the Web, but it says nothing about the meaning of that data. In effect, the Web has developed as a medium for humans without a focus on data that could be processed automatically.

As a result, computers are unable to automatically process the meaning of Web content. For machines to perform useful automatic reasoning tasks on these documents, the language machines used must go beyond the basic semantics of XML Schema. They will require an ontology language, logic connectives, and rule systems.

By introducing these elements, the Semantic Web is intended to be a paradigm shift just as powerful as the original Web. The Semantic Web will bring meaning to the content of Web pages, where software agents roaming from page-to-page can carry out automated tasks.

The Semantic Web will be constructed over the Resource Description Framework (RDF) and Web Ontology Language (OWL). In addition, it will implement logic inference and rule systems. These languages are being developed by the W3C. Data can be defined and linked using RDF and OWL so that there is more effective discovery, automation, integration, and reuse across different applications.

Figure 2-3 illustrates how Semantic Web languages are built upon XML and climbs up the Markup Language Pyramid.

These languages are conceptually richer than HTML and allow representation of the meaning and structure of content (interrelationships between concepts). This makes Web content understandable by software agents, opening the way to a whole new generation of technologies for information processing, retrieval, and analysis.

If a developer publishes data in XML on the Web, it does not require much more effort to take the extra step and publish the data in RDF. By creating ontologies to describe data, intelligent applications will not have to spend time translating various XML schemas.

An ontology defines the terms used to describe and represent an area of knowledge. Although XML Schema is sufficient for exchanging data between

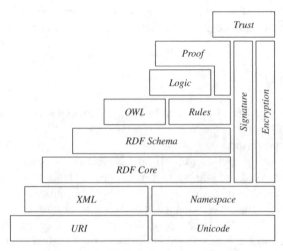

Figure 2-3. Markup language pyramid.

parties who have agreed to the definitions beforehand, their lack of semantics prevents machines from reliably performing this task with new XML vocabularies.

In addition, the ontology of RDF and RDF Schema (RDFS) is very limited (see Chapter 5). The RDF is roughly limited to binary ground predicates and RDF Schema is roughly limited to a subclass hierarchy and a property hierarchy with domain and range definitions.

Adding an Ontology language will permit the development of explicit, formal conceptualizations of models (see Chapter 6). The main requirements of an onotology language include a well-defined syntax, a formal semantics, convenience of expression, an efficient reasoning support system, and sufficient expressive power.

Since the W3C has established that the Semantic Web would require much more expressive power than using RDF and RDFS would offer, the W3C has defined OWL. The layered architecture of the Semantic Web would suggest that one way to develop the necessary ontology language is to extend RDF Schema by using the RDF meaning of classes and properties and adding primitives to support richer expressiveness. However, simply extending RDF Schema would fail to achieve the best combination of expressive power and efficient reasoning. The layered architecture of the Semantic Web promotes the downward compatibility and reuse of software that is achieved only with OWL Full (see Chapter 6), but at the expense of computational intractability.

Both RDF and OWL (DL and Lite, see Chapter 6) are specializations of predicate logic. They provide a syntax that fits well with Web languages. They also define reasonable subsets of logic that offer a trade-off between expressive power and computational complexity.

Semantic Web research has developed from the traditions of AI and ontology languages. Currently, the most important ontology languages on the Web are XML, XML Schema, RDF, RDF Schema, and OWL.

Agents are pieces of software that work autonomously and proactively. In most cases, agent will simply collect and organize information. Agents on the Semantic Web will receive some tasks to perform and seek information from Web resources, while communicating with other Web agents, in order to fulfill its task. Semantic Web agents will utilize metadata, ontologies, and logic to carry out its tasks.

In a closed environment, Semantic Web specifications have already been used to accomplish many tasks, such as data interoperability for business-to-business (B2B) transactions. Many companies have expended resources to translate their internal data syntax for their partners. As the world migrates toward RDF and ontologies, interoperability will become more flexible to new demands.

An inference is a process of using rules to manipulate knowledge to produce new knowledge. Adding logic to the Web means using rules to make inferences and choosing a course of action. The logic must be powerful enough to describe complex properties of objects, but not so powerful that agents can be tricked by a paradox. A combination of mathematical and engineering issues complicates this task. A more detailed presentation on paradoxes on the Web and what is solvable on the Web will be provided in the next few chapters.

Inference Engines for the Semantic Web

Inference engines process the knowledge available in the Semantic Web by deducing new knowledge from already specified knowledge. Higher Order Logic (HOL)-based inference engines have the greatest expressive power among all known logics, such as the characterization of transitive closure. However, higher order logics do not have nice computational properties. There are true statements, which are unprovable (Gödel's Incompleteness Theorem).

Full First-Order Logic based inference engines for specifying axioms requires a full-fledged automated theorem prover, which is semidecidable, but inferencing is computationally not tractable for large amounts of data and axioms.

This means that in an environment like the Web, HOL and FFOL programs would not scale up for handling huge amounts of knowledge. Besides, full first theorem proving would mean maintaining consistency throughout the web, which is impossible.

Predicate calculus is the primary example of logic where syntax and semantics are both first order. From a modeling point of view, DL correspond to Predicate Logic statements with three variables suggesting that modeling is syntactically bound and is a good candidate language for Web logic. Other possibilities for inference engines for the Semantic Web are languages based on Horn Logic, which is another fragment of First-Order Predicate logic (see Fig. 2-2).

In addition, DL and rule systems (e.g., Horn Logic) have different capabilities. Both Descriptive Logic and Horn Logic are critical branches of logic that highlight essential limitations and expressive powers that are central issues to designing the Semantic Web languages. They will be discussed further in Chapters 6–9.

CONCLUSION

For the Semantic Web to provide machine processing capabilities, the logic expressive power of mark-up languages must be balanced against the resulting computational complexity of reasoning. This chapter, examined both the expressive characteristics of logic languages, as well as, their inherit limitations. First-Order Logics (FOL) fragments, such as Descriptive Logic and Horn Logic offer attractive characteristics for Web applications and set the parameters for how expressive Web markup languages can become.

The concept of Artificial Intelligence (AI) and how logic is applied in computer programming was also reviewed. After exploring the basic elements, characteristics, and limitations of logic and suggesting that errors in logic contribute to many significant "bugs" that lead to crashed computer programs, we reviewed how Web architecture is used to partition the delivery of business logic from the user interface. The Web architecture keeps the logic restricted to executable code residing on the server and delivering user interface presentations residing within the markup languages traveling along the Internet. Finally, the implications of using logic within markup languages on the Web through the development of the Semantic Web was discussed.

Our conclusions from this chapter include the idea that logic is the foundation of knowledge representation that can be applied to AI in general and the World Wide Web specially. Logic can provide a high-level language for expressing knowledge and has high expressive power. Logic has a well-understood formal semantics for assigning unambiguous meaning to logic statements. In addition, we saw that proof systems exist that can automatically derive statements syntactically from premises. Predicate logic uniquely offers a sound and complete proof system while higher order logics do not. By tracking the proof to reach its consequence, the logic can provide explanations for the answers.

Currently, complex logic and detailed calculations must be carried out by specially compiled programs residing on Web servers where they are accessed by server page frameworks. The result is highly efficient application programs on the server that must communicate very inefficiently with other proprietary applications using XML in simple ASCII text. In addition, this difficulty for interoperable programs greatly inhibits automation of Web Services. The Semantic Web offers a way to use logic in the form of Descriptive Logic or Horn Logic on the Web.

EXERCISES

2-1. Explain how logic for complex business calculations is currently carried out through .NET and J2EE application servers.

2-2. Explain the difference between FOL and HOL.

2-3. Why is it necessary to consider less powerful expressive languages for the Semantic Web?

2-4. Why is undeciability a concern on the Web?

Website http://escherdroste.math.leidenuniv.nl/ offers the mathematical structure behind Escher's Print Gallery using the Escher and the Droste effect. This mathematical structure answers some questions about Escher's picture, such as: What's in the blurry white hole in the middle? This project is an initiative of Hendrik Lenstra of the Universiteit Leiden and the University of California at Berkeley. Bart de Smit of the Universiteit Leiden runs the project (see Figure 2-1).

Figure 2-4. Escher and the Droste effect (http://escherdroste.math.leidenuniv.nl/)

INTERLUDE #2: TRUTH AND BEAUTY

As John passed with a sour look on his face, Mary looked up from her text book and asked, "Didn't you enjoy the soccer game?"

"How can you even ask that when we lost?" asked John gloomily.

"I think the team performed beautifully, despite the score," said Mary.

This instantly frustrated John and he said, "Do you know Mary that sometimes I find it disarming the way you express objects in terms of beauty. I find that simply accepting something on the basis of its beauty can lead to false conclusions?"

Mary reflected upon this before offering a gambit of her own, "Well John, do you know that sometimes I find that relying on objective truth alone can lead to unattractive conclusions."

John became flustered and reflected his dismay by demanding, "Give me an example."

Without hesitation, Mary said, "Perhaps you will recall that in the late 1920s, mathematicians were quite certain that every well-posed mathematical question had to have a definite answer—either true or false. For example, suppose they claimed that every even number was the sum of two prime numbers," referring to Goldbach's Conjecture, which she had just been studying in her text book. Mary continued, "Mathematicians would seek the truth or falsity of the claim by examining a chain of logical reasoning that would lead in a finite number of steps to prove if the claim were either true or false."

"So mathematicians thought at the time," said John. "Even today most people still do."

"Indeed," said Mary. "But in 1931, logician Kurt Gödel proved that the mathematicians were wrong. He showed that every sufficiently expressive logical system must contain at least one statement that can be neither proved nor disproved following the logical rules of that system. Gödel proved that not every mathematical question has to have a yes or no answer. Even a simple question about numbers may be undecidable. In fact, Gödel proved that there exist questions that while being undecidable by the rules of logical system can be seen to be actually true if we jump outside that system. But they cannot be proven to be true."

"Thank you for that clear explanation," said John. "But isn't such a fact simply a translation into mathematic terms of the famous Liar's Paradox: 'This statement is false.'"

"Well, I think it's a little more complicated than that," said Mary. "But Gödel did identify the problem of self-reference that occurs in the Liar's Paradox. Nevertheless, Gödel's theorem contradicted the thinking of most of the great mathematicians of his time. The result is that one cannot be as certain as the mathematician had desired. See what I mean, Gödel may have found an important *truth*, but it was—well to be frank—rather disappointingly unattractive," concluded Mary.

"On the contrary," countered John, "from my perspective it was the *beauty* of the well-posed mathematical question offered by the mathematicians that was proven to be false."

Mary replied, "I'll have to think about that."

3

TURING: WHAT IS MACHINE INTELLIGENCE?

OVERVIEW

Web intelligence is an issue of philosophy as much as application. It has been suggested that the next generation of Web architecture, the Semantic Web, creates an Artificial Intelligence (AI) application that will make Web content meaningful to computers thereby unleashing a revolution of new abilities. More realistically, however, the Semantic Web will add semantics to the Web along with some limited AI capabilities to produce a more useful Web. The balance between greater logic expressive power and solvable computer reasoning complexity is still being questioned and evaluated.

Alan Turing was one of the great thinkers of the twentieth century, and his contributions in the area of machine intelligence were seminal. This chapter provides an overview of Turing's contributions and discusses some of the key ideas emanating from his work. In addition, we engage in a discussion of the meaning of machine intelligence and offer some perspective on how making content on the Web machine processible will contribute toward Web intelligence.

In Interlude #3 at the end of this chapter, we present a vignette entitled, "Turing's test" to highlight some of these ideas.

WHAT IS MACHINE INTELLIGENCE?

Alan Turing, while acting as the leading cryptography expert to break the German codes during the Second World War, formulated the ideas that emerged after the

Thinking on the Web: Berners-Lee, Gödel, and Turing, by H. Peter Alesso and Craig F. Smith
Copyright © 2006 John Wiley & Sons, Inc.

war as Intelligent Machinery, and are now referred to as AI. Key to this field of study is the definition of what is meant by the terms "thinking" and "intelligence."

Thinking is often ambiguously defined, but generally can be applied to a complex processes that uses concepts, their interrelationships, and inference to produce new knowledge. We can extend the concept of thinking and identify an intelligent individual as one who is capable of accurate memory recall or able to apply logic to extend knowledge.

It is possible to extend the description of intelligence to nonhuman entities as well, such as in AI. But we frequently mean something different than in the case of human intelligence. For example, while one might be quite impressed with the intelligence of a child prodigy who can perform difficult arithmetic calculations quickly and accurately, a computer that could perform the same calculations faster and with greater accuracy would not be considered intelligent.

While it is still not possible to resolve controversial differences of opinion over the nature of human intelligence, it is possible to recognize certain attributes that most would agree reflect the concept. These include such elements as: the ability to learn; the ability to assimilate; the ability to organize and process information; and the ability to apply knowledge to solve complex problems. By extension then, many of these attributes of human intelligence can be traced into the various areas of research in the field of artificial intelligence. Artificial intelligence addresses the basic questions of what it means for a machine to have intelligence.

In 1947, shortly after the end of World War II, English mathematician Alan Turing first started to seriously explore the idea of intelligent machines. By 1956, John McCarthy of MIT coined the term Artificial Intelligence, and by the late 1950s, there were many researchers in AI, most basing their work on programming computers. Eventually, AI became more than a branch of science: it expanded far beyond mathematics and computer science into fields such as philosophy, psychology, and biology.

ALAN TURING

Alan Mathison Turing was one of the great pioneers of the computer field. He designed "The Turing machine" and "Turing's test." As a mathematician he applied the concept of the algorithm to digital computers. His research into the relationships between machines and Nature created the field of AI. His insights opened the door into the information age.

Turing was born in London, U.K., on June 23, 1912 (see Fig. 3-1). He had a difficult childhood, and was separated from his parents for long periods of time. He struggled through his school years, but he excelled in mathematics. He entered King's College, Cambridge, in 1931 to study mathematics.

He took an early interest in the works of von Neumann, Einstein, Eddington, and Russell's *Introduction to Mathematical Philosophy*.

By 1933, Turing's interest in mathematical logic intensified. He suggested that a purely logic-based view of mathematics was inadequate; and that

Figure 3-1. Photo of Alan Turing.

mathematical propositions possessed a variety of interpretations. Turing's achievements at Cambridge were primarily centered on his work in probability theory. However, he began to focus his attention on the question of mathematical decidability. In 1936, he published the paper *On Computable Numbers, with an Application to the Entscheidungsproblem.* Turing introduced the idea of a computational machine, now called the "Turing machine," which in many ways became the basis for modern computing (see Interlude #3). The Turing machine was an abstract device intended to help investigate the extent and limitations of computation. A Turing machine is a "state machine" that can be considered to be in any one of a finite number of states. Instructions for a Turing machine consist of specified conditions under which the machine will transition between one state and another using a precise, finite set of rules (given by a finite table) and depending on a single symbol it read from a tape, representing the state of the machine.

A Turing machine includes a one-dimensional tape, theoretically of infinite length, divided into cells. Each cell contains one symbol, either "0" or "1." The machine has a read–write head to scan a single cell on the tape. This read–write head can move left and right along the tape to scan successive cells.

The action of a Turing machine is determined completely by (*1*) the current state of the machine; (*2*) the symbol in the cell currently being scanned by the head; and (*3*) a table of transition rules, which serves as the "program" for the machine. If the machine reaches a situation in which there is not exactly one transition rule specified, then the machine halts.

In modern terms, the tape represents the memory of the machine, and the read–write head represents the memory bus through which data is accessed (and updated) by the machine. Two important factors are (*1*) the machine's tape is infinite in length; and (*2*) a function will be Turing-computable if there exists a set of instructions that will result in the machine computing the function regardless of how long it takes; that is, the function will be successfully computed in a finite number of steps.

These two assumptions ensure that no computable function will fail to be computable on a Turing machine (i.e., Turing computable) solely because there is insufficient time or memory to complete the computation.

Turing defined a computable number as a real number whose decimal expansion could be produced by a Turing machine. He showed that, although only countable many real numbers are computable, most real numbers are not computable (e.g., irrational numbers). He then described a number that is not computable and remarked that this seemed to be a paradox since he appeared to have described, in finite terms, a number that cannot be described in finite terms. However, Turing understood the source of the apparent paradox. It is impossible to decide (using another Turing machine) whether a Turing machine with a given table of instructions will output an infinite sequence of numbers. Turing's paper contains ideas that have proved of fundamental importance to mathematics and to computer science ever since.

In 1939, he was recruited to work for the British Government breaking the German Enigma codes. Together with W. G. Welchman, Turing developed the Bombe, a machine based on earlier work by Polish mathematicians, which, from late 1940, was decoding messages sent by the Enigma machines of the German Luftwaffe. By the middle of 1941, Turing's statistical approach, together with captured information, had led to the German Navy messages being decoded, using the first practical programmed computer, called Colossus.

In March 1946, Turing submitted a design proposing the Automatic Computing Engine (ACE). Turing's design was a prospectus for a modern computer.

In 1950, Turing published *Computing Machinery and Intelligence* in the journal *Mind*. It is a remarkable work on questions that would become increasingly important as the field of computer science developed. He studied problems that today lie at the heart of artificial intelligence. In his 1950 paper, he suggested what has become known as a Turing's test, still the acid test for recognizing intelligence in a machine. Turing died of cyanide poisoning, an apparent suicide, in 1954.

TURING TEST AND THE LOEBNER PRIZE

In Turing's seminal work entitled *Computing Machinery and Intelligence* more than 50 years ago, he suggested that a computer can be called intelligent if it could deceive a human into believing that it was human. His test—called the Turing test—consists of a person asking a series of questions to both a human subject and a machine (see Interlude #4). The questioning is done via a keyboard so that the questioner has no direct interaction. A machine with true intelligence will pass the Turing test by providing responses that are sufficiently human-like that the questioner cannot determine which responder is human. A scaled down version of the Turing test, known as the Loebner Prize, requires that machines "converse" with testers only on a limited topic in order to demonstrate their intelligence.

JOHN SEARLE'S CHINESE ROOM

While AI enthusiasts have pursued and promoted technologies related to machine intelligence, doubts about the possibility of producing intelligent machines have also continued over the years. In 1980, John Searle, a philosophy professor at the University of California, Berkeley, came up with a thought experiment called the Chinese Room.

The experiment consists of the idea of an English-speaking man in a room with a book of instructions. There is a slot in the wall, through which a paper can be delivered. The instruction book includes directions in English that describe how to manipulate Chinese characters by copying, erasing, and reordering. However, the book says nothing about the meaning of the characters. Someone outside the room puts paper slips into the slot that contains a written story and a question about the story, but all in Chinese. The man inside the room does not speak or read Chinese, but he uses the rule book and follows the instructions. The instructions may tell him to write or erase characters, and by blindly applying the rules, he continues until the instruction book tells him he is done. He passes the final paper with the answer to the original questions (in Chinese characters) out the slot without understanding what it says.

Outside, a Chinese speaker reads the page and understands the answers. This person may even find the answers intelligent and insightful. But the real question is, "Where does the insight reside?" (see Interlude #5).

ARTIFICIAL INTELLIGENCE

How far is AI from reaching human-level intelligence? Some have suggested that human-level intelligence can be achieved by writing large numbers of programs and assembling vast databases of facts in the languages used for expressing knowledge. However, most AI researchers believe that new fundamental ideas are required before true intelligence can be approached.

There are two main lines of AI research. One is biological, based on the idea that since humans are intelligent, AI should study humans and imitate the psychology or physiology of human intelligence. The other is phenomenological, based on studying and formalizing common sense facts about the world and the problems that the world presents to the achievement of goals thereby providing functionality that, in humans, would be considered intelligent behavior, even if the approach used is quite different from what would be found in a human.

Today, AI still means different things to different people. Some confusion arises because the word intelligence is so ill-defined. Artificial intelligence is sometimes described in two ways: strong AI and weak AI. Strong AI asserts that computers can be made to think on a level (at least) equal to humans. Weak AI simply holds that some thinking-like features can be added to computers to make them more useful tools. Examples of Weak AI abound: expert systems, drive-by-wire cars, smart browsers, and speech recognition software. These weak AI components may, when combined, begin to approach some aspects of strong AI.

As participants of the Information Revolution, we could ask by extension, "What is Web intelligence?" For the most part, the World Wide Web can be considered to be a massive information system with interconnected databases and remote applications providing various services. While these services are becoming more and more user oriented, the concept of smart or intelligent applications and services on the Web is still in its infancy.

A classic example of an AI application that many would consider intelligent in some form is computer chess. Over the years, computer chess-playing software has received considerable attention, and such programs are a commercial success for home PCs or on the Web. In addition, most are aware of the highly visible contest between IBMs Deep Blue Supercomputer and the reigning World Chess Champion, Garry Kasparov in May 1997. Millions of chess and computing fans observed this event in real-time where, in a dramatic sixth game victory, Deep Blue beat Kasparov. This was the first time a computer has won a match with a current world champion under tournament conditions.

Computer chess programs generally make use of standardized opening sequences, and end game databases as a knowledge base to simplify these phases of the game. For the middle game, they examine large trees and perform deep searches with pruning to eliminate branches that are evaluated as clearly inferior and to select the most highly favorable move.

MACHINE INTELLIGENCE

Machine intelligence is associated with Machine Learning, Computational Intelligence, Soft-Computing, and Artificial Intelligence. Although these terms are often used interchangeably, they are actually different branches of study.

For example, Artificial Intelligence involves symbolic computation (i.e., the mathematical transformation of symbolic expressions, using computer algorithms), while Soft-Computing (i.e., techniques in computer science and in artificial intelligence, such as Fuzzy logic, Neural networks, and Probabilistic reasoning, that resemble human reasoning more closely than traditional techniques) involves intensive numerical computation. The following subbranches of machine intelligence have particular relevance to the Semantic Web and the idea Web intelligence: computational complexity, descriptive logic, ontology, inference, and software agents.

Although symbolic AI is currently built and incorporated into Semantic Web data representation, there is no doubt that software tool developers will eventually incorporate the soft-computing paradigm as well. The benefit of such a step will be the creation of adaptive software. This would imply that soft-computing applications will have the ability to adapt to changing environments and input.

While the Semantic Web is under development, concepts surrounding machine intelligence will continue to evolve. The extent of the usefulness of the Semantic Web will be tested in various ways, but the controversy involving the meaning of machine intelligence will undoubtedly not end in the foreseeable future.

In the following sections, topics related to semantic networks and description logic, will be discussed and then each of the key machine-intelligence areas identified above will be addressed starting with computational complexity, followed by knowledge representation, Ontology, inference engines, and software agents.

SEMANTIC NETWORKS AND FRAMES

A semantic network or net is a graphic approach to represent knowledge in patterns of interconnected nodes and arcs. Computer applications using semantic networks were first developed for artificial intelligence and machine translation, but earlier versions were also used in the fields of philosophy, psychology, and linguistics. A more complex type of semantic net is sometimes used in expert systems. These are known as frames; frames use a hierarchical structure.

What is common to all semantic networks is a declarative graphic representation that can be used to either represent knowledge or support automated systems for reasoning about knowledge. Some versions are informal, but other versions are formally defined systems of logic. Semantic nets facilitate processing of information and have been found to be useful as modeling tools.

The way that the information is processed, is known as arc traversal. This is used to identify the complex relationships between nodes. One method of obtaining information from the network is though intersection search. This finds relationships between nodes by spreading a pattern of activation out from two nodes and then seeing where they meet.

REASONING WITH SEMANTIC NETWORKS

There is no formal semantics or agreed upon notion of what a given representational structure means. Meaning is assigned only by the nature of the programs that manipulate the network. Most common reasoning schemes use a network fragment as constructed for the query and attempt to match the network. Sets of things in a semantic network are termed types, while individual objects in a semantic network are termed instances. Reasoning on such nets takes place when the network is modified to reflect some process of derived meaning, such as the inheritance of values and relationships.

Semantic nets are important to cognitive science, but are rarely used on their own due to limitations in representing some concepts. The problem is dealing with concepts like "some of" and "all of," which are known as quantifiers. They are impossible to represent in normal semantic nets, and extensions have been proposed to deal with the problem. However, there are still limitations to semantic nets and the only way to get around these is to use a more complex calculus, such as that offered by frames.

Frames offer a more highly structured hierarchy of nodes. Basically, each level in the hierarchy is of a given type, and there are certain options for filling the slot of this node type. In this way, specific knowledge can be represented and manipulated. A lot of work has been done in the field of hypertext network organization. Advocates of hypertext suggest that the ideas relevant to a subject can be represented best by a simple associative network, or web, with multiple interrelationships specified. The idea is that hypertext representation mimics the associative networks of the human brain a notion derived directly from Vannevar Bush's seminal 1945 *Atlantic Monthly* article entitled "As We May Think."

It has long been recognized that hypertext structures mimic semantic networks. Similar to hypertext, semantic networks are composed of nodes and links. Nodes represent concepts, and links represent relationships between them. A hypertext system with arbitrary link types corresponds to a free semantic net. If the hypertext system allows just a limited number of link types, the underlying semantic net is restricted. Semantic nets are tightly coupled to the notion of associative networks.

We can say that, in general, knowledge is stored in the human mind in information packets that are interrelated in a network structure. This view of the organization of the human memory may be used as a model to organize the information in hypertext. The evolution of associative network theory provides the foundation for the development of hypertext structures.

The semantic network formalism can be used as a general inferential representation mechanism of knowledge. Concepts surrounding a starting point are viewed during the process of problem solving. The resulting path indicates a potential relationship between the original concepts. Other inferential mechanisms in semantic networks are inheritance hierarchies and analogical structures. Both draw on the assumption that relevant facts about nodes can be inferred from neighboring nodes.

Frame-based representation adds methods to handle inference to the declarative knowledge representation in semantic networks. Each node in the semantic network (and in the corresponding hypertext structure) is represented as a single frame. Links are defined as slots of frames. Frame-based systems support inheritance, defaults of slot values, integration of truth maintenance, inference engines, and rule-based reasoning.

COMPUTATIONAL COMPLEXITY

Turing's ideas rearding the operation of a general purpose computing machine lead naturally into the question of computability. Computational complexity addresses the issue of the relative computational difficulty of computable functions.

In computational complexity, a single problem is in reality a class of related questions, where each question can be considered a finite-length string. For example, a problem might be to determine the prime factors of a number; this problem could consist of many or even an infinite number of instances of the problem.

The time complexity of a problem is characterized by the number of steps that it takes to solve an instance of the problem as a function of the size of the input (usually measured in bits), using the most efficient algorithm. If a problem instance involves an input value that is n bits long, and the problem can be solved in n^2 steps, we say the problem has a time complexity of n^2. The actual number of steps will depend on exactly what machine computational process is being used. Nevertheless, we generally use the terminology that if the complexity is of order n^2 [or $O(n^2)$] on one typical computer, then it will also have complexity $O(n^2)$ on other computers.

Decision Problems

Much of complexity theory deals with decision problems. A decision problem is a problem where the answer always comes down to Yes or No. For example, the problem to determine whether or not a number is prime can be stated as: given an integer written in binary, return whether it is a prime number or not. A decision problem can be considered to be equivalent to a language, in the sense that it can be considered to be a set of finite-length strings. For a given decision problem, the equivalent language is the set of all strings for which the answer is YES.

Decision problems are often considered because an arbitrary problem can generally be reduced to a decision problem. For example, consider the problem to determine if a given number has a prime factor less than another number (i.e., given integers n and k written in binary, return whether n has any prime factors $< k$). If this problem can be solved with a certain amount of resources, then we can use that solution to solve the problem of determining the prime factors of a number without much more resources (i.e., by conducting a binary search on k until you find the smallest factor of n, then dividing out that factor, and repeat until all the factors are found).

Complexity Classes

Decision problems fall into sets of comparable complexity, called complexity classes. The complexity class P is the set of decision problems that can be solved by a deterministic machine in polynomial time. This class corresponds to an intuitive idea of the problems that can be effectively solved in the worst cases. The complexity class NP is the set of decision problems that can be verified in polynomial time or solved by a nondeterministic machine in polynomial time.

Intractability

Problems that are solvable in theory, but cannot be solved in practice, are called intractable. Although what can be solved "in practice" is open to debate, in general only problems that have polynomial-time solutions are solvable for more than the smallest inputs. Problems that are known to be intractable include those that are exponential-time-complete. If NP is not the same as P, then the NP-complete problems are also intractable.

To see why exponential-time solutions are not usable in practice, consider a problem that requires 2^n operations to solve (where n is the size of the input). For a relatively small input size of $n = 100$, and assuming a computer that can perform 10^{10} operations per second, a solution would take about 4×10^{12} years, far longer than the age of the universe.

DESCRIPTION LOGIC

The question of how best to represent knowledge in a database or information system has long been recognized as a key issue in AI. The main research effort in Knowledge–Representation (KR) is centered on theories and systems for expressing structured knowledge and for accessing and reasoning with it. Description Logics (DL) is an important powerful class of logic-based knowledge–representation languages.

The basic components of DL include a family of knowledge–representation formalisms designed for the representation of and reasoning about semantic networks and frame-based systems. Description Logics are also closely related to Modal Logic (an extension of propositional calculus, which uses operators that express various "modes" of truth, such as: necessarily A, possibly A, probably A, it has always been true that A, it is permissible that A, it is believed that A and DL (a multimodal logic in which there are explicit syntactic constructs, called programs, whose main role is to change the values of variables, thereby changing the truth values of formulas based on program representation), and it has turned out that DLs are also well suited to the representation of and reasoning about database conceptual models, information integration, and ontologies. A variety of different DLs exist with different expressive power and different computational complexity for the corresponding inference problems.

The Semantic Web requires a language that expresses both data and rules for reasoning about the data and allows rules from any existing knowledge–representation system to be imported. Both XML and the RDF are important technologies for developing the Semantic Web. The meaning is expressed by RDF, in which it is encoded in sets of triples, each triple acting as a sentence with a subject, predicate, and object. These triples can be written using XML syntax.

For the Semantic Web to function, computers must have access to structured collections of information (as RDF statements) and sets of inference rules that they can use to conduct automated reasoning. A knowledge–representation language includes language syntax (describes configurations that can constitute sentences) and semantics (determines the facts based upon the sentences). Traditional knowledge–representation systems typically have been centralized, requiring everyone to share exactly the same definition of common concepts. But central control is stifling, and increasing the size produces complexity that rapidly becomes unmanageable. These systems limit the questions that can be asked reliably. In avoiding the problems, traditional knowledge–representation systems narrow their focus and use a limited set of rules for making inferences.

Possible inference engines for the Semantic Web could be based upon Horn logic, which is a fragment of first-order logic (FOL). Horn logic was studied in the area of deductive databases and logic programming and a number of efficient evaluation strategies are available for this fragment of predicate logic. However, integrating Horn rules from different sources distributed on the Web introduces rules that can interfere with each other (see Chapter 8).

ONTOLOGY

If a program wants to compare conceptual information across two knowledge bases on the Web, it has to know when any two given terms are being used to mean the same thing. Ideally, the program must have a way to discover common meanings for whatever knowledge bases it encounters. A solution to this problem is provided by the Semantic Web in the form of collections of information called ontologies. Artificial Intelligence and Web researchers use the term ontology as a document that defines the relations among terms. A typical ontology for the Web uses a taxonomy and a set of inference rules.

The taxonomy defines classes of objects and relations among them. Classes, subclasses, and relations among entities are important tools. We can express a large number of relations among entities by assigning properties to classes and allowing subclasses to inherit such properties.

Inference rules in ontologies may express rules for manipulating information. Inference rules may express the rule: "If a city code is associated with a state code, and an address uses that city code, then that address has the associated state code." A program could then readily deduce, for example, that a Cornell University address, being in Ithaca, must be in New York State, which is in the United States, and therefore should be formatted to U.S. standards.

The real power of the Semantic Web will be realized when people create many programs that collect Web content from diverse sources, automatically process the information, and exchange the results. The effectiveness of software agents will increase exponentially as more machine-readable Web content and automated services become available. The Semantic Web promotes this synergy: even agents that were not expressly designed to work together can transfer semantic data (see Chapter 7).

INFERENCE ENGINES

Inference engines are intended to derive answers from a knowledge base. They are at the core of the expert systems that provide a methodology for reasoning about the information in the knowledge base, and for formulating conclusions. Inference engines process knowledge available in the Semantic Web. They deduce new knowledge from previously established knowledge.

An inference engine controls overall execution of a set of rules. It searches through a knowledge base, attempting to pattern-match facts or knowledge present in memory to the antecedents of rules. If a rule's antecedent is satisfied, the rule is ready to fire and is placed in the agenda. When a rule is ready to fire it means that since the antecedent is satisfied, the consequent can be executed.

Salience is a mechanism used by some expert systems to add a procedural aspect to rule inferencing. Certain rules may be given a higher salience than others, which means that when the inference engine is searching for rules to fire, it places those with a higher salience at the top of the agenda.

SOFTWARE AGENTS

An intelligent agent is a computer system that is situated in some environment, and that is capable of autonomous action and learning in order to meet its design objectives. Agents have the following characteristics: they are reactive—they perceive their environment, and respond; proactive—they exhibit goal-directed behavior; and social—they interact with other agents.

Real-time intelligent agent technology offers a powerful Web tool. Agents are able to act without the intervention of humans or other systems; they have control both over their own internal state and their behavior. Normally, an agent will have a repertoire of actions available to it. So that in complexity domains, agents must be prepared for the possibility of failure. This situation is called nondeterministic. Its set of possible actions represents the agent's capability to modify its environments. Similarly, the action "purchase a house" will fail if insufficient funds area available to do so. Actions therefore have preconditions associated with them, which define the possible situations in which they can be applied.

The key problem facing an agent is that of deciding which of its actions it should perform to satisfy its design objectives. Agent architectures are really software architectures for decision-making systems that are embedded in an environment. The complexity of the decision-making process can be affected by a number of different environmental choices: accessible versus inaccessible, deterministic versus nondeterministic, episodic versus nonepisodic, static versus dynamic, and discrete versus continuous.

The most complex general class of environments consists of those that are inaccessible, nondeterministic, nonepisodic, dynamic, and continuous. For the Semantic Web, providing sufficient expressive power for agents to interact successfully is essential.

ADAPTIVE SOFTWARE

In the 1970s, structured programming made it feasible to build larger scale software systems based on existing specifications. A typical application was a database program that read an input file and produced an output file.

In the 1980s, object-oriented programming made it easier to reorganize for changes, because functionality was split up into separate classes. A typical application was a desktop publishing system using user-initiated events (mouse clicks or menus). The problem with using existing software, however, is that it takes too much time and money to modify, and it is brittle when used in situations for which it was not explicitly designed. Adaptive software design methodologies can help alleviate this problem.

A primary element in adaptive software is realizing that optimization of structured programs is not the only solution to increasingly complex problems. The optimization approach is based on maintaining control to impose order on uncertainty. Imposed order is the product of rigorous engineering discipline and deterministic, cause-and-effect-driven processes. The alternative idea is one of an adaptive mindset, of viewing organizations as complex adaptive systems, and of creating emergent order out of a web of interconnected components.

Complexity involves the number of interacting agents and the speed of agent interaction. For software products, the need for adaptive development arises when there are a great many independent operators—developers, customers, vendors, competitors, stockholders—interacting with each other, fast enough that linear cause and effect rules are no longer sufficient for success. Size and technological complexity are additional factors.

Adaptive software adds a feedback loop that provides information based on performance. The design criteria themselves become a part of the program and the program reconfigures itself as the environment changes. There are significant adaptive software challenges including scaling to large networks and to large numbers of applications. Other challenges include deployable intelligence mechanisms from pattern recognition algorithms to data mining algorithms. For the Semantic Web, adaptive software agents could yield surprising benefits.

LIMITATIONS AND CAPABILITIES

The promising aspects of combining Web Services and intelligent agents on the Semantic Web would be the ability to move from manipulating keywords to understanding and manipulating concepts. The limitations to achieving this would be the development of ontologies and the annotation of content with metadata that may not scale due to computational complexity.

CONCLUSION

This chapter provided an overview of Alan Turing's ideas and a discussion of some of the key ideas emanating from his work. In addition, we engaged in a discussion of the meaning of machine intelligence and offer some perspective of how realistically making the Web machine processable will contribute toward Web intelligence. Some of the more advanced applications on the Web, which include Artificial Intelligence, were explored. Key related concepts essential for understanding what is meant by machine intelligence were also described: machine intelligence, computational complexity, knowledge representation, ontology, inference, and software agents.

From this chapter, it may be concluded that balancing expressive power with reasoning capability may offer useful applications on the Semantic Web that are much less exciting than one might expect from the hype surrounding machine intelligence. In addition, innovations in adaptive software may offer surprising capabilities for Web software agents.

EXERCISES

3-1. Make a list of 10 questions you would ask as part of a Turing test.

3-2. Ask a colleague or classmate these questions and record their answers. Compare the results.

Figure 3-2. This is a "completed" representation of Escher's Print Gallery, which includes the filled-in hole in Figure 1-1, created (http://escherdroste.math.leidenuniv.nl/) by Hendrik Lenstra and Bart de Smit.

INTERLUDE #3: COMPUTING MACHINES

Having had the final word in their last discussion, John was feeling a little smug as he listened to his ipod. Mary sat down next to him on the library steps. Their last class had been on computer design and they were both thinking about just how far the new technology could evolve.

John said, "As you suggested earlier, Gödel was concerned that a logic system had to be consistent and then he determined that no logic system can prove itself to be consistent."

"True," replied Mary. "But it was Turing who built on Gödel's findings. Shortly before World War II, Turing found a way to translate Gödel's logic results about numbers and mathematics into analogous results about calculations and computing machines."

John interrupted, "Yes, Turing was convinced that mathematical problem solving could be reduced to simple steps that could be used to program computer actions."

Mary said, "True. Turing considered the logical steps one goes through in constructing a proof as being the same steps that a human mind follows in a computation." Mary gave John a sideways glance before continuing, "Turing was convinced that the ability to solve this type of mathematical problem is a significant indication of the ability of machines to duplicate human thought."

John dissented, "Wait a minute. We've been here before. Just because machines follow the same logical steps a human uses to solve a calculation doesn't mean that they actually think. Since calculating machines are not biological, it seems unreasonable to me to suggest that machines are capable of actual creative thought. They may be mimicking the logical steps, but are they actually thinking? I think not."

"Therefore, you are not," Mary said with a grin.

John relied, "Hey."

Mary said, "Ok. Seriously, if it were even remotely possible that machines could independently mimic thought that would be significant."

She continued, "Consider Turing's machine. Turing held that a mechanical computer is basically a large number of address locations acting as a memory, together with an executive unit that carries out individual operations of a calculation. These operations represent a program. Let's imagine that I want to use the machine to add two numbers 1 and 2 together. The computing machine would begin with placing a '1' in the first location and a '2' in the second location and then the computer consults a program for how to do addition. The instructions would say gather the numbers from the two locations and perform a summing operation to yield the sum of the two numbers and place the resultant number '3' in the third location. This process could be considered to mimic the operations a human would perform."

John replied solemnly, "Simple rote actions."

Mary added, "Turing's computer consists of two basic elements: an infinitely long tape ruled off into squares, each capable of being inscribed with the symbol '0' or '1,' and a scanning head that can move forward or back one square at a time reading the symbol on that square, either leaving it alone or writing a new symbol on that square. At any step of the operation, the scanning head can be in one of an infinite number of states. The machine has a pointer that is set at one of the letters 'A' 'B' 'C,' and this letter represents the state of the machine. Part of the program tells the machine how to change the pointer setting, depending on what state the machine is currently in and what symbol is on the square of the tape that the head is currently reading."

John nodded slowly as he visualized the machine.

Mary continued, "The action of a Turing machine is determined completely by (1) the current state of the machine; (2) the symbol in the cell currently being scanned by the head; and (3) a table of transition rules, which serves as the "program" for the machine. If the machine reaches a situation in which there is not exactly one transition rule specified, then the machine halts. While it may take a long tape and many steps to carry out sophisticated calculations, anything at all that can be thought of as following from a set of rules, can be calculated in the step by step fashion."

John said, "It is easy to appreciate that Turing's machine is the foundation of the modern computer."

Mary said, "And that leads us to your earlier question about whether a computing machine can have human-like intelligence."

John said, "In general, I would consider 'thinking' to be a complex process that uses concepts and relationships to infer new knowledge. Thinking would involve acts, such as memory recall, arithmetic calculations, puzzle solving, and so on. By extension, the performance of these acts would indicate 'intelligence.' For example, a child who can perform difficult arithmetic calculations quickly would display intelligence. Likewise an individual who has rapid memory recall and who has accumulated sufficient amounts of information to consistently win games such as Scrabble, or Trivial Pursuit, might also be considered to be intelligent."

"Well then," responded Mary, "Why wouldn't a computer that could perform the same calculations as that child, but faster and with greater accuracy be considered intelligent. Or consider a computer with substantial memory storage that is able to answer all those Trivial Pursuit questions. Why can't that computer, be considered intelligent."

John said, "Well human thinking involves complicated interactions within the biological components of the brain. In addition, the processes of communication and learning are also important elements of human intelligence."

Mary replied, "By mentioning intelligent communication you have led us to Turing's test for machine intelligence."

John said, "Ok, but please, let's talk about that tomorrow."

4

BERNERS-LEE: WHAT IS SOLVABLE ON THE WEB?

OVERVIEW

When Tim Berners-Lee was developing the key elements of the World Wide Web, he showed great insight in providing Hypertext Markup Language (HTML) as a simple easy-to-use Web development language. As a result, it was rapidly and widely adopted. To produce Web information required skills that could be learned with a high school level education. Consequently, personal computing merged with global networking to produce the World Wide Web.

The continuing evolution of the Web into a resource with intelligent features, however, presents many new challenges. The solution of the World Wide Web Consortium (W3C) is to provide a new Web architecture that uses additional layers of markup languages that can directly apply logic. However, the addition of ontologies, logic, and rule systems for markup languages means consideration of extremely difficult mathematic and logic consequences, such as paradox, recursion, undecidability, and computational complexity on a global scale. Therefore, it is important to find the correct balance between achieving powerful reasoning with reasonable complexity on the Web. This balance will decide what is solvable on the Web in terms of application logic.

This chapter will briefly review Berners-Lee's contribution in developing the Web. Then, we look at the impact of adding formal logic to Web architecture and present the new markup languages leading to the future Web architecture: the Semantic Web. It concludes with a presentation of complexity theory and rule-based inference engines followed by a discussion of what is solvable on the Web.

Thinking on the Web: Berners-Lee, Gödel, and Turing, by H. Peter Alesso and Craig F. Smith
Copyright © 2006 John Wiley & Sons, Inc.

THE WORLD WIDE WEB

By 1991, three major events converged to accelerate the development of the Information Revolution. These three events were the introduction of the World Wide Web, the widespread availability of the graphical browser, and the unleashing of commercialization on the Internet. The essential power of the World Wide Web turned out to be its universality though the use of HTML. The concept provided the ability to combine words, pictures, and sounds (i.e., to provide multimedia content) on Internet pages. This excited many computer programmers who saw the potential for publishing information on the Internet with the ease of using a word processor, but with the richness of multimedia forms.

Berners-Lee and his collaborators laid the groundwork for the open standards of the Web. Their efforts included inventing and refining the Hypertext Transfer Protocol (HTTP) for linking Web documents, the HTML for formatting Web documents and the Universal Resource Locator (URL) system for addressing Web documents.

TIM BERNERS-LEE

Tim Berners-Lee was born in London, England, in 1955. His parents were computer scientists who met while working on the Ferranti Mark I, the world's first commercially sold computer. He soon developed his parents' interest in computers, and at Queen's College, at Oxford University, he built his first computer from an old television set and a leftover processor.

Berners-Lee studied physics at Oxford, graduated in 1976, and began a career in computing (see Fig. 4-1). Between 1976 and 1980, he worked at Plessey Telecommunications Ltd. followed by D. G. Nash Ltd.

In 1980, he was a software engineer at CERN, the European Particle Physics Laboratory, in Geneva, Switzerland where he learned the laboratory's complicated information system. He wrote a computer program to store information and use random associations that he called, "Enquire-Within-Upon-Everything," or "Enquire." This system provided links between documents.

Hypertext actually began in 1945 when Vannevar Bush, a computer pioneer, wrote an article for the Atlantic Monthly describing a theoretical electromechanical device called a memex, which would make and follow links between documents on microfiche. In the mid-1960s, Ted Nelson drew on Bush's work to develop a software framework called Xanadu and coined the word "hypertext."

In 1968, Douglas Engelbart completed a prototype for an "oNLine System" (NLS), which linked documents through hypertext. He also invented the mouse.

While Enquire proved useful at CERN, Berners-Lee did not publish his work and he left CERN in 1981. In 1984, he returned to CERN, to work on distributed real-time systems for scientific data acquisition and system control.

During this time at CERN, Berners-Lee began to conceive of a different type of Enquire system. The Internet was 15 years old and had proven to be

Figure 4-1. Photo of Tim Berner-Lee.

a reliable networking system, but it was still cumbersome to use. Berners-Lee was looking at ways to simplify the exchange of information. Berners-Lee began to imagine a system that would link up all the computers of his colleagues at CERN, as well as those of CERN's associates in laboratories around the world.

In 1989, Berners-Lee with a team of colleagues developed HTML, an easy-to-learn document coding system that allows users to click onto a link in a document's text and connect to another document. He also created an addressing plan that allowed each Web page to have a specific location known as a URL. Finally, he completed HTTP a system for linking these documents across the Internet. He also wrote the software for the first server and the first Web client browser that would allow any computer user to view and navigate Web pages, as well as create and post their own Web documents.

In the following years, Berners-Lee improved the specifications of URLs, HTTP, and HTML as the technology spread across the Internet.

While many early Web developers became Internet entrepreneurs, Berners-Lee eventually chose an academic and administrative life. He left CERN in the early 1990s and spent research stints at various laboratories, including Xerox's Palo Alto Research Center (PARC), in California, and the Laboratory for Computer Science (CSAIL) at the Massachusetts Institute of Technology (MIT), in Cambridge. He directs the W3C, an open forum of companies and organizations with the mission to lead the Web to its full potential.

HyperText Markup Language is the primary language for formatting Web pages. With HTML, the author describes what a page should look like, what types of fonts to use, what color text should be, where paragraphs begin, and many other attributes of the document.

Hypertext Transfer Protocol

HyperText Transfer Protocol is the network protocol used to deliver files and data on the Web including: HTML files, image files, query results, or anything else. Usually, HTTP takes place through TCP/IP sockets. Socket is the term for the package of subroutines that provide an access path for data transfer through the network.

Like most network protocols, HTTP uses the client–server model: An HTTP client opens a connection and sends a request message to an HTTP server; the server then returns a response message, usually containing the resource that was requested. After delivering the response, the server closes the connection.

A simple HTTP exchange to retrieve the file at the URL, first opens a socket to the host www.somehost.com, at port 80 (the default) and then, sends following through the socket:

```
GET/path/file.html HTTP/1.0
From: someuser@somehost.com
User-Agent: HTTPTool/1.0
```

The server responds with the HTTP protocol file followed by the HTML "hello world" file with the following:

```
HTTP/1.0 200 OK
Date: Fri, 31 Dec 1999 23:59:59 GMT
Content-Type: text/html
Content-Length: 1354

<html>
 <body>
  Hello World
 </body>
</html>
```

This simple process has proven to be not only easy and straightforward, but highly successful as well.

Bridging Web Services

While the W3C continually develops open Web standards, vendors have been customizing their applications for efficient business logic processing through their proprietary server applications. For example, Web Services communicate through open standards including Simple Object Access Protocol (SOAP) and

Web Service Description Language (WSDL), but then the business logic is executed through server pages designed for specialized server frameworks (either Java 2 Platform Enterprise Edition (J2EE) or Microsoft .NET).

Simple Object Access Protocol (SOAP) is an implementation of XML that represents one common set of rules about how data and commands are represented and extended. It consists of three parts: an envelope (a framework for describing what is in a message and how to process it), a set of encoding rules (for expressing instances of application-defined data types), and a convention for representing remote procedure calls and responses. The SOAP messages are fundamentally one-way transmissions from a sender to a receiver using HTTP binding. Simple Object Access Protocol describes commands and parameters that can be passed between browsers and Web Services for both J2EE and .NET platforms.

Web Services Description Language (WSDL) describes networked XML-based services. It provides a way for service providers to describe the format of requests to their systems regardless of the underlying protocol or encoding. It is a part of the effort of Universal Discovery and Description Identification (UDDI) initiative to provide directories and descriptions of such on-line services for electronic business.

Limits of Today's Web

The Web has changed from its original structure of a distributed, high-reliability, open system without a superimposed logic or metadata. Today, the basic information is still displayed as a distributed open system, but the development of portals, such as, Yahoo, Google AOL, and MSN has focused Web entry and led to controlling traffic to partisan sites. In addition, business logic has migrated primarily into two segregated server frameworks: active server pages and java server pages. The result has produced a decentralized Web system with critical proprietary portal-centric nodes and frameworks.

In the future, we can expect significant improvements, such as increased average bandwidth, the use of open standards to facilitate advanced markup languages, the application of metadata, and the use of inference search.

The paradigm of the Web is centered on the client–server interaction, which is a fundamentally asymmetric relationship between providers, who insert content into the Web hypertext (server) and users who essentially read texts or provide answers to questions by filling out forms (clients). The hyperlinks of the Web represent structures of meaning that transcend the meaning represented by individual texts. At present, these Web structures of meaning lack longevity and can only be blindly used, for example by search engines, which at best optimize navigation by taking into account the statistical behavior of Web users.

In effect, the Web has developed as a medium for humans without a focus on data that could be processed automatically. Hypertext Markup Language is not capable of being directly exploited by information retrieval techniques, hence the Web is restricted to manual keyword searches.

The problem at present is that there is no way to construct complex networks of meaningful relations between Web contents. In fact, the providers have no influence on the links to the contents they provide and the users have no impact on the available access structures to the content. As a result, some of today's basic Web limitations include search, database support, interoperable applications, intelligent business logic, automation, security, and trust.

An important framework for creating meaningful Web links can be provided by the Semantic Web: the automated creation of links between machine-understandable metadata. Such semantic linking will not be restricted to the use of specifically prepared metadata sets, but will exploit the meaningful structure of the Web itself in order to provide a content-based semantic access to information.

THE SEMANTIC WEB ROADMAP

The inventor of the World Wide Web, Tim Berners-Lee, and his W3C team work to develop, extend, and standardize the Web's markup languages and tools. In addition, what they are designing is the next generation Web architecture: the Semantic Web.

Currently, the objective of the Semantic Web architecture is to provide a knowledge representation of linked data in order to allow machine processing on a global scale. This involves moving the Web from a repository of data without logic to a level where it is possible to express logic through knowledge-representation systems. The vision for the Semantic Web is to augment the existing Web with resources more easily interpreted by programs and intelligent agents.

A defining application for the Semantic Web will be a more effective search capability. While today's search engines index HTML pages to find many answers and cover a huge part of the Web, they return many irrelevant pieces of information. There is no notion of "correctness" to such searches.

The difficulty of semantic search is perhaps its most important limitation. With the current state of the Web, there are two methods of gaining broader information about documents. The first is to use a directory, or portal site, manually constructed by searching the Web and then categorizing pages and links. The problem with this approach is that directories take a tremendous effort to maintain. Finding new links, updating old ones, and maintaining the database technology, all add to a portal's administrative burden and operating costs. The second method uses automatic Web crawling and indexing systems.

Consequently, searching the World Wide Web can be frustrating. The result of having better standard metadata could be a Web where users and agents could directly tap the latent information in linked and related pages. This would be a powerful paradigm greatly improving the intelligent use of Web resources.

By contrast, logic engines have typically been able to restrict their output to that which is a provably correct answer, but have suffered from the inability to go through the mass of connected data across the Web to construct valid answers.

If an engine of the future combines a reasoning engine with a search engine, it may actually be able to produce useful results. It will be able to reach out to indexes that contain very complete lists of all occurrences of a given term, and then use logic to weed out all but those that can be of use in solving the given problem.

If the Semantic Web can bring structure and meaningful content to the Web, it will create an environment where software agents can carry out sophisticated tasks for users. The first steps in weaving the Semantic Web with the existing Web are already under way. In the near future, these developments will provide new functionality as machines become better able to "understand" and process the data.

For the Semantic Web to function, computers must have access to structured collections of information and sets of inference rules that they can use to conduct automated reasoning. Artificial Intelligence researchers have long studied such systems and have produced today's knowledge representation. Knowledge representation is currently in a state comparable to that of hypertext before the advent of the Web.

The objective of the Semantic Web therefore, is to provide a framework that expresses both data and rules for reasoning for Web-based knowledge representation. Adding logic to the Web means using rules to make inferences, choose courses of action, and answering questions. A combination of mathematical and engineering issues complicates this task. The logic must be powerful enough to describe complex properties of objects, but not so powerful that agents can be tricked by being asked to consider a paradox.

The development of the Semantic Web is proceeding in a step-by-step approach building one layer on top of another. Two important technologies for developing the Semantic Web are already in place: eXtensible Markup Language (XML) and the Resource Description Framework (RDF) (see Fig. 2-3).

Building one layer upon another requires each layer to have downward compatibity and upward partial understanding. Downward compatibility means that agents are fully aware of a layer to interpret and use information written at a lower level. Upward partial understanding means that agents take at least partial advantage of information at higher levels. For example, an agent aware of RDF and RDF Schema semantics can interpret knowledge written in OWL, by disregarding all but RDF and RDF Schema elements.

eXtensible Markup Language lets everyone create their own tags. Scripts, or programs, can make use of these tags in sophisticated ways, but the script writer has to know how the page writer uses each tag. In short, XML allows users to add arbitrary structure to their documents, but says nothing about what the structure means.

Why is so XML important? Just as HTML is an open standard that allows information exchange and display over the Internet, XML is an open standard that allows data to be exchanged between applications over the Web. XML is the bridge to exchange data between the two main software development frameworks over the Web: J2EE and .NET. We can consider XML as a highly functional subset of SGML, but as a result, it is a meta-language that allows users to design their own markup languages.

Resource Description Framework

Resource Description Framework contains the concept of an assertion and allows assertions about assertions. Meta-assertions make it possible to do rudimentary checks on a document (see Chapter 5).

Resource Description Framework is a model of statements made about resources and associated URI. Its statements have a uniform structure of three parts: subject, predicate, and object.

For example,

> "The book [subject] has the title [predicate] *Gödel, Escher, Bach: An Eternal Golden Braid* [object]."

With RDF we can express statements in a formal way that software agents can read and act on. It lets us express a collection of statements as a graph, as a series of (subject, predicate, object) triples, or even in XML form. The first form is the most convenient for communication between people, the second for efficient processing, and the third for flexible communication with agent software.

The next steps up the Language Pyramid of Web markup languages, which address ontology and services languages are: Web Ontology Language (OWL), Semantic Web Rule Language (SWRL), and OWL-Services (OWL-S).

Ontology

An ontology is an agreement between agents that exchange information. The agreement is a model for structuring and interpreting exchanged data and a vocabulary that constrains these exchanges. Using ontology, agents can exchange vast quantities of data and consistently interpret it. Furthermore, they can infer new information by applying the ontology logical rules.

A nontrivial ontology will allow logical inconsistencies, and as Gödel pointed out in his Incompleteness Theorem: in any axiomatic system it is possible to create propositions that cannot be proved or disproved. This does not negate the usefulness of ontologies; however, it does mean ontologies, like everything else, have their limitations.

In the AI community, the ability to infer new information from existing data is of fundamental importance, and this is sometimes misinterpreted as a defining feature of ontology. In fact, many ontologies only weakly support this capability. Ontology is also sometimes narrowly defined to mean hierarchical taxonomies or constrained vocabularies, but ontology may also contain assertions about how data can be structured and interpreted.

The leading ontology system using RDF is Web Ontology Language (called OWL) (see Chapter 6).

Web Ontology Language allows us to formally express ontologies. The RDF provides some classification and rules, but OWL goes much further. In fact, one way to look at OWL is as the business rules for the Semantic Web, yet it is much more flexible than most business rule languages.

Most of OWLs power comes from primitives for expressing classifications. The OWL provides a toolbox of class expressions, which bring the power of mathematical logic and set theory to the tricky and important task of mapping ontologies through classifications.

Web Ontology Language

In 2003, the W3C began final unification of the disparate ontology efforts into a standardizing ontology and called it the OWL. This language is a vocabulary extension of RDF and is currently evolving into the semantic markup language for publishing and sharing ontologies on the World Wide Web.

Web Ontology Language facilitates greater machine readability of Web content than that supported by XML, RDF, and RDFS by providing additional vocabulary along with formal semantics. It comes in several flavors as three increasingly expressive sublanguages: OWL Lite, OWL DL, and OWL Full. By offering three flavors, OWL hopes to attract a broad following. Chapter 6 returns to detailed presentation of OWL.

Making an Inference

In Artificial Intelligence, scientists recognize that although computers are beginning to overtake the human brain in terms of sheer processing speed and storage capacity, they still cannot approach the level of human intelligence in terms of general purpose cognitive capability. At least one reason for this is that the brain does not stubbornly store and categorize every scrap of every detail that we use as the basis of thought. The brain can make connections between partially stored information, and assemble this into intelligence.

The Semantic Web will not be possible until software agents have the means to figure out some things by themselves. Fortunately, artificial intelligence gives us two tools to help make this possible. First, knowledge representation is a field that defines how we might represent, in computers, some of what is stored between our ears. Second, inference is a way of using formal logic to approximate further knowledge from what is already known. An inference engine is a software application that processes the knowledge to derive resulting conclusions.

Computational Complexity for Large Networks

Knowledge representation, search, and software agents are all severely limited by the complexity of their particular applications. This section, will explore various complexity limitations affecting the Semantic Web.

A problem is solved when it is resolved or explained. On the other hand, an unsolvable problem is one for which you have a proof that a solution cannot be reached. The theory of the difficulty of solving general classes of problems is called computational complexity.

Computational-complexity theory establishes how much of a resource (e.g., time, space, parallelism, or randomness) is required to solve certain classes of computations. Some of the most common classifications include

- P: Problems that can be solved in polynomial time. An example problem in P is the task of sorting a list of numbers. Since by systematically swapping any disordered pair the task can be accomplished within quadratic time, the problem is considered to be in P.
- NP: Problems are "nondeterministic in polynomial time." A problem is NP if a selected (or guessed) trial solution can be quickly (in polynomial time) tested to determine if it is correct.
- PSPACE: Problems that can be solved using an amount of memory that is limited as a polynomial in the input size, regardless of how much time the solution takes.
- EXPTIME: Problems that can be solved in exponential time. This class contains problems most likely to be encountered, including everything in the previous three classes.
- UNDECIDABLE: For some problems, it can be proved that there is no algorithm that always solves them, no matter how much time or space is allowed.

Whether a certain statement of First-Order Logic (FOL) is provable as a theorem is one example of the undecidable classification; and whether a polynomial equation in several variables has integer solutions is another. While humans solve problems in these domains all the time, it is not certain that arbitrary problems in these domains can always be solved. This is relevant for AI since it is important to establish the boundaries for problem solutions.

In the 1960s, computer scientists Steve Cook and Richard Karp developed the theory of NP-complete problem domains. Problems in these domains are solvable, but take an exponential amount of time in proportion to its size. Humans often solve problems in NP-complete domains in times much shorter than is guaranteed by the general algorithms, but, in general, cannot solve them quickly.

NP-complete problems are encountered frequently in AI. Alternatives to addressing them include the following:

- Using a heuristic. If the problem cannot be quickly solved deterministically in a reasonable time, a heuristic method may be used in certain cases.
- Accepting an approximate instead of an exact solution. In some cases, there is probably a fast algorithm that does not solve the problem exactly, but comes up with an acceptable approximate solution.
- Using an exponential time solution anyway. If an exact solution is necessary, an exponential time algorithm may be the best approach.
- Redefining the problem. Normally, the NP-complete problem is based on an abstraction of the real world. Revising the abstraction to eliminate unnecessary details may make the difference between a P and an NP problem.

Evaluating different knowledge-representation methodologies is highly dependent on the issue of scaling semantic applications for the Web. The complexity introduced with each methodology will have to be closely analyzed.

SWRL and Rule-Based Inference Engines

The OWL language creates statements for knowledge bases that are interpreted by inference engines utilizing powerful sets of rules. The Semantic Web Rule Language (SWRL) expresses these rules as modular stand-alone units in a declarative way (see Chapter 8). This language is XML-based and has an abstract syntax for defining various concrete sub-languages serving different purposes. The semantics of SWRL is a straightforward extension of the first-order model-theoretic semantics of OWL-DL. Since, like RDF and OWL, SWRL is based on classical two-valued logic, it cannot deal with partial information and with closed predicates. It will, however, play an important role in facilitating business rules and interactions over the Web.

In general, rules may be considered at three abstraction levels (business domain, platform independent, platform specific).

- At the business domain level, rules are statements that express parts of a business policy in a declarative manner, typically using a natural language. Generally, rules are self-contained knowledge units that contain a form of reasoning. They may specify static or dynamic integrity constraints, derivations, or reactions.
- At the platform-independent level, rules are formal statements, expressed in some formalism, which can be directly mapped to executable statements of a software platform. These business rule categories are checks/assertions for constraint rules, views for derivation rules, and triggers for reaction rules.
- At the platform-specific level, rules are statements in a specific executable language. Given the linguistic richness and the complex dynamics of business domains, it should be clear that any specific mathematical account of rules, such as classical logic Horn clauses, must be viewed as a limited descriptive theory that captures just a certain fragment of the entire conceptual space of rules.

Rule-Based Systems

Rule-based systems use symbolic representation and inference mechanisms to reach conclusions from facts and rules. Certainty factors and truth maintenance allow rules to deal with uncertainty. However, rules are cumbersome as a way of encoding relational knowledge and knowledge about objects.

The term "expert system" can be considered a particular type of knowledge-based system. Expert systems are applications that make decisions in real-life situations, which would otherwise be performed by a human expert. Expert systems can take many different forms. In general, they are programs designed to mimic human performance at specialized, constrained problem-solving tasks. Frequently, they are constructed as a collection of IF-THEN production rules combined with a reasoning engine that applies those rules, either in a forward or backward direction, to a specific problem.

A key element of an expert system is the acquisition of the body of knowledge that is contained within the system. Such information is normally extracted from human experts, and is frequently in the form of rules of thumb or heuristic information, rather than statements of absolute fact. Simply put, an expert system contains knowledge derived from an expert in some narrow domain. This knowledge is used to help individuals using the expert system to solve some problem.

The traditional definition of a computer program is usually:

$$Algorithm + data\ structures = program$$

In an expert system, this definition changes to

$$Inference\ engine + knowledge = expert\ system$$

Inference Engines

An inference engine controls overall execution of a set of rules to process the knowledge available on the Semantic Web and deduce new knowledge. It searches through a knowledge base, attempting to match patterns of facts, or knowledge, to the antecedents of rules. If a rule's precursors are satisfied, the consequence can be executed. As a result, we can relate inference to computers in the same way we would relate reason to humans.

There are two types of knowledge chaining: forward and backward. In forward chaining, the expert system is given data and chains forward to reach a conclusion. In backward chaining, the expert system is given a hypothesis and backtracks to check if it is valid.

Most knowledge-representation systems distinguish between inference "rules" and other information. In a knowledge-representation system the following properties are required: a compact syntax; a well-defined semantics; a sufficiently expressive power to represent human knowledge; an efficient, powerful, and understandable reasoning mechanism; and a usable and large knowledge base. However, it has proven difficult to achieve the third and fourth properties simultaneously.

All logical data on the Web should to be expressed directly or indirectly in terms of the Semantic Web, though different machines that use data from the Web will use different algorithms and different sets of inference rules. In some cases, these will be powerful AI systems and in others they will be simple document conversion systems. The results should be provably correct against the same basic minimalist rules.

As a result, the Semantic Web will require consistency. Applications will have to be consistent.

Semantic Web Services

Using the new generation of Web markup languages, such as OWL, an ontology for Web Services, called OWL-S could facilitate automated functions.

The following are the fundamental automatic Web Service OWL-S tasks: discovery, invocation, composition and interoperation, and execution monitoring. OWL-S will provide descriptors for the automatic execution of services (see Chapter 9).

LOGIC ON THE SEMANTIC WEB

The goal of the Semantic Web is different from most systems of logic. The Semantic Web's goal is to create a unifying system where a subset is constrained to provide the tractability and efficiency necessary for real applications. However, the Semantic Web itself does not actually define a reasoning engine, but rather follows a proof of a theorem.

This mimics an important comparison between conventional hypertext systems and the original Web design. The original Web design dropped link consistency in favor of expressive flexibility and scalability. The result allowed individual Web sites to have a strict hierarchical order or matrix structure, but it did not require it of the Web as a whole.

As a result, a Semantic Web would actually be a proof validator rather than a theorem prover. In other words, the Semantic Web cannot find answers, it cannot even check that an answer is correct, but it can follow a simple explanation that an answer is correct. The Semantic Web as a source of data would permit many kinds of automated reasoning systems to function, but it would not be a reasoning system itself.

Philosophically, the Semantic Web produces more than a set of rules for manipulation of formulas. It defines documents on the Web having significant meaning. Therefore it is not sufficient to demonstrate that one can constrain the Semantic Web to make it isomorphic to a particular algebra.

Intractability and Undecidability

The world is full of undecidable statements and intractable problems, but the Semantic Web is capable of expressing them.

Knowledge-representation systems require a trade-off between their expressive power and their computational complexity. For example, if a knowledge-representation system is a first-order predicate calculus, then the problem of deciding what an agent could logically deduce is unsolvable.

An agent may have various kinds of reasoning engines, and various amounts of connectivity, storage space, access to indexes, and processing power that will determine what it may deduce. Knowing that a certain algorithm may be a nondeterministic polynomial in the size of the entire Web may not be helpful. Practical computability may be assured by the existence of know shortcuts, such as precompiled indexes and definitive exclusive lists.

A goal of logicians has long been to find languages in which all sentences were either true or false, and provably so. This involves trying to restrict the language so as to avoid the possibility of self-contradictory statements that cannot be categorized as a true or not true.

On the Semantic Web, however, we are already operating with a mass of untrustworthy data and restrictions on usage. Clearly, a self-contradictory statement is not useful, but there is no harm in the language being powerful enough to express it. A typical response of a system that finds a self-contradictory statement, such as, "that statement is false," might be to cease to trust information from that source.

Things will get really interesting when inference systems can acquire knowledge in a goal-oriented fashion, that is, knowledge acquisition bots. We could see proof engines operating on known-consistent knowledge bases. As a result, before the Semantic Web can become a reality it faces challenges including

- Complexity: Semantics are complex, and it will not be easy to use.
- Abuse: Practices like metatag spamming, and even trademark hijacking, are subject to abuse. Semantic Web technologies will need a mostly automated system for establishing trust.
- Proprietary Technology: Because of the diversity in developers and development tools, Semantic Web technology will have to be technically open for implementation and use.

Semantic Web Capabilities and Limitations

The Semantic Web promises to make Web content machine-understandable, allowing agents and applications to access a variety of heterogeneous resources, processing and integrating the content, and producing added value for the user. The Semantic Web aims to provide an extra machine-understandable layer, which will considerably simplify programming and maintenance effort for knowledge-based Web Services.

Current technology at research centers allows many of the functionalities the Semantic Web promises such as software agents accessing and integrating content from distributed heterogeneous Web resources. However, these applications are really ad hoc solutions using wrapper technology. A wrapper is a program that accesses an existing Website and extracts the needed information. Wrappers are screen scrapers in the sense that they parse the HTML source of a page, using heuristics to localize and extract the relevant information. Not surprisingly, wrappers have high construction and maintenance costs since much testing is needed to guarantee robust extraction; and each time the Website changes, the wrapper has to be updated accordingly.

The main power of Semantic Web languages is that anyone can create one, simply by publishing RDF triplets with URIs. We have already seen that RDF Schema and OWL are very powerful languages. One of the main challenges the Semantic

Web community faces for the construction of innovative and knowledge-based Web Services is to reduce the programming effort while keeping the Web preparation task as small as possible.

CONCLUSION

This chapter presented a brief overview of Tim Berners-Lee and his role developing of the Web and Web Services. Then, we looked at the impact of adding formal logic to the Web architecture and presented the competition between open markup languages and proprietary server frameworks. This led to the evaluation of the future Web architecture: the Semantic Web. This chapter concludes with a presentation of complexity theory and rule-based inference engines followed by a discussion of what is solvable on the Web.

From this chapter, it may be concluded that the Semantic Web will have to balance the excessive power of its ontology languages with the efficient reasoning capabilities it offers in order to become successful.

EXERCISES

4-1. Estimate the number of Web sites on the Web today.

4-2. Discuss how the number of nodes on the Web creates computational complexity that limits the ability to develop logic proof systems.

Figure 4-2. Zooming into Figure 3-2 to create a blowup by a factor 2.
(http://escherdroste.math.leidenuniv.nl/).

INTERLUDE #4: TURING'S TEST

The next day, Mary was once again sitting on the library steps when John came by and joined her to resume their conversation.

"Well, after our last discussion on Turing's machine you should already have considered the next step."

John said, "By the next step, I expect you mean determining just how intelligent the Turing machine could become?"

Mary said, "Yes, and Turing was obliging in suggesting a test to evaluate just such a case. The Turing test is a behavioral approach to determining whether or not a machine is intelligent."

John said, "And can you state the conditions of the test?"

Mary said, "Of course. Originally, Alan Turing proposed that conversation was the key to judging intelligence. In his test, a judge has conversations (via teletype) with two subjects, one human, the other a machine. The conversations can be about anything, and would proceed for a set period of time (e.g., 1 h). If, at the end of this time, the judge cannot distinguish the machine from the human on the basis of the conversation, then Turing argued that we would have to say that the machine was intelligent."

John said, "There are a number of different views about the utility of the Turing test. Some researchers argue that it is the benchmark test of what John Searle calls strong AI, and as a result is crucial to defining intelligence. Other experts take the position that the Turing test is too weak to be useful in this way, because many different systems can generate correct behaviors for incorrect reasons."

Mary said, "That true. Some famous examples of this are Weizenbaum's ELIZA program and Colby's PARRY program. These "chatbot" programs were designed to converse as much like people as possible, and they did a pretty good job, as long as the test was limited in time."

John said, "The controversy around the Turning test is that it doesn't seem to be very general and it defines intelligence purely in terms of behavior. Thus the Turing test may not in itself be an adequate test of intelligence. Conversation is not the ultimate display of intelligence, and real thinking is not indicated by spitting out sentences, and that is all the computer is programmed to do."

Mary frowned, but did not respond.

John said, "The Turing test focuses too much on the behavior of conversation. Just because I am speaking to a student who speaks broken English, it does not follow that the student is not intelligent. Just because a computer program sometimes miscues and says something that makes no sense does not necessarily mean it is not intelligent. On the other hand, a person who has an extensive knowledge in a small area can seem to be very smart due to this knowledge. This doesn't necessarily imply intelligence either, since it says nothing about the person's ability to learn, handle a new situation, or to merely converse about some other subject. In the end, conversational skills are not the ultimate sign of intelligence, even where communication media are pervasive."

Mary said, "Wait a minute. Let's consider the purpose of building artificial intelligence. Are we trying to simulate human minds in order to experiment about how they work? Or are we interested solely in the end result? If we are only interested in the consequences of a program's execution, its output, then perhaps the Turing test is applicable. In this case, it doesn't matter how the program arrived at the response, but merely the fact that the output matched, to some degree, the output that would be expected from a human. The appearance of intelligence could be sustained by a program that had merely a large enough database of preprogrammed responses and a good pattern recognizer that could trigger the appropriate output."

John said, "We both need to think about this some more."

PART II

WEB ONTOLOGY AND LOGIC

Before we can achieve anything approaching artificial intelligence or 'thinking' on the Web, the next generation Web architecture must be able to support the basic elements of logic and automation.

In Part II, Web Ontology and Logic are presented: the solution of the World Wide Web Consortium (W3C) to deliver Semantic Web architecture built upon layers of open markup languages. The Semantic Web will support machine-processing capabilities that will automate Web applications and services. Berners-Lee has suggested that Web technologies would benefit from integration of the Semantic Web's meaningful content with Web Services' business logic.

For the Semantic Web to provide intelligent features and capabilities, it will have to trade off the expressive power of new logic languages against the computational complexity of processing large semantic networks. The layered language approach of the W3C seeks to implement a balanced approach toward building the Semantic Web.

Agents on the Semantic Web will perform tasks by seeking information from Web resources while communicating with other Web agents. Agents are simply pieces of software that work autonomously and proactively. In most cases, agents will simply collect and organize information by utilizing metadata, ontologies, and logic.

Chapter 5 begins our presentation of Semantic Web markup languages by introducing Resource Description Framework (RDF). Chapter 6 describes the Web Ontology Language (OWL). In Chapter 7, ontology engineering is introduced, while in Chapter 8, logic, inference, and rule systems are discussed.

Thinking on the Web: Berners-Lee, Gödel, and Turing, by H. Peter Alesso and Craig F. Smith
Copyright © 2006 John Wiley & Sons, Inc.

Chapter 9 presents the current state of development for the Semantic Web Rule Language (SWRL).

Achieving powerful reasoning with reasonable complexity is the ultimate goal. The challenge is finding the best layering of ontology, logic, and rule markup languages for the Semantic Web that will offer solutions to the most useful Web applications. These include accomplishing important tasks automatically on the Web, such as search, query, and information acquisition for collaborative Web applications and services. In Chapter 10, we present Semantic Web applications in general. Chapter 11 details Semantic Web Services and Chapter 12 offers the latest in semantic search technology.

Chapter 13 discusses semantic patterns and adoptive software that may play an important role in automation on the Web. Chapter 14 summarizes the state of semantic tools. Finally, in Chapter 15, the challenges and opportunities for the Semantic Web in the near future are summarized.

5

RESOURCE DESCRIPTION FRAMEWORK

OVERVIEW

The eXtensible Markup Language (XML) is a universal meta-language for defining markup. It provides a uniform framework for exchanging data between applications. It builds upon the original and most basic layer of the Web, Hypertext Markup Language (HTML). However, XML does not provide a mechanism to deal with the semantics (the meaning) of data.

Resource Description Framework (RDF) was developed by the World Wide Web Consortium (W3C) for Web-based metadata in order to build and extend XML. The goal of RDF is to make work easier for autonomous agents and automated services by supplying a rudimentary semantic capability.

The RDF is a format for data that uses a simple relational model that allows structured and semistructured data to be mixed, exported, and shared across different applications. It is a data model for objects and relationships between them and is constructed with an object-attribute-value triple called a statement. While XML provides interoperability within one application (e.g., producing and exchanging bank statements) using a given schema, RDF provides interoperability *across* applications (e.g., importing bank statements into a tax calculating program).

This chapter highlights some basic characteristics of HTML and XML. Then, we introduce RDF and present fundamental concepts, such as resources, properties, and statements. We define the subject, predicate, and object as the RDF triplet and illustrate it as a graph. Then, we introduce RDF Schema (RDFS) and provide illustrative examples. Finally, our conclusions about the utility of RDF and RDFS for meeting the requirements of the Semantic Web are summarized.

Thinking on the Web: Berners-Lee, Gödel, and Turing, by H. Peter Alesso and Craig F. Smith
Copyright © 2006 John Wiley & Sons, Inc.

HTML LANGUAGE

In 1990, when Tim Berners-Lee laid the foundation for the World Wide Web, he included three primary components: HTTP (Hypertext Transfer Protocol), URLs (Universal Resource Locators), and HTML (Hypertext Markup Language).

These three components represented the essential ingredients leading to the explosive growth of the World Wide Web. The original idea behind HTML was a modest one. Browsers, such as Internet Explorer or Netscape Navigator, could view information on Web pages written in HTML. The HTML program can be written to a simple text file that is recognized by a browser application and can also be called embedded script programming. As a result, it was so easy that it could be mastered by a high school student in a day.

The following listing of HTML markup tags is a HTML "Hello World" example consisting of root tags (<HTML>), head tags (<HEAD>), and body tags (<BODY>) with the displayed information wedged in between the appropriate tags:

```
<HTML>
 <HEAD>
  <TITLE>My Title</TITLE>
 </HEAD>
 <BODY>
   Hello World
 </BODY>
</HTML>
```

As the Web flourished and use of HTML became widespread, the limitations of the language began to foil continued progress. As more content moved to the Web, those creating browsers realized that this simple markup language needed more capability. In particular, Web applications, such as Web Services, required a means to explicitly manipulate data. This motivated the development of XML.

XML LANGUAGE

The HTML program is not extensible. That is, it has specifically designed tags that require universal agreement before changes can be made. Although over the years, Microsoft was able to add tags that work only in Internet Explorer, and Netscape was able to add tags that work only in Navigator, Web site developers had no way of adding their own tags. The solution was XML. Proposed in late 1996 by the W3C, it offered developers a way to identify and manipulate their own structured data.

The XML document simplified the process of defining and using metadata. The very nature of XML is that of a structured document representing the information to be exchanged, as well as the metadata encapsulating its meaning. As a result, XML provides a good representation of extensible, hierarchical, formatted information, and its required encoded metadata.

XML is not a replacement, but rather a complementary technology to HTML. While XML is already widely used across the Web today, it is still a relatively new technology. The XML is a meta language, which means it is a language used to create other languages. It can provide a basic structure and set of rules for developing other markup languages. By using XML, it is possible to create a unique markup language to model just about any kind of information.

Markup text, in general, needs to be differentiated from the rest of the document text by delimiters. Just as in HTML, the angle brackets (<>) and the names they enclose are delimiters called tags. Tags demarcate and label the parts of the document and add other information that helps define the structure. The XML document lets you name the tags anything you want, unlike HTML, which limits you to predefined tag names. You can choose element names that make sense in the context of the document. Tag names are case-sensitive, although either case may be used as long as the opening and closing tag names are consistent.

The text between the tags is the content of the document, raw information that may be the body of a message, a title, or a field of data. The markup and the content complement each other, creating an information entity with partitioned labeled data in a handy package.

In its simplest form, an XML document is comprised of one or more named elements organized into a nested hierarchy. An element consists of an opening tag, some data, and a closing tag. For any given element, the name of the opening tag must match that of the closing tag. A closing tag is identical to an opening tag except that the less-than symbol (<) is immediately followed by a forward-slash (/). Keeping this simple view, we can construct the major portions of the XML document to include the following six ingredients: (*1*) XML declaration (required), (*2*) Document Type Definition (or XML Schema), (*3*) elements (required), (*4*) attributes, (*5*) entity, and (*6*) notations.

The top of an XML document contains special information called the document prolog. At its simplest, the prolog merely says that this is an XML document and declares the version of XML being used. The XML declaration is an announcement to the XML processor that this document is marked up in XML. The declaration begins with the five-character delimiter "<?xml" followed by some number of property definitions each of which has a property name and value in quotes. The declaration ends with the two-character closing delimiter "?>."

The Document Type Definition (DTD) is used for validating the XML document. A DTD is a collection of parameters that describe a document type and includes specific information about the sequence, frequency, and hierarchy of the XML document's elements, attributes, and character data.

The beginning of an XML document starts with the prolog that can hold additional information that nails down such details as the DTD being used, declarations of special pieces of text, the text encoding, and instructions to XML processors.

An example of a well-formed XML declaration is

```
<?xml version="1.0" encoding="iso-8859-1" standalone="yes"?>
```

Following the XML declaration is a document type declaration that links to a DTD in a separate file. This is followed by a set of declarations. These parts together comprise the prolog. A simple XML "Hello World" example follows:

```
<?xml version="1.0"?>
<!DOCTYPE message [
<!ELEMENT message (#PCDATA)>
]>
 <message>
  Hello World!
 </message>
```

The text between the tags; <message>···</message>; is the Hello World text.

In addition, XML is both a powerful and essential language for Web Services. It is the open standard that allows data to be exchanged between applications and databases over the Web. As such, XML is the interoperable bridge for exchanging data between Java and Window frameworks that support today's Web Services. Yet, despite the recognition of XMLs importance today, its does not offer semantics and logic capabilities. The next step up the markup language pyramid is RDF, which begins to establish a basis for semantics on the Web.

RDF LANGUAGE

The XML tags can often add meaning to data, however, actually understanding the tags is meaningful only to humans. For example, given the following segment of XML markup tags:

```
<book>
 <title>Gödel, Escher, Bach: An Eternal Golden Braid<title>
</book>
```

A human might infer that: "The book has the title *Gödel, Escher, Bach: An Eternal Golden Braid*." This simple grammatical sentence is understood to contain three basic parts: a subject [The book], a predicate [has title], and an object [*Gödel, Escher, Bach: An Eternal Golden Braid*]. A machine, however, could not make this inference based upon the XML alone.

We could, however, prepare an eXtensible Stylesheet Language Transform (XSLT) style sheet to transform the XML markup to display the following string:

The book has the title *Gödel, Escher, Bach: An Eternal Golden Braid*.

Regardless, the computer would not take action based upon this string (e.g., checking to see related titles, prices, availability, etc.) without additional explicit programming.

For machines to do more automatically, it is necessary to go beyond the notion of the HTML display model, or XML data model, toward a "meaning" model. This is where RDF and metadata can provide new machine-processing capabilities built upon XML technology.

What is metadata? It is information about other data. Building upon XML, the W3C developed the RDF metadata standard. The goal was to add semantics defined on top of XML.

While RDF is actually built upon a very simple model and it can support very large-scale information processing. An RDF document can delineate precise relationships between vocabulary items by constructing a grammatical representation. Assertions in different RDF documents can be combined to provide far more information together than they could separately. As a result, RDF provides a powerful and flexible query structure.

RDF Triple

The RDF model is based on statements made about resources that can be anything with an associated URI (Universal Resource Identifier). The basic RDF model produces a triple, where a resource (the subject) is linked through an arc labeled with a property (the predicate) to a value (the object).

The RDF statements can be represented as

A resource[subject] has a property[predicate] with a specific value[object].

Which can be reduced to a triple:

(subject, predicate, object).

And subject, predicate, and object can be defined in terms of resources, properties, and value as:

Subject: The resource (a person, place, or thing) that the statement describes. A RDF resource can be anything in the data model (document, user, product, etc) and is uniquely identified by a URI. A URI can be a URL (Universal Resource Locator).

Predicate: The property (name, city, title, color, shape, characteristic) of the subject (person, place, or thing) and is uniquely identified by a URI.

Object: The value (Douglas R. Hofstadter, San Jose, "*Gödel, Escher, Bach: An Eternal Golden Braid*," blue, circle, strong) can be specified for the property (name, city, title, color, shape, characteristic), which describes the subject (person, place, or thing). This value can be any valid RDF data type. (RDF supports all of the XML data types.)

This simple model of the triple with URIs used by RDF to describe information has many advantages. One of the most important is that any data model can be reduced to a common storage format based on a triple. This makes RDF ideal for aggregating disparate data models because all the data from all models can be treated the same. This means that information can be combined from many sources and processed as if it came from a single source.

The RDF relationships can be between two resources or between a resource and a literal. These relationships form arcs. The RDF arc can be graphically represented where the subject is shown as an oval, the predicate as a connecting arc or line, and the object as an oval. Graphs are easy to read and the directed arc removes any possibility of confusion over what are the subject and the objects.

Let us examine a very simple statement and identify the components that comprise an RDF model. Example 5-1 considers a simple RDF statement:

EXAMPLE 5-1. Consider this sentence as an RDF Statement

"The book has the title *Gödel, Escher, Bach: An Eternal Golden Braid*."

"The book [subject] has the title [predicate] *Gödel, Escher, Bach: An Eternal Golden Braid* [object]."

This can be represented as the triple:

(The book, has the title, *Gödel, Escher, Bach: An Eternal Golden Braid*).

Figure 5-1 shows the corresponding graph for the Example 5-1 triple. It is a directed graph with labeled nodes and labeled arcs. The arc is directed from the resource (the subject) to the value (the object), and this kind of graph is recognized in the AI community as a semantic net.

We can think of the triple (x, P, y) as a logical formula $P(x, y)$ where the binary predicate P relates the object x to the object y.

Applying this to our triple:

(The book, has the title, *Gödel, Escher, Bach: An Eternal Golden Braid*)

produces a logical formula:

'has the title' (The book, *Gödel, Escher, Bach: An Eternal Golden Braid*)

where the binary predicate (P):

'has the title'

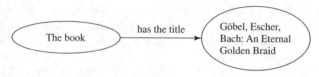

Figure 5-1. Graphical representation of the RDF statement of "The book has the title *Gödel, Escher, Bach: An Eternal Golden Braid*."

relates the object (x):

The book

to the object (y):

Gödel, Escher, Bach: An Eternal Golden Braid.

Think of a collection of interrelated RDF statements represented as a graph of interconnected nodes. The nodes are connected via various relationships. For example, let us say each node represents a person. Each person might be related to another person because they are siblings, parents, spouses, friends, or employees. Each interconnection is labeled with the relationship name. Another type of relationship is the physical properties of a node, such as the name or job of a person (see the Friend of a Friend application at the end of this chapter).

The RDF is used in this manner to describe these relationships. It does not actually include the nodes directly, but it does indirectly since the relationships point to the nodes. At any time, we could introduce a new node, such as a newborn child, and all that is needed is for us to add the appropriate relationship for the two parents.

BASIC ELEMENTS

Most of the elements of RDF concern classes, properties, and instances of classes. This section presents the language components essential to introducing these elements.

Syntax

Both RDF and RDF Schema (RDFS) use XML-based syntax.

The RDF system provides a means of describing the relationships among resources in terms of named properties and values. Since RDF and XML were developed about the same time, RDF was defined as an excellent complement to XML. Encoding RDF triples in XML makes an object portable across platforms and interoperable among applications. Because RDF data can be expressed using XML syntax, it can be passed over the Web as a document and parsed using existing XML-based software. This combination of RDF and XML enables individuals or programs to locate, retrieve, process, store, or manage the information objects that comprise a Semantic Web site.

Header

An RDF Document looks very much like all XML documents in terms of elements, tags, and namespaces. An RDF document starts with a header including the root element as an "rdf:RDF" element that also specifies a number of namespaces. It then defines properties and classes.

TABLE 5-1. RDF Document Parts

Document Parts	RDF Document
Header–XML Syntax declaration	`<?xml version="1.0"?>`
Root element tag	`<rdf:RDF`
XML namespaces for rdf and dc, as well as, the URLs where they are defined.	`xmlns:rdf=http://www.w3.org/1999/02/` `22-rdf-syntax-ns#xmlns:dc=` `"http://purl.org/dc/elements/1.1/">`
Inserting the Triple (subject, predicate, object) within the code.	`<rdf:Description rdf:about="`**SUBJECT**`">` `<dc:`**PREDICATE**`>`**"OBJECT"**`</dc:`**PREDICATE**`>` `</rdf:Description>`
End of root element indicates end of RDF document.	`</rdf:RDF>`

Table 5-1 illustrates the parts of an RDF document (header, XML syntax, root element, namespace, the RDF triple, and the end element) and its serialization as an XML document.

Namespaces

The namespace mechanism of XML is also used in RDF. However, in XML, namespaces are only used to remove ambiguities. In RDF, external namespaces are expected to be RDF documents defining resources, which are used to import RDF documents. This allows reuse of resources and enables others to add additional features for the resources producing a large distributed collection of knowledge.

To add a namespace to an RDF document, a namespace attribute can be added anywhere in the document, but is usually added to the RDF tag itself. The namespace declaration for RDF vocabularies usually points to a URI of the RDF Schema document for the vocabulary. We can add a namespace as:

```
<rdf:RDF xmlns:rdf="http://www.w3.org/1999/02/22-rdf-syntax-ns#">
```

The namespace declaration for RDF vocabularies points to the URI of the RDF Schema document for the vocabulary. Note, the prefix for the RDF Syntax is given as "rdf," the RDF Schema is given as "rdfs," and the Dublin Core schema (a special publication ontology) is given as "dc."

Description

The "rdf:about" attribute of the element "rdf:Description" is equivalent to that of an ID attribute, but is often used to suggest the object may be defined elsewhere. A set of RDF statements form a large graph relating things to other things through their properties.

The content of "rdf:Description" elements are called property elements. Descriptions may be defined within other descriptions producing nested descriptions. Further definition of ID is found through the "rdf:resource" attribute and the "rdf:type" element introduces structure to the rdf document.

While RDF is required to be well formed, it does not require XML-style validation. The RDF parsers do not use Document Type Definitions (DTDs) or XML Schema to ensure that the RDF is valid.

Data Types

Sometimes it is useful to be able to identify what kind of thing a resource is, much like how object-oriented systems use classes. The RDF system uses a type for this purpose. While there are two very general types, a resource and a literal, every resource may be given a precise type. For example, the resource "John" might be given a type of "Person." The value of the type should be another resource that would mean that more information could be associated with the type itself.

As with other properties, types can be specified with a triple:

```
<http://www.web-iq.com/people/John>,
        rdf:type, <http://xmlns.com/wordnet/1.6/Person>
```

The resource <http://xmlns.com/wordnet/1.6/Person> is used to represent a person. The URI is from WordNet, which provides resource URIs for words. The predicate is rdf:type, which is in the RDF namespace since the "type" predicate is built-in to RDF. The full name is

```
'http://www.w3.org/1999/02/22-rdf-syntax-ns#type'.
```

Also, the attribute rdf:datatype="&xsd;integer" indicates the data type defines the range as an integer. The RDF uses XML data types that includes a wide range of data types. In addition, RDF allows any externally defined data typing scheme.

Now we will use Table 5-1 and serialize Example 5-1: "The book has the title *Gödel, Escher, Bach: An Eternal Golden Braid*," as:

```
<?xml version="1.0"?>
<rdf:RDF
  xmlns:rdf=http://www.w3.org/1999/02/22-rdf-syntax-ns#
  xmlns:dc="http://purl.org/dc/elements/1.1/">
 <rdf:Description rdf:about="http://www.amazon.com/books">
  <dc:title>Gödel, Escher, Bach: An Eternal Golden Braid</dc:title>
 </rdf:Description>
</rdf:RDF>
```

Note: dc stands for Dublin Core: a well-established RDF vocabulary for publications (see http://dublincore.org/).

Vocabularies

What kind of vocabularies can be used to model business resources using the syntax of RDF? The answer is any kind of business resource. Because RDF creates domain-specific vocabularies that are then used to model resources, we can use RDF to model business-specific resources. The only limitation is the need for industry cooperation in developing an interoperable vocabulary.

We can consider RDF as a way of recording information about resources. The RDF can be serialized using XML for specific business domains using a set of elements defined within the rule of the RDF data model and constrained through RDF syntax, vocabulary, and schema. The RDF recorded in XML is a powerful tool. By using XML we have access to a great number of existing XML applications, such as parsers and APIs. However, RDF provides the same level of functionality to XML as the relational data model adds to commercial databases and RDF provides predefined data grammar that can be used for business information.

The way to start defining the vocabulary for a business is to first create domain elements and their properties within the given business scope. Defining the business elements for a new system is the same process as being defined for use within a more traditional relational database. Following the existing data-modeling techniques, first describe the major entities and their properties, then describe how these entities are related to one another. Once the elements for the vocabulary are defined, they can be compared to existing Web resource domain vocabulary for matches.

Classes and Properties

The RDF and RDF Schema (RDFS) classes and properties can be found at: **RDF W3C specifications:**
RDF Model and Syntax Specification:

http://www.w3.org/TR/1999/REC-rdf-syntax-19990222/

RDFS Specification:

http://www.w3.org/TR/2003/WD-rdf-schema-20030123/

We provide a summary of RDF and RDFS classes and properties in Tables 5-3 and 5-4 respectively after we discuss RDFS.

Collections

A collection is considered to be a finite grouping of items with a given terminator. Within RDF, a collection is defined through the use of rdf:parseType = "Collection" and through listing the collected resources within the collection block.

Reification

The RDF allows us to make statements about statements using a reification mechanism. This is particularly useful to describe belief or trust in other statements.

Example 5-2 discusses the interpretation of multiple statements in relationship to RDF statements.

EXAMPLE 5-2. Interpreting Multiple Sentences as an RDF Statement.
Let us start with five simple facts that we wish to represent as RDF triplets.

1. The name of this URI (mailto: Hofstadter@yahoo.com) is Douglas R. Hofstadter.
2. The type of this URI (mailto: Hofstadter@yahoo.com) is a person.
3. The author of this URI (mailto: Hofstadter@yahoo.com) is isbn:0465026567.
4. The id of this URI (isbn:0465026567) is a book.
5. The title of this URI (isbn:0465026567) is *Gödel, Escher, Bach: An Eternal Golden Braid.*

Alternatively,

1. URI (mailto: Hofstadter@yahoo.com) is the name Douglas R. Hofstadter.
2. This URI (mailto: Hofstadter@yahoo.com) is a type of person.
3. This URI (mailto: Hofstadter@yahoo.com) is an author of isbn:0465026567.
4. URI (isbn:0465026567) is the identity of a book.
5. URI (isbn:0465026567) has the title of *Gödel, Escher, Bach: An Eternal Golden Braid.*

We represent these five facts as RDF triplets in Table 5-2. Then, in Figure 5-2, the information in this table is illustrated as a graph.

Figure 5-2 illustrates the simple individual RDF statements as five simple directed graphs with subject, predicates, and objects.

Then in Figure 5-3, we draw a composite graph that represents all the statements in an efficient form.

TABLE 5-2. RDF Triplet Data Table

Subject	Predicate	Object
mailto:Hofstadter@yahoo.com	name	Douglas R. Hofstadter
mailto:Hofstadter@yahoo.com	type	Person
mailto:Hofstadter@yahoo.com	author-of	isbn: 0465026567
isbn:0465026567	type	book
isbn:0465026567	title	*Gödel, Escher, Bach: An Eternal Golden Braid*

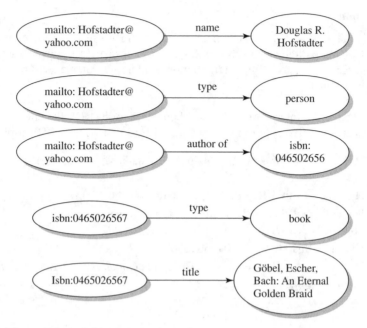

Figure 5-2. Individual graphs for each triplet statement of Example 5-2.

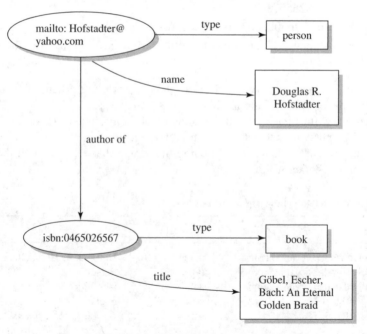

Figure 5-3. Merged RDF graph for Example 5-2.

The serialized form of the RDF document for this example can be written as:
Serialization of RDF Statement as

```
<?xml version="1.0"?>
<Class rdf:ID="book"
       xmlns:rdf="http://www.w3.org/1999/02/22-rdf-syntax-ns#"
       xmlns="uri">
<title>Gödel, Escher, Bach: An Eternal Golden Braid</title>
  ...
</Class>
```

In any RDF graph, a subgraph would be a subset of the triples contained in the graph. Each triple is its own unique RDF graph (see Fig. 5-2). The union of two or more graphs is a new graph called a merged graph (see Fig. 5-3).

RDF SCHEMA

The RDF provides a simple yet powerful model for describing information including a basic directed graph, but the semantics (meaning of the information) is described using RDFS. The purpose of RDFS is to provide an XML vocabulary that can express classes and their (subclass) relationships, as well as to define properties associated with classes.

The RDF Schemas are focused on defining taxonomies (class hierarchies) that in turn facilitate inference and search. This Schema is actually a primitive ontology language (see Chapter 6).

Classes and Properties

To describe a specific domain, we specify the "things" we want to talk about. We can talk about either individual objects (resources) or classes that define types of objects.

A class can be considered as a set of elements. Individual objects that belong to a class are instances of the class. The relationship between instances and classes in RDF is expressed by "rdf:type." An important use of classes is to restrict what can be stated in an RDF document using Schema.

When a relationship exists between two things, we can express it as a class. The subject of any property is a domain of the property. The object of the class is called the range of a property. A property can have many domains and ranges.

The three most important RDF concepts are "Resource" (rdfs:Resource), "Class" (rdfs:Class), and "Property" (rdf:Property). These are all "classes." Class is in the rdfs namespace. Property is in the rdf namespace. For example, all terms in RDF are types of resources. We just use the rdf:type property, to declare that something is a "type" of something else as following:

```
rdfs:Resource rdf:type rdfs:Class.
rdfs:Class  rdf:type  rdfs:Class.
```

```
rdf:Property rdf:type rdfs:Class.
rdf:type rdf:type rdf:Property.
```

This means that "Resource is a type of Class, Class is a type of Class, Property is a type of Class, and type is a type of Property."

For example, the rdf:ID provides a name for the class while the conjunction (AND) of two subClassOf statements is a subset of the intersection of the classes:

```
<rdfs:Class rdf:ID="Set1 AND Set 2">
    <rdfs:subClassOf rdf:resource="#Set1"/>
    <rdfs:subClassOf rdf:resource="#Set2"/>
</rdfs:Class>
```

Both RDF and RDFS Classes are presented in Table 5-3.
We have listed the RDF and RDFS properties in Table 5-4.

Class Hierarchies and Inheritance

Once classes are established, the relationship between them must be established through subclasses, superclasses, and so on.

Suppose we have the following simple related classes (e.g., ontology, see Chapter 6) for polygons that are plane figures with three or more sides:

1. all quadrilaterals are polygons
2. all polygons are shapes
3. squares are quadrilaterals

In predicate logic, we can express these simple related classes (ontology) as

TABLE 5-3. RDF and RDFS Classes

Class Name	Comment
rdfs:Resource	Class of all resources
rdfs:Literal	Class of all literals (strings)
rdfs:XMLLiteral	The class of XML literals
rdfs:Class	Class of all classes
rdf:Property	Class of all properties
rdfs:Datatype	Class of datatypes
rdf:Statement	Class of all reified RDF statements
rdf:Bag	An unordered collection
rdf:Seq	An ordered collection
rdf:Alt	A collection of alternatives
rdfs:Container	This represents the set Containers
rdfs:ContainerMembershipProperty	The container membership properties, rdf:1, rdf:2, ..., all of which are subproperties of 'member'
rdf:List	The class of RDF Lists

TABLE 5-4. RDF and RDFS Properties

Property Name	Comment
rdf:type	Related a resource to its class
rdfs:subClassOf	Indicates membership of a class
rdfs:subPropertyOf	Indicates specialization of properties
rdfs:domain	A domain class for a property type
rdfs:range	A range class for a property type
rdfs:label	Provides a human-readable version of a resource name.
rdfs:comment	Use this for descriptions.
rdfs:member	A member of a container.
rdf:first	The first item in an RDF list. Also often called the head.
rdf:rest	The rest of an RDF list after the first item, called the tail.
rdfs:seeAlso	A resource that provides information about the subject resource
rdfs:isDefinedBy	Indicates the namespace of a resource.
rdf:value	Identifies the principal value (usually a string) of a property when the property value is a structured resource.
rdf:subject	The subject of an RDF statement.
rdf:predicate	The predicate of an RDF statement.
rdf:object	The object of an RDF statement.

1. quadrilaterals(X) → polygons(X)
2. polygons(X) → shapes(X)
3. quadrilaterals (squares)

And now from this knowledge the following conclusions can be deduced:

1. polygons (squares)
2. shapes (squares)
3. quadrilateral(X) → shapes(X)

The hierarchy relationship of classes is shown in Figure 5-4 for the simple related classes (ontology) of shapes.

Consider the range restriction that organization charts can only include quadrilaterals and suppose that we want to use squares in an organization chart application. Our restriction actually prohibits squares from being used. The reason is because there is no statement specifying that squares are also a member of the polygon class. What we need is for a square to inherit the ability to use the class of polygons. This is accomplished through RDFS.

The RDFS fixes the semantics of "is a subclass of." Now the meaning can be used to process software. As a result, RDF Schema is a primitive ontology language.

Object oriented programming also use classes, inheritance, and properties, however, in RDFS, properties are defined globally and it is possible to define new properties that apply to an existing class without changing that class.

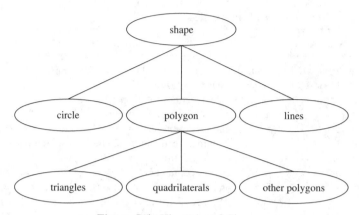

Figure 5-4. Hierarchy of Classes.

Property Hierarchies

Just as hierarchy for classes can be defined, so can properties.

RDF and RDFS Layers

Consider the RDF statement

"Nuclear Physics is taught by Professor Smith."

The schema for this contains classes and properties shown in Figure 5-5, which separates the layers of RDF from RDFS.

Let us consider the following classes: "academic staff" and "courses." If a course "c" is taught by academic staff "a" then "c" also involves "a." We can consider the class "academic staff" having subclasses: professor, associate professor, and assistant professor designated by subClassOf (see Fig. 5-5).

In addition, property hierarchies consider, "its taught by" is a subproperty of "involves" (see Fig. 5-5).

Figure 5-5 shows that the blocks are properties, ellipses in the RDFS layer represent classes, while ellipses in the RDF layer are instances. The RDFS is therefore able to express the ingredients: subClassOf, Class, Property, subPropertyOf, Resource, and so on.

Constraints on Properties

The constraints on properties are introduced through "rdfs:domain" and "rdfs:range." The property "rdfs:domain" restricts the set of *resources* that may have a given property (i.e., its domain). The "rdfs:range" property restricts the set of *values* for a given property (i.e., its range). The domain and range force subjects and objects of a property to be a certain type.

Figure 5-6 shows some relationships between modeling primitives in RDFS.

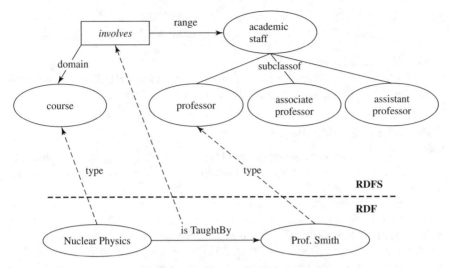

Figure 5-5. RDF and RDFS separate layers.

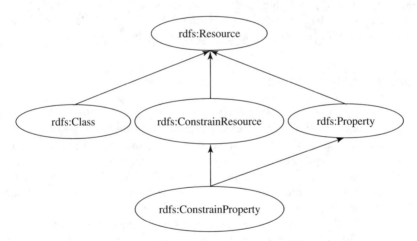

Figure 5-6. Subclass hierarchy for some RDFS primitives.

RDF and RDFS Semantics

In order to make the semantics of RDF and RDFS unambiguous and machine accessible, the formal language of predicate logic can be used to axiomatically represent RDF and RDFS. Then, automatic reasoning with RDF and RDFS becomes possible, even though a first-order logic proof system is required.

The inference system supporting the semantic of RDF and RDFS directly uses the RDF triplets. This inference system consists of rules of the form:

IF   S contains certain triples
THEN   add to S certain additional triples

(where S is an arbitrary set of triples).

The entire set of inference rules can be found in the RDF specification. A simple RDF inference engine example is presented in Chapter 8.

RDF and RDFS Limitations

The RDF uses only binary properties. This restriction is important because we often use predicates with two or more arguments. Fortunately, RDF allows such predicates to be simulated.

Another RDF limitation results from properties as special kinds of resources. The properties themselves can be used as the object in an object-attribute-value statement. This flexibility can lead to modelers becoming confused.

Also, the reification mechanism is very powerful, but may be misplaced in the RDF language, since making statements about statements is complex.

The RDF promotes the use of standardized vocabularies, standardized types (classes) and standardized properties. While RDF XML-based syntax is well suited for machine processing, it is not user-friendly.

To summarize, RDF is not an optimal modeling language. However, it is an accepted standard upon which subsequent ontology languages can build.

XQUERY: XML QUERY LANGUAGE

In order to get access to information applications we can use an XML-based query language called XQuery. XQuery provides two forms of query specific to retrieval of concepts and data. As such, an XQuery interface is tuned to support the semantics and additional expressiveness over relational data structures.

XQuery provides a common query layer to the Semantic Web "stack": enabling developers to use a familiar grammar as the mechanism for discovering logic, rules, data, and documents.

XQuery is a W3C query standard, it is a query language that uses the structure of XML intelligently and can express queries across many kinds of data, whether physically stored in XML or viewed as XML via middleware.

Friend of a Friend Application

Many communities, such as companies, professional organizations, and social groupings, have proliferated on the Internet. The Friend of a Friend (FOAF) RDF vocabulary, originated by Dan Brickley and Libby Miller, gives a basic expression for community membership. The FOAF project describes people and their basic properties, such as name, email address, and so on.

Friend of a Friend allows the expression of personal information and relationships. As a result, search engines can find people with similar interests through

FOAF. It is a useful building block for creating information systems that support online communities.

Friend of a Friend is simply an RDF vocabulary. You can create FOAF files on your Web server and share the URLs so that software can use the information. The creation of FOAF data is decentralized since it allows many to contribute independently. An example application that uses these files might be a community directory where members maintain their own records. However, the interesting parts of FOAF come into play when the data is aggregated and can then be cross-linked.

The FOAF has the potential to become an important tool in managing communities. In addition to providing simple directory services, information from FOAF is accessible in many ways.

For the naming of people, the email address (mailto:) is a convenient URI scheme to use. A naive approach might lead a developer to write down, for example: mailto: alesso@web-iq.com lives in the USA.

While a person may have multiple email addresses, the principle of using an email address to identify a person is reasonable. While we can never create a global name for a person, we could reasonably assume that all descriptions of a person that included this person's email address.

So, you might correctly write: "The person with the email address mailto: alesso@web-iq.com lives in the USA." The result is building a web of relationships that can combine in a useful way of relating specific information about unique individuals.

In order to combine information about particular individuals, the assumption is made that an email address is an unambiguous property and that only one person owns a particular mailbox. We illustrate this as an RDF document.

A sample FOAF description of the author.

```
<rdf:RDF
    xmlns:rdf="http://www.w3.org/1999/02/22-rdf-syntax-ns#"
    xmlns:foaf="http://xmlns.com/foaf/0.1/">

<foaf:Person>
    <foaf:name>H. Peter Alesso</foaf:name>
    <foaf:mbox rdf:resource="mailto:alesso@web-iq.com"/>
</foaf:Person>

</rdf:RDF>
```

Rich-Site Summary

One of the latest episodes in the personal Web publishing trend is weblogs, which often have a very personal and informal tone. One of the technologies that underpins this form of publishing is Rich-Site Summary or RSS, an XML document that contains metadata about content items on a site. Part of its appeal is the way you can connect your content to the larger Web, enabling others to find you more easily.

Many communities have proliferated on the Web, from companies to professional organizations to social groupings. The FOAF is simply an RDF vocabulary. Its typical use is akin to that of RSS: We create one or more FOAF files on your Web server and share the URLs so software can use the information inside the file. The creation of FOAF data is decentralized. An example application that uses these files might be a community directory where members maintain their own records. However, as with RSS, the interesting parts of FOAF come into play when the data is aggregated and can then be explored and cross-linked.

CONCLUSION

This chapter highlighted some characteristics of HTML and XML before we introduced Resource Description Framework (RDF) and presented fundamental concepts, such as resources, properties, and statements. The subject, predicate, and object was defined as the RDF triplet and was illustrated as a graph. Then, we introduced RDF Schema (RDFS) and provided illustrative examples.

Currently, the ontology related languages on the Web are XML (provides a surface syntax for structured documents but includes no semantic constraints), XML Schema (restricts the structure of XML documents), RDF (a data object model for objects and relations between them), and RDFS (a vocabulary description language for describing properties and classes of RDF resources).

From this chapter, you may conclude that although RDF and RDFS form building blocks for defining the Semantic Web, together they still lacked sufficient expressive power. For example, they cannot define: *(1)* the properties of properties, *(2)* necessary and sufficient conditions for class membership, or *(3)* equivalence and disjointness of classes. In addition, the only constraints expressible are domain and range constraints on properties. As a result, the semantics have remained weakly specified.

In addition, RDFS is an object-oriented type system that acts as a minimal ontology modeling language, however, for the Semantic Web we will need a more powerful ontology layer on top of RDF/RDFS. Chapter 6 presents the Web Ontology Language (OWL), which will offer greater expressive power and efficient reasoning capability.

EXERCISES

5-1. Map an RDF statement onto a relational database model.

5-2. Compare rdfd:subClassOf with the type extensions used in XML Schema.

5-3. Write an ontology about geography including cities, counties, states, and so on.

5-4. What is the relationship between "is parent of" and "is child of"?

Figure 5-7. Zooming in Figure 3-2 to create a blow up of the filled in picture by a factor 4 (http://escherdroste.math.leidenuniv.nl/).

INTERLUDE #5: THE CHINESE ROOM

Mary said, "Hi, John. I was just thinking of you while I was sorting out my new project assignment."

John said, "Isn't that curious? I was just hoping you had already figured out the easiest approach to getting it done."

Mary said, "That reminds me of a thought I wanted to share with you. I have been puzzling over these revisions to our class project and wondering how something as seemingly abstract as a language represented through a string of symbols can actually convey meaning?"

John said, "I know what you mean. I'm still puzzling over how a computer that seems able to rearrange patterns of 0's and 1's can ever acquire an understanding of their meaning. I guess it is easier to appreciate how humans can attach meaning to patterns, but when we try to visualize a machine obtaining understanding I too get lost."

Mary said, "Do you recall John R. Searle's Chinese Room problem?"

John said, "Mmmm, as I remember it, a man is in a room with a book of rules. Chinese sentences are passed under the door to him. The man uses the book of rules to process the sentences. The rules tell him to transcribe some Chinese characters onto a paper and pass on the resulting Chinese sentences as his reply to the message. Since the man is only following the book of rule he does not need to understand Chinese. Searle stated that a computer program carrying out these same rules wouldn't understand Chinese either, and therefore he concluded that no computer program can understand anything it is processing. He also argued something about biology being necessary for understanding."

Mary said, "Yes, you got it. The Chinese room represents a kind of Turing test where we can't reliably tell the difference between a machine's response and a human's response. We use the same closed room and communication scheme of the Imitation Game. But in this case, you sit in the closed room together with a book containing symbols while a symbols specialist types in expressions. When you see the input symbols you open your book, find the corresponding passage and copy out the symbols indicated as the correct reply. After several exchanges of this sort, the symbols specialist has no reason to believe that he isn't communicating with another specialist. But in fact there is only that someone in the room and you don't understand the symbols. You are merely responding mechanically and using the prepared book of correct responses. To you the strings are equally meaningless as to a computer."

John said, "So what is at issue here is that if the someone inside had no understanding of what the symbols mean, then the Turing machine can't understand the symbols the computer repeats either. And if there is no understanding then there can be no thinking. Neither you nor the machine is thinking because neither actually understands what the string of symbol means. So where is the semantics, either in the machine or the room? There is no semantics. There is only syntax of manipulated symbols."

Mary said, "It seems to me that one point of view is that an observer outside the room would say that you passed the Turing test by giving correct responses to the input symbols submitted. But another view is that while you were sitting inside the room there was no actual understanding hence no thought, but only symbol manipulation."

John said, "So what is it to understand Chinese? Understanding Chinese involves being able to translate Chinese sentences into some internal representation and to reason with the internal representation and some knowledge base. However, there is considerable thought involved in pre-packaging the dictionary book. Suppose that we had built an elaborate branching tree for a computer instead of a dictionary book. Then the computer would have answered all the input symbols correctly, but what is wrong with the tree structure is that the Turing's Test is not about the behavior it produces, but the way it produces it."

Mary said, "I believe the answer is to correctly define the "system" as consisting of the combination of the man and the book of rules; together they form a system that shows an understanding of Chinese."

John said, "That is something concrete that I can think about."

6

WEB ONTOLOGY LANGUAGE

OVERVIEW

Although eXtensible Markup Language (XML) Schema is sufficient for exchanging data between parties who have agreed to the definitions beforehand, the lack of semantics prevents machines from reliably performing this task with new XML vocabularies. In addition, the expressive power of Resource Description Framework (RDF) and RDF Schema (RDFS) is very limited. RDF is roughly limited to binary ground predicates and RDF Schema is roughly limited to a subclass hierarchy and a property hierarchy with domain and range definitions.

For machines to perform useful automatic reasoning tasks on Web documents, the language machines use must go beyond the basic semantics of XML Schema and RDF Schema. They will require a more expressive and reasoning ontology language; as a result, the World Wide Web Consortium (W3C) has defined Web Ontology Language (called OWL).

Web Ontology Language enhances RDF with more vocabulary for describing properties and classes, including relations between classes (e.g., disjointedness), cardinality (e.g., exactly one), equality, richer typing of properties, characteristics of properties (e.g., symmetry), and enumerated classes.

First, this chapter describes the requirements for OWL and its relationship with RDFS. Then OWL is introduced and each of the three OWL versions currently available: Lite, DL, and Full. Some comparisons of OWL and RDFS are made along with several illustrative examples.

Thinking on the Web: Berners-Lee, Gödel, and Turing, by H. Peter Alesso and Craig F. Smith
Copyright © 2006 John Wiley & Sons, Inc.

ONTOLOGY LANGUAGE

Ontology formally describes a list of terms and the relationships between them in order to represent an area of knowledge. The terms represent important concepts, such as classes of objects. Besides subclass relationships, ontologies may include information, such as properties, value restrictions, disjoint statements, and specifications of logical relationships between objects.

To compare conceptual information across two knowledge bases on the Web, a program must know when any two given terms are being used to mean the same thing. Ideally, the program must have a way to discover common meanings. A solution to this problem is to collect information into ontologies. Artificial Intelligence and Web researchers use the term "ontology" as a document that defines the relations among terms. While the term "taxonomy" defines classes of objects and relationships among them, a typical ontology for the Web uses a taxonomy plus a set of inference rules to produce new knowledge. On the Web, ontologies provide a shared understanding.

Ontologies are usually expressed in a logic-based language, so that accurate, consistent, and meaningful distinctions can be made among the classes, properties, and relations. Some ontology tools can perform automated reasoning using the ontologies, and thus provide advanced services to intelligent applications, such as conceptual (semantic) search and retrieval, software agents, speech understanding, knowledge management, intelligent databases, and e-commerce.

OWL was developed in 2003, when the W3C began final unification of the disparate international ontology efforts into a standardized ontology. Web Ontology Language is designed to express a wide variety of knowledge, as well as provide for an efficient means to reason with it in order to express the most important kinds of knowledge. Using an ontology with a rule-based system, we can reach logic inferences about Web information.

OWL can be used to describe the classes and relations between classes that are inherent in Web documents and applications. It is able to formalize a domain by defining classes and properties of those classes, define individuals and assert properties about them, and reason about these classes through semantics and rules.

A set of XML statements by itself does not allow us to reach a conclusion about any other XML statements. To employ XML to generate new data, we need knowledge embedded in some proprietary procedural code that exists as a server page on a remote server. However, a set of OWL statements by itself can allow us to reach a conclusion about another OWL statement.

OWL ontology documents are designed to be modular and independent. They can be combined dynamically to provide additional meaning if required. As an example, if there is additional need to include information about a shipping concept in a manufacturing system, the application can add use of the shipping ontology dynamically.

Web Ontology Language ontology documents have a logical consistency to them. They provide machine-based systems with the ability to interpret the declared relationships within them. More importantly, they also allow mathematical techniques to be applied that can interpret and calculate the relationships that are implied within the logical formulations. These inferences make the use of OWL ontologies tractable and realistic for organizations, drastically reducing the amount of information that has to be modeled, encoded, or worked around by systems engineers and integrators. Being able to standardize the definition of real-world concepts becomes very powerful as we investigate knowledge that spans across multiple domains.

ONTOLOGY LANGUAGE REQUIREMENTS

An ontology language permits the development of explicit, formal conceptualizations of models. The main requirements of an onotology language are a well-defined syntax, a formal semantics, convenience of expression, an efficient reasoning support system, and sufficient expressive power.

A necessary condition for machine-processing is a well-define syntax. As a result, OWL has been built upon RDF and RDFS and has the same XML-based syntax.

A formal semantics precisely describes the meaning of knowledge and allows users to reason about knowledge. Semantics is a prerequisite for reasoning support that allows consistency checks, checks for unintended relationships, and automatic classification of instances in classes.

A formal semantics and reasoning support can be provided through mapping an onotology language to a known logical formalism. The OWL is partially mapped on description logic (see Chapter 2), which is a subset of predicate logic for which efficient reasoning support is possible.

Limitation of Expressive Power of RDF Schema

Both RDF and RDF Schema allow some ontology knowledge representation. The main modeling primitives of RDF–RDFS are concerned with the organization of vocabularies in typed hierarchies. However, some of the missing necessary features are local scope of properties, disjointness of classes, Boolean combinations of classes, cardinality of restrictions, and special characteristics of properties.

Therefore, an ontology language that is richer than RDF Schema with respect to these additional features is needed. In designing this language, the trade-off is between expressive power and efficient reasoning support. The richer the language the more inefficient the reasoning support becomes. Therefore, compromises must be reached between a language that can support efficient reasoners while being sufficiently expressive to incorporate classes of ontology and knowledge.

COMPATIBILITY OF OWL AND RDF/RDFS

The layered architecture of the Semantic Web would suggest that one way to develop the necessary ontology language is to extend RDF Schema by using the RDF meaning of classes and properties (`rdfs:classes`, etc.) and adding primitives to support richer expressiveness. However, simply extending RDF Schema would fail to achieve the best combination of expressive power and efficient reasoning.

The W3C has defined OWL to include three different sublanguages (OWL Full, OWL DL, OWL Lite) in order to offer different balances of expressive power and efficient reasoning.

OWL Full

The entire language is called OWL Full and it uses all the primitives and allows their combination with RDF and RDFS. The OWL Full supports maximum expressiveness and the syntactic freedom of RDF, but has no computational guarantees. For example, in OWL Full, a class can be treated simultaneously as a collection of individuals and as an individual in its own right. It is intended to be used in situations where very high expressiveness is more important than being able to guarantee the decidability or computational completeness of the language (see Chapter 2). Therefore it may be impossible to perform automated reasoning on OWL Full ontologies.

The advantage of OWL Full is that it is fully compatible with RDF syntax and semantics. Any legal RDF document is also a legal OWL Full document. Any valid RDF–RDFS conclusion is also a valid OWL Full conclusion. The disadvantage of OWL Full is that the language is undecidable, and therefore cannot provide complete (or efficient) reasoning support.

OWL DL

Web Ontology Language DL (Descriptive Logic) is a sublanguage of OWL Full that restricts how the constructors from OWL and RDF can be used. This ensures that the language is related to description logic. Description Logics are a decidable fragment of First-Order Logic (FOL) (see Chapter 2), and are therefore amenable to automated reasoning.

The OWL DL supports strong expressiveness while retaining computational completeness and decidability. It is therefore possible to automatically compute the classification hierarchy and check for inconsistencies in an ontology that conforms to OWL DL.

The advantage of this sublanguage is efficient reasoning support. The disadvantage is the loss of full compatibility with RDF. However, every legal OWL DL document is a legal RDF document.

OWL Lite

Further restricting OWL DL produces a subset of the language called OWL Lite, which excludes enumerated classes, disjointness statements, and arbitrary

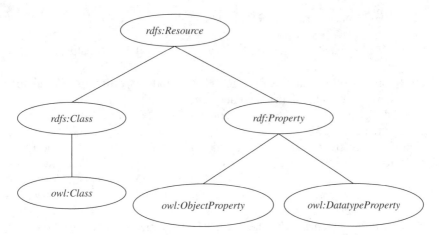

Figure 6-1. The OWL and RDF–RDFS subclass relationships.

cardinality. The OWL Lite supports a classification hierarchy and simple constraints. It is simpler for tool support and provides a quick migration path for taxonomies. While this language is easier to comprehend it is less expressive. The choice between OWL Lite and OWL DL depends on the extent of requirements for expressive constructs. All sublanguages of OWL use RDF for their syntax and instances are declared as in RDF (see Fig. 6-1).

The layered architecture of the Semantic Web promotes the downward compatibility and reuse of software. It is only achieved with OWL Full, but at the expense of computational tractability.

THE OWL LANGUAGE

A key problem in achieving interoperability over the Web is recognizing when two pieces of data referring to the same thing, even though different terminology is being used. OWL may be used to bridge this "terminology gap."

Specifically, ontology includes four concepts that form the basis of an OWL document: (*1*) classes, (*2*) relationships between classes, (*3*) properties of classes, and (*4*) constraints on relationships between the classes and properties of classes.

As a result, an OWL document identifies:

- Class hierarchy: Defines class–subclass relationships.
- Synonym: Identifies equivalent classes and equivalent properties.
- Class association: Maps one or more classes to one or more classes, through the use of a property (i.e., domain/range).
- Property metadata: Contains metadata for properties.
- Class definition: Specifies the composition of classes.

The W3C Specification for OWL

The OWL Syntax Specification http://www.w3.org/TR/owl-features/

Web Ontology Language defines the classes and properties, as well as their relationship to each other in the document, consequently, they are extremely similar to RDF Schema (see Fig. 6-1). For example, an `owl:Class` element categorizes elements that are classes.

The OWL reference document provides a formal specification of the OWL. Unlike RDF, the OWL vocabulary is quite large. Like RDF, OWL makes use of elements from RDFS. However, OWL has several concepts unique to it, such as Boolean combination of class expressions and property restrictions, which add a layer of reasoning to applications. Both the RDFS and OWL are compatible, which is why there are RDFS elements within the OWL element set.

BASIC ELEMENTS

Most of the elements of an OWL ontology concern classes, properties, instances of classes, and relationships between these instances. This section presents the language components essential to introducing these elements.

Syntax

The OWL builds on RDF and RDFS and uses RDFs XML-based syntax. However, because RDF syntax is not very readable, other syntactic forms for OWL have also been proposed: an XML-base syntax that does not follow RDF, an abstract syntax, and a graphical syntax based upon UML (Universal Modeling Language).

Header

An OWL document contains an OWL ontology and is an RDF document with elements, tags, and namespaces. An OWL document starts with a header that identifies the root element as an `rdf:RDF` element, which also specifies a number of namespaces. Then the document defines properties and classes as shown in Table 6-1.

OWL Namespace and Ontology Elements

After the OWL header, the document includes the definitions for classes and properties of the ontology. The OWL classes define entities through properties.

An OWL ontology begins with assertions grouped under the `owl:Ontology` element. This section could also include import statements. The element

TABLE 6-1. OWL Document Parts

Document Parts	OWL Document
Header	
XML Syntax	`<?xml version="1.0" encoding="UTF-8"?>`
Root element	`<rdf:RDF`
Namespace	`xmlns:iq = "http://www.web-iq.com">`
	`xmlns:owl = "http://www.w3.org/2002/07/owl#"`
	`xmlns:rdf = "http://www.w3.org/1999/02/22-rdf-syntax-ns#"`
	`xmlns:rdfs = "http://www.w3.org/1999/02/22-rdf-schema#"`
	`xmlns:dc = "http://purl.org/dc/elements/1.1/"`
	`xmlns:xsd = "http://www.w3.org/2000/1/XMLSchema#">`
OWL properties	`<owl:Ontology rdf:about = "http://www.amazon.com">`
and classes	`<owl:versionInfo>`
	`$ID: Overview.html`
	`</owl:versionInfo>`
	`<dc:creator> Douglas R. Hofstadter </dc:creator>`
	`<dc:title> Gödel, Escher, Bach: An Eternal Golden Braid`
	`</dc:title>`
End of OWL	`</owl:Ontology>`
End of RDF	`</rdf:RDF>`

`owl:imports` can be used to list other ontologies whose content are part of the current ontology. An import section includes an `rdf:resource` attribute that identifies a separate RDF resource providing definitions used by the ontology. This may include the schema for the ontology.

Dublin Core (dc) elements are included in the header to provide title, creator, and other information since the ontology is a published resource. The dc was designed to document metadata about published resources.

Simple Classes and Individuals

Many uses of an ontology will depend on the ability to reason about individuals. In order to do this we need to have a mechanism to describe the classes that individuals belong to and the properties that they inherit by virtue of class membership. We can always assert specific properties about individuals, but much of the power of ontologies comes from class-based reasoning.

Sometimes we want to emphasize the distinction between a class as an object and a class as a set containing elements. We call the set of individuals that are members of a class the extension of the class.

The most basic concept corresponds to classes that are the roots of a taxonomic tree. Every individual in the OWL world is a member of the class `owl:Thing`. Thus each user defined class is implicitly a subclass of `owl:Thing`. Domain specific root classes are defined by simply declaring a named class. The OWL also defines the empty class, `owl:Nothing`.

The OWL classes are interpreted as sets that contain individuals. They are described using formal (mathematical) descriptions that state precisely the requirements for membership of the class. For example, the class Dog would contain all the individuals that are dogs in our domain of interest. Classes may be organized into a superclass–subclass hierarchy.

For example, consider the classes Animal and Dog: Dog might be a subclass of Animal (so Animal is the superclass of Dog). This says that, "All dogs are animals," "All members of the class Dog are members of the class Animal," "Being a Dog implies that you're an Animal," and "Dog is subsumed by Animal." One of the key features of OWL DL is that these superclass–subclass relationships can be computed automatically by a reasoner.

Examples of the OWL vocabularies include (*1*) subClassOf: This OWL element is used to assert that one class of items is a subset of another class of items. Example: Dog is a subClassOf Animal, and (*2*) equivalentProperty: This OWL element is used to assert that one property is equivalent to another. Example: Quardruped is an equivalentProperty to "four-legged."

Class Elements

Classes are defined using an owl:Class element. An example of an OWL class "computer" is defined with a subclass "laptop" as

```
<owl:Class rdf:ID="Computer">
   <rdfs:subClassOf rdf:resource="#laptop"/>
</owl:Class>
```

We can also specify that the class is disjoint using owl:disjointWith elements, These elements are included in the definition or by referring to the ID using rdf:about which is an inherited mechanism from RDF.

Equivalence of classes is defined with owl:equivelentClass.

Property

A property in RDF provides information about the entity it is describing. Property characteristics increase our ability to understand the inferred information within the data.

The RDF Schema provides three ways to characterize a property: (*1*) range: Used to indicate the possible values for a property; (*2*) domain: Used to associate a property with a class; and (*3*) subPropertyOf: Used to specialize a property.

The OWL documents can use rdfs:range, rdfs:domain, and rdfs:subPropertyOf as well. An OWL property is very similar to an RDFS property. They both share the same use of rdfs:domain and rdfs:range, but OWL adds some constraints.

Properties let us assert general facts about the members of classes and specific facts about individuals. A property is a binary relation. There are two kinds of

OWL property: object properties that relate object to other objects and data type properties that relate objects to datatype values.

When we define a property there are a number of ways to restrict the relation. The domain and range can be specified. The property can be defined to be a specialization (subproperty) of an existing property

Note that the use of range and domain information in OWL is different from type information in a programming language. Among other things, types are used to check consistency in a programming language. In OWL, a range may be used to infer a type.

Properties and Datatypes

Properties are distinguished according to whether they relate individuals to individuals (object properties) or individuals to datatypes (datatype properties). Datatype properties may range over strings or they may make use of simple types defined in accordance with XML Schema datatypes.

The OWL uses some of the many built-in XML Schema datatypes. References to these datatypes are by means of the URI reference for the datatype, http://www.w3.org/2001/XMLSchema.

Property Restrictions

In general, an `owl:Restriction` element contains an `owl:onProperty` element and one or more restriction declarations. One restriction could be the kind sof values the property can take, such as `owl:allValuesFrom`.

Boolean Combinations

Boolean combinations, such as union, intersection, and complement of classes are power elements. They can be nested arbitrarily.

Instances

Instances of classes are declared just as in RDF:

```
<rdf:Description rdf:ID="123456">
 <rdf:type rdf:resource="computer"/>
</rdf:Description>
```

OWL Lite Specific Property Examples

In OWL Lite it is possible to specify property characteristics, which provides a powerful mechanism for enhanced reasoning about a property. The following special identifiers can be used to provide information concerning properties and their values:

- `inverseOf`: One property may be stated to be the inverse of another property.
- `TransitiveProperty`: Properties may be stated to be transitive.
- `SymmetricProperty`: Properties may be stated to be symmetric.
- `FunctionalProperty`: Properties may be stated to have a unique value.
- `InverseFunctionalProperty`: Properties may be stated to be inverse functional.

In addition to designating property characteristics, it is possible to further constrain the range of a property in specific contexts in a variety of ways. The OWL Lite allows restrictions to be placed on how properties can be used by instances of a class. The following two restrictions limit which values can be used while the cardinality restrictions limit how many values can be used.

- `allValuesFrom`: The restriction `allValuesFrom` is stated on a property with respect to a class.
- `someValuesFrom`: The restriction `someValuesFrom` is stated on a property with respect to a class. A particular class may have a restriction on a property that at least one value for that property is of a certain type.
- `minCardinality`: Cardinality is stated on a property with respect to a particular class. If a `minCardinality` of 1 is stated on a property with respect to a class, then any instance of that class will be related to at least one individual by that property. This restriction is another way of saying that the property is required to have a value for all instances of the class.
- `maxCardinality`: Cardinality is stated on a property with respect to a particular class. If a `maxCardinality` of 1 is stated on a property with respect to a class, then any instance of that class will be related to at most one

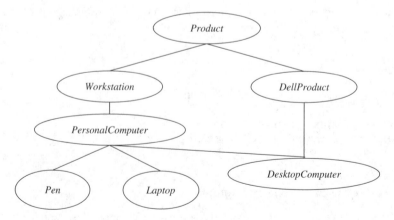

Figure 6-2. Classes and subclasses of the computer ontology.

individual by that property. A `maxCardinality` 1 restriction is sometimes called a functional or unique property.

- `cardinality`: Cardinality is provided as a convenience when it is useful to state that a property on a class has both `minCardinality` 0 and `maxCardinality` 0 or both `minCardinality` 1 and `maxCardinality` 1.

- `intersectionOf`: OWL Lite allows intersections of named classes and restrictions.

OWL EXAMPLE: COMPUTE ONTOLOGY

This example presents several OWL features for a computer ontology.

The classes and subclasses are shown in Figure 6-2. The serialization for the computer ontology is

```
<[DOCTYPE owl [
 <!ENTITY xsd "http://www.w3.org/2001/XMLSchema#">
]>

<rdf:RDF
 xmlns:rdf="http://www.w3.org/1999/02/22-rdf-syntax-ns#"
 xmlns:rdfs="http://www.w3.org/200/01/rdf-schema#"
 xmlns:xsd="http://www.w3.org/2001/XMLSchema#"
 xmlns:owl="http://www.w3.org/2002/07/owl#"
 xmlns="http://www.web-iq.com/computer.owl#">

<owl:Ontology rdf:about="">
<owl:versionInfo>
Example
</owl:versionInfo>
</owl:Ontology>

<owl:Class rdf:ID="Product">
</owl:Class>

<owl:Class rdf:ID="Workstation">
<rdfs:label>Device</rdfs:label>
<rdfs:subClassOf rdf:resource="#product"/>
</owl:Class>

<owl:Class rdf:ID="DellProducts">
<rdfs:label>Dell Devices</rdfs:label>
<owl:intersectionOf rdf:parseType="Collection">
<owl:Class rdf:about "#product"/>
<owl:Restriction>
<owl:onProperty rdf:resource="#manufactured_by"/>
<owl:hasValue rdf:datatype="&xsd;string">
DELL
```

```
</owl:hasValue>
</owl:Restriction>
</owl:Intersection>
</owl:Class>

<owl:Class rdf:ID="PersonalComputer">
 <rdfs:subClassOf rdf:resource="#workstation"/>
</owl:Class>

<owl:Class rdf:ID="Laptop">
 <rdfs:subClassOf rdf:resource="#personalcomputer"/>
</owl:Class>

<owl:Class rdf:ID="DesktopComputer">
 <rdfs:subClassOf rdf:resource="#personalcomputer"/>
 <rdfs:subClassOf rdf:resource="#dellproduct"/>
</owl:Class>

<owl:Class rdf:ID="Pen">
 <rdfs:subClassOf rdf:resource="#personalcomputer"/>
</owl:Class>

<owl:DatatypeProperty rdf:ID= "manufactured_by">
 <rdf:domain rdf:resource= "#product"/>
 <rdf:range rdf:resource ="&xsd:string"/>
</owl:DatatypeProperty>

<owl:DatatypeProperty rdf:ID= "price">
 <rdf:domain rdf:resource= "#product"/>
 <rdf:range rdf:resource ="&xsd:string"/>
</owl:DatatypeProperty>

</rdf:RDF>
```

This onotology demonstrates siblings in a hierarchy may not be disjoint.

ONTOLOGY EXAMPLE: BIRTHPLACE

In this example, asking the question: What is the birthplace of George Washington? helps to illustrate several OWL facilities.

Suppose we search the Web and find three documents that provide information about George Washington's birthplace. The first document states that George Washington was born in Virginia, the second document said he was born in the Mother State, while the third document stated that George Washington was born in the Old Dominion State. Historically, these are all referring to the same location, but how could OWL help equate their meaning on the Web?

Consider the RDF, which defines a person, ontology, and birthplace.

What is the birthplace of George Washington?

RDF Statements:

```
<Person rdf:about="http://www.person.org# GeorgeWashington ">
  <birthplace rdf:about="http://www.states.org#Virginia"/>
</Person>
<Person rdf:about="http://www.person.org# GeorgeWashington ">
  <birthplace rdf:resource="http://www.history.org# Mother State "/>
</Person>
<Person rdf:about="http://www.person.org# GeorgeWashington ">
  <birthplace rdf:resource="http://www.tourism.org# Old Dominion
        State"/>
</Person>
```

Figure 6-3, represents the OWL Ontology showing that the person OWL ontology indicates a Person with only one birthplace location.

Figure 6-3 specifies that a subject Resource has exactly one value. The OWL properties that relate a resource to exactly one other resource are said to have a cardinality = 1. Therefore this example requires: "A person has exactly one birthplace location."

As a result, applying the person OWL ontology results in the interpretation of the rules that makes the following inference:

Inference: Virginia, Mother State, and Old Dominion State, are actually the same location.

This example demonstrates that:

An OWL instance document can be enhanced with an OWL property to indicate that it is the same as another instance.

OWL provides the capability to construct taxonomies (class hierarchies). Such taxonomies can be used to dynamically understand how entities in an RDF instance relate to other entities.

OWL provides the capability to specify that a subject can have only one value.

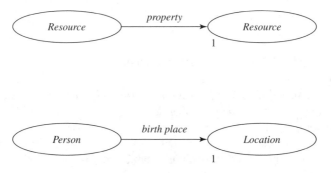

Figure 6-3. Birthplace ontology.

OWL facilitates a dynamic understanding of the semantics of data.

APPLYING OWL

This section identifies several OWL applications: Web portal, multimedia semantics, and corporate sites.

Web portals can define an ontology for the community to allow more intelligent syndication. The ontology can provide a terminology for describing content and terms about other terms. These definitions allow inferences that allow users to obtain search results that are impossible to obtain from conventional retrieval systems.

The OWL also can be used to provide semantic annotations for collections of images, audio and video. Multimedia ontologies can be of two types: media-specific or content-specific. Media-specific ontologies could have taxonomies of different media types and describe properties of different media. For example, video may include properties to identify the length of the clip and scene breaks. Content-specific ontologies could describe the subject of the resource, such as the setting or participants. Since such ontologies are not specific to the media, they could be reused by other documents that deal with the same domain.

Company Web pages often contain press releases, product offerings, corporate procedures, product comparisons, white papers, and process descriptions. Ontologies can be used to index these documents and provide a better means of retrieval. Also, a typical problem is that they may not share terminology with the authors of the desired content. For such problems, it would be useful for each class of user to have different ontologies of terms, but have each ontology interrelated so translations can be performed automatically.

There are >8 billion pages on the Web, and the potential application of the Semantic Web to embedded devices and agents indicates that even larger amounts of information eventually must be handled. The OWL language should support reasoning systems that scale well. However, the language should also be as expressive as possible, so that users can state the kinds of knowledge important to their applications.

OWL CAPABILITIES AND LIMITATIONS

The OWL language offers the following features: less chance of misinterpretation, understanding each other's data's semantics, and OWL uses existing XML syntax to express semantics.

There are many reasons for keeping the OWL semantic information separate from the application. The OWL document can be extensible, reusable, and avoids misinterpretation.

Some OWL applications have encountered problems attaching semantics on a per-application basis or with burying semantic definitions within each application.

This can lead to duplicate effort since each application must express the semantics and variability of its own interpretation.

Additional OWL problems include no ad hoc discovery and exploitation, thus an application may not be able to effectively process new data when it is encountered. This can result in a brittle application. A better approach would be to provide semantic definitions for applications and express them in a standard vocabulary.

CONCLUSION

This chapter presented an introduction to the Web Ontology Language and each of the three OWL versions currently available: Lite, DL, and Full. Some comparisons of OWL and RDFS were made and several illustrative examples are included. Finally, the basis of using this markup language for supporting the development of the Semantic Web was discussed.

From this chapter, we may conclude: OWL is the W3C standard for Web ontologies and provides the semantics of knowledge that can be processed in a machine-accessible way. The OWL builds on RDF and RDF Schema. Formal semantics and reasoning support for OWL is based on predicate logic and descriptive logics. The OWL is offered in three flavors to allow developers to evaluate trade-offs between expressive power and efficient reasoning. For example, OWL Full has a very high expressiveness, but is unable to guarantee the decidability or computational completeness of the language. Therefore it may be impossible to perform automated reasoning on OWL Full ontologies. While OWL is sufficiently rich to be applied, extensions are being developed for further features of logic and rules. The OWL-Services is needed for automatic Web Services.

EXERCISES

6-1. State how to identify two classes as disjoint.

6-2. Consider a graph with nodes and edges. Let an edge e from node a to node b be edge(a,b). Define a binary predicate path that is true for nodes c and d, if and only if, there is a path c to d in the graph.

6-3. Determine which constructs of RDFS and OWL can be expressed with monotonic rules.

Figure 6-4. Zooming in Figure 3-2 to create a blow up by a factor 8. (http://escherdroste.math.leidenuniv.nl/).

INTERLUDE #6: MACHINES AND BRAINS

John and Mary were walking across campus toward their afternoon class when Mary felt compelled to renew their ongoing debate over machine intelligence.

Mary said, "The deeper problem we should be addressing is whether the performance of machine processing is similar to how a human brain thinks."

John said, "I still don't see how writing and erasing 0s and 1s on a tape has anything to do with thinking. How can you believe that a symbol writing machine bears a resemblance to the thought processes of the human brain? Brains are not machines."

Mary said, "Well, before I disagree with you, let me review some basic features of the physical makeup of the brain. I think you'll see then how its structure is captured in the structure of a computing machine. The human brain is composed of a very large number of neurons; 10 billion or more. These neurons are connected to each other through a dense network of axons and dendrites which behave just like "wires." The resulting brain structure resembles something like a giant telephone switching network."

John looked reproachfully at Mary and replied, "You can't be serious—my brain is a giant telephone switching network?"

Mary said, "Mine too. The neuron is a kind of switch that can be either ON or OFF, which is determined by the signal it receives from other connected neurons. The neurons fire like a trigger being pulled. The only difference is that each neuron may have many signals from other neurons coming into it. But an individual neuron has only one output going to one other neuron. Some of the input channels are excitatory, which is like putting pressure on the trigger while other inputs are inhibitory reducing trigger tension. If the net sum of all the positive and negative inputs exceeds a certain threshold then the neuron fires a pulse into its output channel. Otherwise it remains OFF. Many neurophysiologists believe that the patterns created in the brain by these neuron firings form an important part of the human thought process."

John said, "Oh, I see! You are forming an analogy between the computer machine and a brain on the basis of electric impulses. They both involve the storage of large numbers of elements: 0s and 1s states for the compute and ON and OFF states for the brain."

Mary said, "You've got it. Moreover, both the computer and the brain process these data according to patterns."

John said, "Patterns? That sounds like you are returning to your chess playing analogy for pattern recognition."

Mary said, "It *is* relevant. The brain stores its data in the form of patterns created by firing neurons. Each pattern is just a listing of the firing of its associated neurons in ON or OFF states. These patterns are associated with thought states in ways no one understands. The computer on the other hand stores data in sequences of 0s and 1s, which is equivalent to the ON and OFF states. In both cases there is a way to modify what is stored in an individual memory location. This produces output by either causing different neurons to fire in the brain or by executing an instruction in a machine. The question you might ask, however, is does the technological limitations of the machine prevent it from achieving the same degree of pattern recognition as in the brain."

John said "Perhaps. But in addition, I am concerned about what the brain components do. That means we need to understand the cortex where higher human cognition takes place."

Mary said, "Of course and the neocortex, as well. In 1943, Warren McCulloch; a neurophysiologist, and his student Walter Pitts published an article about how the operation of groups neurons connected with other neurons might be duplicating purely logical elements. The model regards a neuron as being activated and then firing another neuron in the same way a logical sequence can imply the truth or falsity of some other proposition. We can picture the analogy between neurons and logic in engineering terms as signals that either pass or fail to pass through electrical circuits. It's only a small step from this to the elements of a computer."

John said, "Surely you are not implying that data stored in machines or even the ON–OFF neuron patterns in brains can be called "thoughts."

Mary said, "There was a famous Dartmouth Conference in 1956 that split the AI community into two camps. The "Top-down" group held that cognition was a high level phenomenon that could be "skimmed off" the top so as to create a similar intelligence in a machine, but it required the right silicon surrogates for the symbols of the brain. The competing "Bottom-Up" group held that the actual structure of the human brain is important for producing cognitive activity. Therefore one needed to mimic this structure in hardware for AI. The "Top-down" group gained some advantage in the 1970s."

John said, "Well, we can't observe mental phenomena directly, so we can't actually resolve a theory of thinking. The only resolution we can make comes from a conceptual investigation of how we use word like "apple" and "love." These words only gain meaning from a life experience and not through stored states."

Mary said, "I'll have to think about this experience."

7

ONTOLOGY ENGINEERING

OVERVIEW

The field of Philosophy originally defined the word ontology to represent the concept of existence. It is the theory of objects and their interrelationships. As used in information science, the term ontology frequently refers to a hierarchical data structure containing the relevant objects and their relationships, as well as the rules within that domain.

In the field of Artificial Intelligence (AI), ontology applications have been developed for knowledge management, natural language processing, e-Commerce, education, and new emerging technologies such as the Semantic Web. The Semantic Web requires the construction of ontologies for its various representation languages, query languages, and inference technologies.

This chapter presents the basic methodology for designing and building ontologies. In addition, ontology matching and mapping, which are essential to knowledge representations, are described.

ONTOLOGY ENGINEERING

Ontology is the formal specification of terms within a domain and their relationships. It defines a common vocabulary for the sharing of information that can be used by both humans and computers. Ontologies can be in the form of lists of words; taxonomies, database schema, frame languages and logics. The main difference between these forms is their expressive power. Ontology together with a set of concept instances constitutes a knowledge base.

If a program is designed to compare conceptual information across two knowledge bases on the Web, it must know when any two terms are being used to mean the same thing. Ideally, the program must have a way to discover common meanings for whatever knowledge bases it encounters. Typically, an ontology on the Web will combine a taxonomy with a set of inference rules.

Taxonomy is defined as a set of classes of objects and their relationships. These classes, subclasses, and their relationships are important tools for manipulating information. Their relations are described by assigning properties to classes and allowing subclasses to inherit these properties. An ontology then is a taxonomy plus inference.

Ontology inference rules allow manipulation of conceptual information. The most important ontology relationship is the subsumption link (e.g., subtype and supertype link).

When a network of concepts is represented by a tree, it rigorously defines the taxonomy. While ontology can sometimes be modularized as a set of trees, some advocate that all ontology should be taxonomic, but others favor a lattice structure. For example, ontology rigorously defines a Thesaurus structure when it uses the related-to link in addition to the subsumption link.

Ontology engineering seeks a common vocabulary through a data collection process that includes discussions, interviews, document analysis, and questionnaires. Existing ontologies on a subject are discovered, assessed, and reused as much as possible to avoid "reinventing the wheel." As part of this process, ontologies are designed as living objects with a maintenance cycle.

Ontology Applications

The simplest ontology consists of a simple taxonomy with a single relation. Categories of ontology applications can be grouped as

- Neutral Authoring: The author of an object in a single language translates into a different format for use in alternative applications.
- Ontology as Specification: Ontology of a given domain is created and used as a basis for specification and development of some software. This approach allows documentation, maintenance, reliability and knowledge (re)use.
- Common Access to Information: Information in an inaccessible format becomes intelligible by providing a shared understanding of the terms, or by mapping between sets of terms.
- Ontology-Based Search: Ontology is used for searching an information repository.

CONSTRUCTING ONTOLOGY

Ontology permits sharing common understanding of the structure of information among people and software agents. Since there is no unique model for a particular domain, ontology development is best achieved through an iterative process.

Objects and their relationships reflect the basic concepts within an ontology. An iterative approach for building ontologies starts with a rough first pass through the main processes as follows:

- First, set the scope. The development of an ontology should start by defining its domain and scope. Several basic questions are helpful at this point: What will the ontology cover? How will the ontology be used? What questions does the ontology answer? Who will use and maintain the ontology? The answers may change as we proceed, but they help limit the scope of the model.

- Second, evaluate reuse. Check to see if existing ontologies can be refined and extended. Reusing existing ontologies will help to interact with other applications and vocabularies. Many knowledge-representation systems can import and export ontologies directly for reuse.

- Third, enumerate terms. It is useful to list all terms, what they address, and what properties they have. Initially, a comprehensive list of terms is useful without regard for overlapping concepts. Nouns can form the basis for class names, and verbs can form the basis for property names.

- Fourth, define the taxonomy. There are several possible approaches in developing a class hierarchy: a top-down process starts by defining general concepts in the domain. A bottom-up development process starts with the definition of the most specific classes, the levels of the hierarchy, with subsequent grouping of these classes into more general concepts. A combination development process combines the top-down and bottom-up approaches: define the more salient concepts first and then generalize them appropriately.

- Fifth, define properties. The classes alone will not provide enough information to answer questions. We must also describe the internal structure of concepts. While attaching properties to classes one should establish the domain and range. Property constraints (facets) describe or limit the set of possible values for a frame slot.

- Sixth, define facets. Up to this point the ontology resembles a RDFS without any primitives from OWL. In this step, the properties add cardinality, values, and characteristics that will enrich their definitions.

- Seventh, the slots can have different facets describing the value type, allowed values, the number of the values (cardinality), and other features of the values. Slot cardinality: the number of values a slot has. Slot value type: the type of values a slot has. Minimum and maximum value: a range of values for a numeric slot. Default value: the value a slot has unless explicitly specified otherwise.

- Eighth, define instances. The next step is to create individual instances of classes in the hierarchy. Defining an individual instance of a class requires choosing a class, creating an individual instance of that class, and filling in the slot values.

- Finally, check for anomalies. The Web-Ontology Language allows the possibility of detecting inconsistencies within the ontology. Anomalies, such as incompatible domain and range definitions for transitive, symmetric, or inverse properties may occur.

Ontologies can be constructed by iterating through this process.

ONTOLOGY DEVELOPMENT TOOLS

Below is a list of some of the most common editors used for building ontologies:

- DAG-Edit provides an interface to browse, query and edit vocabularies with a DAG data structure: http://www.geneontology.org/#dagedit.
- Protege 2000 is the most widely used tool for creating ontologies and knowledge bases: http://protege.stanford.edu/index.shtml.
- WonderTools is an index for selecting an ontology-building tool: http://www.swi.psy.uva.nl/wondertools/.
- WebOnto is a Java applet coupled with a Web server that allows users to browse and edit knowledge models: http://kmi.open.ac.uk/projects/webonto/.

ONTOLOGY "SPOT" EXAMPLE

Portions of the following example for the "spot" ontology were taken from http://www.charlestoncore.org/ont/example/index.html.

The spot ontology consists of three owl:Classes (spot, ellipse, and point) and six rdf:Properties (shape, center, x-position, y-position, x-radius, y-radius). Together, these vocabularies can be used to describe a spot. Figure 7-1 organizes the relationships for these elements.

Classes

The three OWL classes are

Spot: A two dimensional (2D) "spot" defined as a closed region on the plane.

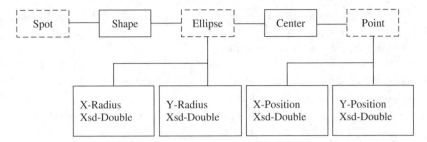

Figure 7-1. Example ontology.

Point: A point is defined as a location on a Cartesian plane. It has two attributes; its x-position and y-position on an implicit coordinate system of the plane.

Ellipse: Ellipse here is defined as a circle stretched along either the x- or y-axis of a coordinate system. The major and minor axes of an Ellipse parallel the coordinates of the implicit coordinate system (see Fig. 7-2).

Properties

The six RDF properties are

Shape: A Spot assumes a shape of an Ellipse. Therefore the domain of shape is Spot and the range of Spot is Ellipse.

Center: The center is the center point of the Ellipse. It has a rdfs:domain of Ellipse and a rdfs:range of Point.

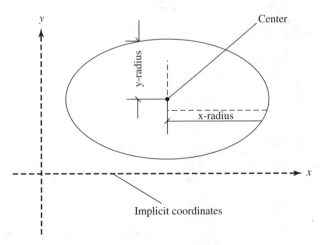

Figure 7-2. Ellipse definition.

x-Position: An *x*-position is an owl:Datatype property that has a domain of Point. Its value (of type xsd:double) is the distance from the origin on the *x*-axis of the coordinate system.

y-Position: A *y*-position is a owl:Datatype property that has a domain of Point. Its value (of type xsd:double) is the distance from the origin on the *y*-axis of the coordinate system.

x-Radius: *x*-radius is a owl:Datatype property that has a rdfs:domain of Ellipse. It is the radius parallel to the *x*-axis of the coordinate system (see Fig. 7-2).

y-Radius: A *y*-radius is a owl:Datatype property that has a rdfs:domain of Ellipse. It is the radius parallel to the *y*-axis of the coordinate system (see Fig. 7-2)

The OWL file for this ontology example (see http://www.charlestoncore.org/ont/example/index.html) is as follows:

```
<?xml version="1.0" encoding="iso-8859-1" ?>
 <!DOCTYPE rdf:RDF (...)>
<rdf:RDF xmlns="http:// example#"
  xmlns:example="http:// example#" xmlns:rdf=
         "http://www.w3.org/1999/02/22-rdf-syntax-ns#"
  xmlns:rdfs="http://www.w3.org/2000/01/rdf-schema#"
  xmlns:xsd="http://www.w3.org/2001/XMLSchema#"
  xmlns:owl="http://www.w3.org/2002/07/owl#"
         xmlns:dc="http://purl.org/dc/elements/1.1/"
  xml:base="http:// /example">
<owl:Ontology rdf:about="">
<rdfs:isDefinedBy rdf:resource="http:// example/" />
<dc:author>Smith</dc:author>
<dc:title>Example Ontology</dc:title>
<rdfs:comment>This file defines a partial ontology in
       OWL</rdfs:comment>
<owl:versionInfo>2005</owl:versionInfo>
  </owl:Ontology>
<owl:Class rdf:ID="Spot" />
<owl:Class rdf:ID="Ellipse" />
<owl:Class rdf:ID="Point" />
<owl:ObjectProperty rdf:ID="shape">
<rdfs:domain rdf:resource="#Spot" />
<rdfs:range rdf:resource="#Ellipse" />
  </owl:ObjectProperty>
<owl:ObjectProperty rdf:ID="center">
<rdfs:domain rdf:resource="#Ellipse" />
<rdfs:range rdf:resource="#Point" />
  </owl:ObjectProperty>
<owl:DatatypeProperty rdf:ID="x-radius">
<rdfs:domain rdf:resource="#Ellipse" />
<rdfs:range rdf:resource= "http://www.w3.org/2001/XMLSchema#double"/>
  </owl:DatatypeProperty>
<owl:DatatypeProperty rdf:ID="y-radius">
<rdfs:domain rdf:resource="#Ellipse" />
```

```
<rdfs:range rdf:resource= "http://www.w3.org/2001/XMLSchema#double"/>
   </owl:DatatypeProperty>
<owl:DatatypeProperty rdf:ID="x-position">
<rdfs:domain rdf:resource="#Point" />
<rdfs:range rdf:resource= "http://www.w3.org/2001/XMLSchema#double"/>
   </owl:DatatypeProperty>
<owl:DatatypeProperty rdf:ID="y-position">
<rdfs:domain rdf:resource="#Point" />
<rdfs:range rdf:resource= "http://www.w3.org/2001/XMLSchema#double"/>
   </owl:DatatypeProperty>
   </rdf:RDF>
```

ONTOLOGY METHODS

Several approaches for developing ontologies have been attempted in the last two decades. In 1990, Lenat and Guha proposed the general process steps. In 1995, the first guidelines were proposed on the basis of the Enterprise Ontology and the TOVE (TOronto Virtual Enterprise) project. At the 12th European Conference for Artificial Intelligence in 1996, a method to build an ontology in the domain of electrical networks was proposed. The methodology Methontology appeared at about the same time. A few years later, the On-To-Knowledge methodology was developed.

The Cyc Knowledge Base (see http://www.cyc.com/) was designed to accommodate all of human knowledge and contains about 100,000 concept types used in the rules and facts encoded in its knowledge base. The method used to build the Cyc consisted of three phases. The first phase manually codified articles and pieces of knowledge containing common sense knowledge implicit in different sources. The second and third phase consisted of acquiring new common sense knowledge using natural language or machine learning tools.

The Electronic Dictionary Research (ERD) project in Japan has developed a dictionary with over 400,000 concepts, with their mappings to both English and Japanese words. Although the EDR project has many more concepts than Cyc, it does not provide as much detail for each one (see http://www.iijnet.or.jp/edr/).

WordNet is a hierarchy of 166,000 word form and sense pairs. WordNet does not have as much detail as Cyc or as broad coverage as EDR, but it is the most widely used ontology for natural language processing, largely because it has long been easily accessible over the Internet (see http://www.cogsci.princeton.edu/~wn/).

Cyc has the most detailed axioms and definitions; it is an example of an axiomatized or formal ontology. Both EDR and WordNet are usually considered terminological ontologies. The difference between a terminological ontology and a formal ontology is one of degree: as more axioms are added to a terminological ontology, it may evolve into a formal or axiomatized ontology.

The main concepts in the ontology development include: a top-down approach, in which the most abstract concepts are identified first, and then, specialized into more specific concepts; a bottom-up approach, in which the most specific concepts are identified first and then generalized into more abstract concepts; and a middle-out approach, in which the most important concepts are identified first and then generalized and specialized into other concepts.

Methontology was created in the Artificial Intelligence Lab from the Technical University of Madrid (UPM). It was designed to build ontologies either from scratch, reusing other ontologies as they are, or by a process of reengineering them. The Methontology framework enables the construction of ontologies at the knowledge level. It includes the identification of the ontology development process, a life cycle based on evolving prototypes, and particular techniques to carry out each activity. The ontology development process identifies which tasks should be performed when building ontologies (scheduling, control, quality assurance, specification, knowledge acquisition, conceptualization, integration, formalization, implementation, evaluation, maintenance, documentation, and configuration management).

The life cycle identifies the stages through which the ontology passes during its lifetime, as well as the interdependencies with the life cycle of other ontologies. Finally, the methodology specifies the techniques used in each activity, the products that each activity outputs, and how they have to be evaluated. The main phase in the ontology development process using the Methontology approach is the conceptualization phase.

By comparison, the On-To-Knowledge methodology includes the identification of goals that should be achieved by knowledge management tools and is based on an analysis of usage scenarios. The steps proposed by the methodology are kickoff: where ontology requirements are captured and specified, competency questions are identified, potentially reusable ontologies are studied, and a first draft version of the ontology is built; refinement: where a mature and application oriented ontology is produced; evaluation: where the requirements and competency questions are checked, and the ontology is tested in the application environment; and finally ontology maintenance.

ONTOLOGY SHARING AND MERGING

Knowledge representation is the application of logic and ontology to the task of constructing automated models. Each of the following three fields contributes to knowledge representation:

- Logic: Different implementations support different subsets and variations of logic. Sharing information between implementations can usually be done automatically if the information can be expressed a common subset.
- Ontology: Different systems may use different names for the same kinds of objects; or they may use the same names for different kinds.
- Computation: Even when the names and definitions are identical, computational or implementation side effects may produce different behaviors in different systems. In some implementations, the order of entering rules may

have inferences that impact computations. Sometimes, the side effects may cause an endless loop.

Although these three aspects of knowledge representation pose different kinds of problems, they are interdependent. Standardizing the terminology used to classify and find the information is important. For artificial intelligence, where the emphasis is on computer processing, effort has been directed to precise axioms suitable for extended computation and deduction.

ONTOLOGY LIBRARIES

Scientists should be able to access a global, distributed knowledge base of scientific data that appears to be integrated, locally available, and is easy to search. Data is obtained by multiple instruments, using various protocols in differing vocabularies using assumptions that may be inconsistent, incomplete, evolving, and distributed. Currently, there are existing ontology libraries including

- DAML ontology library (www.daml.org/ontologies).
- Ontolingua ontology library (www.ksl.stanford.edu/software/ontolingua/).
- Protégé ontology library (protege.stanford.edu/plugins.html).

Available upper ontologies include

- IEEE Standard Upper Ontology (suo.ieee.org).
- Cyc (www.cyc.com).

Available general ontologies include

- (www.dmoz.org).
- WordNet (www.cogsci.princeton.edu/~wn/).
- Domain-specific ontologies.
- UMLS Semantic Net.
- GO (Gene Ontology) (www.geneontology.org).
- Chemical Markup Language, CML.

ONTOLOGY MATCHING

Ontology provides a vocabulary and specification of the meaning of objects that encompasses several conceptual models: including classifications, databases, and axiom theories. However, in the open Semantic Web environment different ontologies may be defined.

Ontology matching finds correspondences between ontology objects. These include ontology merging, query answering, and data translation. Thus, ontology matching enables data interoperate.

Today ontology matching is still largely labor-intensive and error-prone. As a result, manual matching has become a key bottleneck.

String Matching

String matching can help in processing ontology matching. String matching is used in text processing, information retrieval, and pattern matching. There are many string matching methods including "edit distance" for measuring the similarities of two strings.

Let us consider two strings; S1 and S2. If we use limited steps of character edit operations (insertions, deletions, and substitutions), S1 can be transformed into S2 in an edit sequence. The edit distance defines the weight of an edit sequence.

The existing ontology files on the Web (e.g., http://www.daml.org/ontologies) show that people usually use similar elements to build ontologies, although the complexity and terminology may be different. This is because there are established names and properties to describe a concept.

The value of string matching lies in its utility to estimate the lexical similarity. However, we also need to consider the real meaning of the words and the context. In addition, there are some words that are similar in alphabet form while they have different meaning such as, "too" and "to." Hence, it is not enough to use only string matching.

Another approach to improve the performance is called normalization. Since "edit distance" does not consider the lengths of the strings compared. This may produce a side effect: a pair of long strings that differ only in one character may get the same edit distance as that of a pair of short strings. For example, suppose two words whose lengths are both 300 only differ in one character. Suppose further that another pair of strings whose lengths are both 3 also differ in one character. Now by traditional methods computing their edit distance, we will get exactly the same value. However, this is an unfair result since the long strings should get a higher value. In this case, we would use an efficient uniform-cost normalized edit distance.

Comparing Ontologies

Ontology can be represented in a taxonomy tree where each node represents a concept with its attributes. In comparison to the ontology O1 in Figure 7-1, we can make an alternative "spot" ontology called O2, where the only difference is that the term "point" in O1 has been replaced by "origin" in O2.

The aim of ontology matching is to map the semantically equivalent elements. In this case, this is a one-to-one mapping of the simplest type. We can also map the different types of elements: for example, a particular relation maps to a particular attribute. Mapping can be more complex if we want to map the combination of some elements to a specific element.

An approach for semantic search can be based on text categorization for ontology mapping that compares element by element, and then determines a similarity metric on a per pair basis. Matched items are those whose similarity values are greater than a determined threshold.

Similarity measures play a very significant role in ontology matching. All ontologies in the real world not only specify the conceptualization by logical structures, but also refer to terms restricted by natural languages use. For the two ontologies, O1 and O2, we could compute a similarity measure and use that measure to decide whether the onologies match. And we could also apply the notion of the joint probability distribution between any two concepts as a similarity measure.

ONTOLOGY MAPPING

Ontology mapping enables interoperability among different sources in the Semantic Web. It is required for combing distributed and heterogeneous ontologies. Ontology mapping transforms the source ontology into the target ontology based on semantic relations. There are three mapping approaches for combing distributed and heterogeneous ontologies:

1. Mapping between local ontologies.
2. Mapping between integrated global ontology and local ontologies.
3. Mapping for ontology merging, integration, or alignment.

Ontology merge, integration, and alignment can be considered as ontology reuse processes.

Ontology merge is the process of generating a single, coherent ontology from two or more existing and different ontologies on the same subject. Ontology integration is the process of generating a single ontology from two or more differing ontologies in different subjects. Ontology alignment creates links between two original ontologies.

ONTOLOGY MAPPING TOOLS

This section reviews three types of ontology mapping tools and provide an example of each.

For ontology mapping between local ontologies, an example mapping tool is GLUE. GLUE is a system that semiautomatically creates ontology mapping using machine learning techniques. Given two ontologies, GLUE finds the most similar concept in the other ontology. For similarity measurement between two concepts, GLUE calculates the joint probability distribution of the concepts. The GLUE uses a multistrategy learning approach for finding joint probability distribution.

GLUE has a Content Learner and Name Learner, and a Meta Learner. The Content Learner exploits the frequencies of words in the textual content of an instance in order to make predictions and uses the Naïve Bayes's theorem. The Name Learner uses the full name of the input instance. The Meta-learner combines the predictions of base learners and assigns weight to base learners based on how much it trusts that learner's predictions.

For ontology mappings between source ontology and integrated global ontology, an example tool is Learning Source Description (LSD). In LSD, Schema can be viewed as ontologies with restricted relationship types. Therefore, the mediated schema can be considered as a global ontology. The LSD system uses a multistrategy learning two phase approach: training and matching. In the matching phase, prediction combiner combines meta-learner's prediction and match the schema of new input source to the mediated schema. This process can be considered as ontology mapping between information sources and a global ontology.

For ontology mapping in ontology merging, alignment, and integration, an example tool is OntoMorph. OntoMorph provides a powerful rule language for specifying mappings, and facilitates ontology merging and the rapid generation of knowledge base translators. It combines two syntactic rewriting and semantic rewriting. Syntactic rewriting is done through pattern-directed rewrite rules for sentence-level transformation based on pattern matching. Semantic rewriting is done through semantic models and logical inference.

CONCLUSION

This chapter presented the basic issues for designing and building ontologies. The development of the Semantic Web and semantic search requires much more development in ontology engineering. Areas, such as ontology matching and mapping, were prsented.

EXERCISES

7-1. Describe an ontology with the domain of your university faculty, with teachers, courses, and departments. Use an inference engine to validate your ontology and check for inconsistencies.

7-2. Create an ontology that describes the executive branch of government using the Protégé editor.

Figure 7-3. Zooms in on Figure 3-2 to create a blow up of the filled in picture by a factor of 16 (http://escherdroste.math.leidenuniv.nl/).

INTERLUDE #7: MACHINES AND MEANING

"A penny for your thoughts?" asked Mary as she sat down next to John in the auditorium.

John said, "That's just it. What are thoughts?"

Mary said with a sigh, "Oh, you're still thinking about machine intelligence. Have you come round to my way of thinking yet?"

"No, I still don't believe that machines will ever be truly intelligent. So I guess," John added, "we remain in conflict, although our conflict is the conflict of ideas."

"Well said, but conflict can be a good thing." Mary said, "A competition of ideas improves the meaning of the message."

John said, "The meaning that a human extracts from a message is something very different from what is meaningful to a machine. How are words related to reality and how do thoughts relate to language?"

Mary said, "Those are important questions for machine intelligence."

"There's more. The importance of social intercourse to understanding language, the special characteristics of the human brain, and the nuance within a figure of speech are all obstacles to developing machine thinking," John ended defiantly.

Mary said, "Nonsense—each of those obstacles could be overcome by envisioning thinking in terms of a 'thought language'."

John said, "What do you mean by a 'thought language'? How would that work?"

"Well," Mary said pursing her lips, "I'm not exactly sure."

John said, "Ha."

Mary said, "Just a minute, I said I wasn't exactly sure, I didn't say that I didn't have any ideas. Actually, there are two possible approaches."

"Two!" John said, "Two?"

Mary said, "Yes. First, let's consider a thought language that is based on pictures. I can hold an apple in my hands. That's what's called "manifest." In Latin, manifest means literally "what you hold in your hand." I can look directly at the physical object "apple" and form a picture image of the "apple" that represents the word "apple." The picture representation of language mirrors the physical world and we can use it to form linguistic propositions that represent facts. As a result, picture language can directly relate our physical reality to the logical structure of language."

"Perhaps a picture language could represent the words for 'things'," John said making quotation marks in the air with his fingers. "But many concepts we hold dear aren't manifest. Words representing ideas and feelings certainly aren't manifest."

Mary said, "Words are only sounds until they become associated with an object. And they could just as easily be associated with an action or a feeling. The way sounds come to have meaning is through repetitive exposure to spoken language in context of a relationship."

John said, "The rote learning of behaviorism is too limited an explanation for learning language. Language exists to help people communicate, but part of human communication is nonverbal. And this nonverbal communication starts from childhood. Consider the parent who says to her child, "See the cat, this is a cat," or opens up a book and says, "Find the ball." The infant will learn that a unique combination of sounds to signify the cat or the ball. As soon as the infant makes the connection between the object and the sounds, then those sounds become a word. That's how meaning comes to words, by making the association between the sound and the object. But an infant who heard spoken words only from a radio would never really come to understand the meaning of words. That's why I can't learn a language by listening to a foreign language radio station. There's no context."

Mary said, "However, in the beginning of our lives, just as you said, sounds become words through repetitive training by the parent or teacher making the connection between the sound and an object, or the sound and a behavior, or the sound and a feeling. And later in life, we make the further association between the sounds, the physical representation of the object, and the written word. And these associations are maintained through synaptic combinations of neurons in the brain that fire when an appropriate stimuli is introduced. At least in principle, it seems possible that meaning could be coded into a machine just as in the neural circuits of our brains."

"Now it is my turn to say, 'nonsense'." John said. "Where do you find the meaning of the word 'apple' in symbols? How can 0 s and 1 s actually mean 'apple.' You could code the word apple as 0 and 1 characters, but that doesn't codify the meaning as well. It is the practice of language to produce the meaning of the word 'apple.' If the computer is playing any language game at all it isn't any game played by humans. Meaning must reside in social practice not logic. Machines only move symbols around. When humans learn they add to their definitions of the meaning of 'something.' Through that learning we modify our behavior accordingly. As result, humans can change their mind."

Mary said, "True a computer will only display actual intelligence when it is able to modify its own programs materially. Adoptive and self-altering software have a long way to go to reach an effective level in this regard. However, I still support the logical possibility of thinking machines."

John said, "Are you saying that we should build a computer to mimic the human brain in some way or should we duplicate the brain electronically?"

Mary said, "What's the difference? Unless you hold that there is something special about material constituent matter of human beings that can't be captured by electronic circuits. I don't believe that there is anything special about the matter humans are made of."

John replied, "Humph. Let's get back to your picture language as a thought language."

Mary said, "Ok."

John said, "Doesn't thinking require some symbolic representation of real-world objects?"

Mary said, "Yes. I agree with that."

John said, "Well then, how would you explain what the feeling of a parent's 'love' means? I can think of one great example where the word love differentiates love as a possession and love as an emotional attachment. In the story about Solomon's solution to the two mothers who claimed the same infant as their own. One mother's child had died and she had taken another mother's child as her possession. No one except the two mothers really knew whose baby this was. When presented to Solomon, he said, Cut the child in half and give half to each woman. The true mother who loved the child in the emotional sense was willing to give up the child so that the child would live. That's a great example of the difference between the word 'love' as possession and the word 'love' in its truest emotional meaning. How could you program that distinction into a computer?"

Mary said, "The distinction you presented in the parable was complex, detailed, and rather involved even for me to understand your meaning. I could envision a long involved, but plausible, process for 'educating' a machine. Consider the possibility that every normal child has the basic grammar of all languages in its brain from birth. Even small children can form sentences easily. Essentially children already 'know' the correct structure of sentences. A child has a basic template of sentence structure. Perhaps, there is a part of our brain that is specifically wired for language. This language-specific part of the brain can implement any human language. This basic structure gets programmed by their education to specific applications so that a child in Boston speaks his parent's English and the Chinese born grows up to speak her parent's Chinese. Further the language part of the brain is wired to carry out basic operations of language, such as distinguishing verbs from nouns, stringing sound together to create words in sequential order to form sentences. This would appear to suggest the existence of a sort of universal grammar underlying all human languages—acting as a 'thought language'."

John said, "If you were correct then there would be a deep underlying structure common to all languages, rather than a simple surface structure determined by the particular language spoken. I think your universal language theory suffers from a defect highlighted in the picture theory of language. The basic problem is that it assumes the human mind contains a kind of storage of symbols, with each symbol representing a linguistic atom. Then a type of logic calculus combines symbols into creating linguistic sentences that can be verbalized. The calculus would be an inherent structure in universal grammar and for picture language the calculus would be a neurological implementation of logical propositions. But language is much more. Language is a social phenomenon unique to humans."

Mary said, "That leads me to my second possible approach to universal language—a rule based language. But perhaps we had better discuss that later, the professor is about to start his lecture."

John said, "Good thinking."

8

LOGIC, RULES, AND INFERENCE

OVERVIEW

The architecture of the Semantic Web is comprised of a series of layers that form a hierarchy of content and logic. The ontology layer defines knowledge about content, concepts, and relationships. Currently, the RDF Schema (RDFS) is recognized as an ontology language that provides classes, properties, sub-superclasses, range, and domain. However, RDFS has no localized range and domain constraints, no cardinality constraints, no provision for negation, and no transitive, inverse, or symmetrical properties. As a result, RDFS is unable to provide sufficient expressive power for machine processing on the Semantic Web.

To expand the expressive capabilities of RDFS, three versions of the Web Ontology Language (OWL) have been developed: OWL Full is the union of OWL syntax and RDF, but it is undecidable, and therefore cannot provide complete reasoning support. The OWL Descriptive Logic (DL) is a sublanguage of OWL Full that has efficient reasoning support, but is not fully compatible with RDF. Web Ontology Language Lite is an "easier-to-implement" subset of OWL DL.

Both RDF and OWL DL are specializations of predicate logic (also known as first-order logic (FOL)) that are used for Web knowledge representation. They provide a syntax that promotes their use on the Web in the form of tags, where OWL DL and OWL Lite correspond roughly to a descriptive logic that is a subset of predicate logic for which there exists adequate proof systems. Another subset of predicate logic with efficient proof systems is the rule system Horn Logic.

Thinking on the Web: Berners-Lee, Gödel, and Turing, by H. Peter Alesso and Craig F. Smith
Copyright © 2006 John Wiley & Sons, Inc.

The choice of OWL version and complementary rule systems will dictate the resulting computational complexity of the Semantic Web.

This chapter explains how logic and rules are used on the Semantic Web to create inferences that manipulate and produce new knowledge. In addition, an example of a simple RDF inference engine is provided.

LOGIC AND INFERENCE

Logic is the study of the principles of reasoning. As such, it constructs formal languages for expressing knowledge, semantics, and automatic reasoners to deduce (infer) conclusions.

Logic forms the foundation of Knowledge-Representation (KR), which has been applied to Artificial Intelligence (AI) in general and the World Wide Web in particular. Logic provides a high-level language for expressing knowledge and has high expressive power. In addition, KR has a well-understood formal semantics for assigning unambiguous meaning to logic statements.

Predicate (or first-order) logic, as a mathematical construct, offers a complete proof system with consequences. Predicate logic is formulated as a set of axioms and rules that can be used to derive a complete set of true statements (or proofs). As a result, with predicate logic we can track proofs to reach their consequences and also logically analyze hypothetical answers or statements of truth to determine their validity. Proof systems can be used to automatically derive statements syntactically from premises. Given a set of premises, such systems can analyze the logical consequences that arise within the system.

Both RDF and OWL (DL and Lite) incorporate capabilities to express predicate logic that provide a syntax that fits well with Web languages. They offer a trade-off between expressive power and computational complexity (see Chapter 2). Other subsets of predicate logic with efficient proof systems include rules systems (e.g., Horn Logic or definite logic programs).

The Semantic Web language pyramid shown in Figure 2-2 identifies how the ontology and logic layers fit together. An automatic reasoning system would be formed on top of the ontology structure and it would make new inferences through logic and proofs.

The top layer of the stack addresses issues of trust. This component of the Semantic Web has not progressed far beyond a vision of allowing people to ask questions of the trustworthiness of the information on the Web, in order to provide an assurance of its quality.

Inference Rules

In logic, a rule is a scheme for constructing valid inferences. These schemes establish syntactic relations between a set of formulas called premises and an assertion called a conclusion. New true assertions can be reached from already known ones.

There are two forms of deductively valid argument: modus ponens (Latin for "the affirming mode") and modus tollens (the denying mode). Chapter 2 presented prominent examples of rules of inference in propositional logic starting with the rules of modus ponens and modus tollens. For first-order predicate logic, rules of inference are needed to deal with logical quantifiers.

Related proof systems are formed from a set of rules, which can be chained together to form proofs, or derivations. If premises are left unsatisfied in the derivation, then the derivation is a proof of a conditional statement: "*if* the premises hold, *then* the conclusion holds."

Inference rules may also be stated in this form: (*1*) some premises; (*2*) a turnstile symbol ⊢, which means "infers," "proves," or "concludes"; and (*3*) a conclusion. The turnstile symbolizes the executive power. The implication symbol → indicates *potential* inference and it is a logical operator.

For the Semantic Web, logic can be used by software agents to make decisions and select a path of action. For example, a shopping agent may approve a discount for a customer because of the rule:

$$\text{RepeatCustomer}(X) \rightarrow \text{discount}(25\%)$$

where repeat customers are identified from the company database.

This involves rules of the form "IF (condition), THEN (conclusion)." With only a finite number of comparisons, we are required to reach a conclusion. This means that the logic will be tractable and the tools to execute it will be efficient reasoning tools.

In addition, since the logic provides traceable steps in obtaining and backtracking a conclusion, we can analyze the explanation for the premises and inference rules used to reach the conclusion. Explanations are useful because they establish validated proofs for the Semantic Web agents that provide credibility for their results.

Axioms of a theory are assertions that are assumed to be true without proof. In terms of semantics, axioms are valid assertions. Axioms are usually regarded as starting points for applying rules of inference and generating a set of conclusions.

Rules of inference, or *transformation rules*, are rules that one can use to infer a conclusion from a premise to create an argument. A set of rules can be used to infer any valid conclusion if it is complete, while never inferring an invalid conclusion, if it is sound.

Rules can be either conditional or biconditional. Conditional rules, or *rules of inference*, are rules that one can use to infer the first type of statement from the second, but where the second cannot be inferred from the first. With biconditional rules, in contrast, both inference directions are valid.

Conditional Transformation Rules

We will use letters p, q, r, s, etc. as propositional variables.

An argument is Modus ponens if it has the following form (P1 refers to the first premise; P2 to the second premise: C to the conclusion):

(P1) if p then q
(P2) p
(C) q

Example:

(P1) If Socrates is human then Socrates is mortal.
(P2) Socrates is human.
(C) Socrates is mortal.

Which can be represented as Modus ponens:

$$[(p \rightarrow q) \wedge p] \rightarrow [q]$$

An argument is Modus tollens if it has the following form:

(P1) if p then q
(P2) not-q
(C) not-p

Example:

(P1) If Socrates is human then Socrates is mortal.
(P2) Socrates is not mortal.
(C) Socrates is not human.

In both cases, the order of the premises is immaterial (e.g., in modus tollens "not-q" could come first instead of "if p then q").
Modus tollens

$$[(p \rightarrow q) \wedge \neg q] \rightarrow [\neg p]$$

An argument is a disjunctive syllogism if it has either of the following forms:

(P1) p or q (P1) p or q
(P2) not-p (P2) not-q
(C) q (C) p

The order of the premises is immaterial (e.g., "not-q" could come first instead of "p or q").

This argument form derives its name from the fact that its major premise is a "disjunction," that is, a proposition of the form "p or q." The propositions p and q are called the "disjuncts" of the disjunction "p or q."

In logic, the disjunction "*p* or *q*" is interpreted as the claim that not both *p* and *q* are false; that is, that at least one of them is true. Thus a disjunction is held to be true even when both its disjuncts are true. For example, the proposition "either John ate breakfast this morning or he went running this morning" is true even if John did both. Of course, the disjunction will also be true if John only did one of the two. But if he did neither, then the disjunction is false.

Examples of disjunctive syllogism:

(P1) John ate breakfast or he went running.

(P2) John did not eat breakfast.

(C) John went running.

(P1) John ate breakfast or he went running.

(P2) John did not go running.

(C) John ate breakfast.

Conjunction introduction (or conjunction) is represented as

$$[(p) \wedge (q)] \rightarrow [p \wedge q]$$

Biconditional Transformation Rules

Biconditional rules, or *rules of replacement*, are rules that one can use to infer the first type of statement from the second, or vice versa.

Double negative elimination is represented as

$$[\neg\neg p] \leftrightarrow [p]$$

Tautology is represented as

$$[p] \leftrightarrow [p \vee p]$$

MONOTONIC AND NONMONOTONIC RULES

If a conclusion remains valid after new information becomes available within predicate logic, then we refer to this case as a monotonic rule. If, however, the conclusion may become invalid with the introduction of new knowledge, then the case is called a nonmonotonic rule.

The Semantic Web will express knowledge in a machine accessible way using RDF and OWL, and then exchange rules across different applications using XML-based rule languages. A subset of predicate logic, Horn logic is the basis of monotonic rules.

Nonmonotonic rules are useful where information is unavailable. These rules can be overridden by contrary evidence presented by other rules. Priorities are helpful to resolve some conflicts between nonmonotonic rules. The XML-based languages can be used to represent rules.

DESCRIPTIVE LOGIC

Descriptive logic is a family of logic based on knowledge-representation formalisms that is a descendant of semantic networks. It can describe the domain in terms of concepts (classes), roles (properties, relationships), and individuals. Descriptive logic is distinguished by being a formal semantic that has decidable fragments of FOL and has provisions of inference services. Descriptive logics allow specifying a terminological hierarchy using a restricted set of first-order formulas. They usually have nice computational properties (often decidable and tractable), but the inference services are restricted.

Inference and Classes

We can make inferences about relationships between classes, in particular subsumption between classes. Recall that A subsumes B when it is the case that any instance of B must necessarily be an instance of A.

Inference and Individuals

We can make inferences about the individuals, in particular inferring that particular individuals must be instances of particular classes. This can be because of subsumption relationships between classes, or because of the relationships between individuals.

The Unique Name Assumption (UNA) says that any two individuals with different names are different individuals. Many DL reasoners assume UNA, but OWL semantics does not make use of the UNA. Instead there are mechanisms in the language (owl:differentFrom and owl:AllDifferent) that allow us to assert that individuals are different.

Closed and Open Worlds

Reasoning in DLs is monotonic. This means that if we know that x is an instance of A, then adding more information to the model cannot cause this to become false. We cannot assume that if we do not know something, then it is false. This is due to the Open World Assumption (OWA).

Simple Common Logic

Computer-understandable ontologies are represented in logical languages, such as the W3C OWL and the draft ISO standard, SCL (Simple Common Logic). However, logical languages are only a means to express content. It is the information being imparted in the statements that drives how the individual words are selected and sequenced into sentences. It is not the language (or logic) that makes the difference, but how it is used. Ontology is one way to use language and logic more effectively.

Simple Common Logic (SCL) is a proposal for a unified semantic framework for expressing full first-order logical (FFOL) content for transmission on the Web. Simple Common Logic was recently submitted for ISO standardization as Common Logic, and has been incorporated into the OMG Ontology Definition Metamodel (ODM) standard. The SCL extends conventional first-order notations in various ways and is the candidate formalism for expressing content that is currently represented in both description logics and rule languages.

INFERENCE ENGINES

An expert system has three levels of organization: a working memory, an inference engine, and a knowledge base. The inference engine is the control of the execution of reasoning rules. This means that it can be used to deduce new knowledge from existing information.

The inference engine is the core of an expert system and acts as the generic control mechanism that applies the axiomatic knowledge from the knowledge base to the task-specific data to reach some conclusion.

Two techniques for drawing inferences are general logic-based inference engines and specialized algorithms.

Many realistic Web applications will operate agent-to-agent without human intervention to spot glitches in reasoning. Therefore developers will need to have complete confidence in reasoner otherwise they will cease to trust the results. Doubting unexpected results makes a reasoner useless.

How the Inference Engine Works

In simple rule-based systems, there are two kinds of inference, forward and backward chaining.

Forward Chaining

In forward chaining, the data is put into working memory. This triggers rules whose conditions match the new data. These rules then perform their actions. The actions may add new data to memory, thus triggering more rules, and so on. This is also called data-directed inference, because inference is triggered by the arrival of new data in working memory.

Consider iterating continuously though the following set of rules until you reach a conclusion:

> Rule 1: IF A and C   THEN F
> Rule 2: IF A and E   THEN G
> Rule 3: IF B   THEN E
> Rule 4: IF G   THEN D

To prove that D is true, given that A and B are true, we start with Rule 1 and go on down the list until a rule that "fires" is found. In this case, Rule 3 is the only one that fires in the first iteration. At the end of the first iteration, it can be concluded that A, B, and E are true. This information is used in the second iteration.

In the second iteration, Rule 2 fires adding the information that G is true. This extra information causes Rule 4 to fire, proving that D is true.

This is the method of forward chaining, where one proceeds from a given situation toward a desired goal, adding new assertions along the way. This strategy is appropriate in situations where data are expensive to collect and few are available.

Backward Chaining

In backward chaining the system needs to know the value of a piece of data. It searches for rules whose conclusions mention this data. Before it can use the rules, it must test their conditions. This may entail discovering the value of more pieces of data, and so on. This is also called goal-directed inference, or hypothesis driven, because inferences are not performed until the system is made to prove a particular goal.

In backward chaining, we start with the desired goal and then attempt to find evidence for proving the goal. Using the forward chaining example, the strategy to prove that D is true would be the following.

First, find the rule that proves D. This is Rule 4. The subgoal is then to prove that G is true. Rule 2 meets the subgoal, and as it is already known that A is true, therefore the next subgoal is to show that E is true. Rule 3 provides the next subgoal of proving that B is true. But the fact that B is true is one of the given assertions. Therefore, E is true, which implies that G is true, which in turn implies that D is true.

Backward chaining is useful in situations where the amount of data is large and where a specific characteristic of the system is of interest. Typical situations include medical diagnosis or fault finding in electrical equipment.

Some expert systems use more complex methods, for example, mixtures of forward and backward chaining. Some have probability factors attached to rules. Yet others store their rules in frames, and trigger them when an object is recognized as matching that frame.

Tree Searches

A knowledge base can be represented as a branching network or tree. There is a large number of tree searching algorithms available in the existing literature. However, the two basic approaches are depth-first search and breadth-first search.

The depth-first search algorithm begins at a node that represents either the given data (forward chaining) or the desired goal (backward chaining). It then checks to see if the left-most (or first) node beneath the initial node (call this node A) is a terminal node (i.e., it is proven or a goal). If not, it establishes node A on a list of subgoals outstanding. It then starts with node A and looks at the first node below it, and so on. If there are no more lower level nodes, and a terminal node has not been reached, it starts from the last node on the outstanding list and takes the next route of descent to the right.

Breadth-first search starts by expanding all the nodes one level below the first node. Then it systematically expands each of these nodes until a solution is reached or else the tree is completely expanded. This process finds the shortest path from the initial assertion to a solution. However, such a search in large solution spaces can lead to huge computational costs due to an explosion in the number of nodes at a low level in the tree.

There are other methods of making inferences that use a combination of two or more of the above techniques. Depending on the number of given facts and the number of plausible inferences, some of these methods may be better than others in terms of time, memory, and cost of the solution path (see Chapter 12 for Semantic Search Technology).

Full First-Order Logic Inference Engines

Using full first-order logic for specifying axioms requires a full-fledged automated theorem prover. First-order logic is semidecidable and inferencing is computationally intractable for large amounts of data and axioms.

This means that in an environment such as the Web, these programs would not scale up for handling huge amounts of knowledge. Besides, full first theorem proving would mean maintaining consistency throughout the Web, which is impossible.

The approach taken by CYCORPs CYC (see http://www.cyc.com/products. html) is different. Their approach consists of roughly 1 MB of axioms using the first-order framework. The CYC organizes its axioms in contexts and maintains consistency just for one context, and it limits deductions to a few steps. Compared to future Web architecture, CYC is still small.

An interactive theorem prover is not suitable for automated agents since they rely on user interaction. However, they may be useful to construct proofs, which can be validated by automated agents.

Closed World Machine

The Closed World Machine (CWM) (www.w3.org/2000/10/swap/doc/cwm.html) inference engine written in Python by Tim Berners-Lee and Dan Connolly is a popular Semantic Web program. It is a general-purpose data processor for the Semantic Web and is a forward-chaining reasoner that can be used for querying, checking, transforming, and filtering information. Its core language is RDF, extended to include rules.

RDF INFERENCE ENGINE

This section presents the elements of a simple RDF inference engine. RDF is a system meant for stating meta-information through triples composed of a subject, a property, and an object. The subject and object can be either a designation like a URL or a set of another triple. Triples form a simple directed graph.

Figure 8-1 shows a simple RDF example. The first triple says that Smith owns a computer and the second says that there is a computer made by Apple. The third drawing, however, is composed of two triples, and it says that Smith owns a computer made by Apple.

Suppose these triples were placed in a database. Now we can conduct a query as in Figure 8-2.

In the first query, the question is who owns a computer? The answer is "Smith." In the second query, the question is What make of computer are defined in the

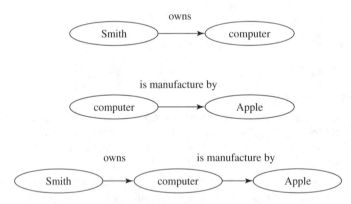

Figure 8-1. RDF statements.

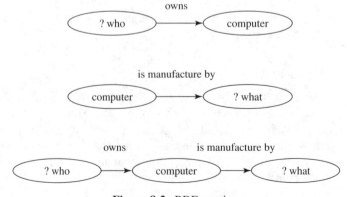

Figure 8-2. RDF queries.

database? The third query, however asks who owns a computer and what is the make of that computer?

The query is a graph containing variables that can be matched with the graph in Figure 8-1. Should the graph in the database be more extended, it would have to be matched with a subgraph. So, generally for executing an RDF query what has to be done is called "subgraph matching."

Following the data model for RDF the two queries are in fact equal because a sequence of statements is implicitly a conjunction. Figure 8-3 illustrates this.

Let us make a rule: If X owns a computer, then X must buy software. How do we represent such a rule? Figure 8-3 gives the graph representation of a rule.

The nodes of the rule form a triple set. Here there is one antecedent, but there could be more. There is only one consequent. (Rules with more than one consequent can be reduced to rules with one consequent.) Figure 8-4 gives a query that will match with the consequent of the rule.

The desired answer is John must buy software. The query of Figure 8-4 is matched with the consequent of the rule. Now an action has to be taken: The antecedents of the rule have to be added to the database with the variables replaced with the necessary values (substitution). Then the query has to be continued with the antecedent of the rule.

The question now is Who owns a computer? This is equal to a query described earlier. A rule subgraph is treated differently from nonrule subgraphs.

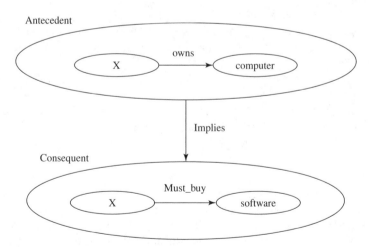

Figure 8-3. Graph representation of a rule.

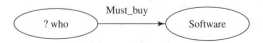

Figure 8-4. Query that matches with a rule.

A triple can be modeled as a predicate: triple(subject, property, object). A set of triples equals a list of triples and a connected graph is decomposed into a set of triples. For our example this gives

Triple(John, owns, computer).
Triple(computer, make, Apple).

This sequence is equivalent to: [Triple(John, owns, computer). Triple(computer, make, Apple).]

From Figure 8-2 the triples are

Triple(?who, owns, computer).
Triple(computer, make, ?what).

This sequence is equivalent to: [Triple(?who, owns, computer). Triple(computer, make, ?what).]

From Figure 8-3 the triple is Triple([Triple(X, owns, computer)], implies, [Triple(X, must_buy, software)]).

From Figure 8-4 the triple is Triple(?who, must_buy, software).

A unification algorithm for RDF can handle subgraph matching and embedded rules by the term "subgraph matching with rules." The unification algorithm divides the sequence of RDF statements into sets where each set constitutes a connected subgraph. This is called a tripleset that is done for the database and for the query. Then the algorithm matches each tripleset of the query with each tripleset of the database. Each triple of a tripleset of the query is matched with each triple of the tripleset of the database. All the triples of the query set must be unified with a triple from the database. If one triple is a rule, then unification will use the mechanism for rules.

The modeling of a triple by owns(John, computer) is not correct because the predicate can be a variable too.

The unication algorithm can be declared by triples and rules. It can do inferencing about properties of graphs. A complex description of the nodes is possible because each node can be a graph itself.

Agents

Agents are pieces of software that work autonomously and proactively. In most cases, an agent will simply collect and organize information. Agents on the Semantic Web will receive some tasks to perform and seek information from Web resources, while communicating with other Web agents, in order to fulfill its task. Semantic Web agents will utilize metadata, ontologies, and logic to carry out its tasks.

The Semantic Web and Artificial Intelligence

Many of the technologies necessary for the Semantic Web build upon the area of Artificial Intelligence (AI). The past difficulties in achieving AI objectives in software applications has led to disappointment. But on the Semantic Web partial solutions will work. Even if an intelligent agent is not able to come to all the conclusions that a human counterpart could reach, the agent will still contribute to a superior Web. The goal of the Semantic Web is to assist human users in online activities and not to replace them.

There is no need to achieve AI at levels higher than are already available in order to meet basic Semantic Web requirements.

CONCLUSION

This chapter introduced the process of forming an inference by using rules to manipulate knowledge to produce new knowledge. In addition, we presented the structure of inference engines and identified existing inference engines on the Web. We discussed agents on the Semantic Web.

From this chapter, we may conclude that ontologies will play a key role by providing vocabulary for semantic markup. Web Ontology Language is a DL based ontology language designed for the Web that exploits the existing standards of XML RDFS. Improved scale is necessary since reasoning is difficult and Web ontologies may grow very large. Good empirical evidence of scalability–tractability for conceptual reasoning with DL systems is necessary. The DLs are a family of object-oriented KR formalisms related to frames and Semantic networks. Descriptive Logic provides formal foundations and reasoning support. Reasoning is important because understanding is closely related to reasoning.

Chapter 9 introduces a specific rule systems language, the Semantic Web Rule Language.

EXERCISES

8-1. Identify the following argument's premises and conclusions. "I think she's in law school; she's always lugging around a pile of law books."

8-2. Definition: An argument is valid if and only if it is absolutely impossible that simultaneously (a) all its premises are true and (b) its conclusion is false. Is the following argument valid: "All human beings are mortal, and Socrates is a human being. Therefore, Socrates is mortal." Explain.

8-3. Multiple choice: If the premises of an argument are true and its conclusion is also true. Then which of the following holds: (a) The argument must be valid. (b) The argument must be sound. (c) The argument must be valid and sound. (d) None of the above.

8-4. Test the validity of the following arguments. Symbolize the propositions and use either a truth table or an informal proof. If Mary loves cats, then John loves dogs. John does not love dogs. Therefore Mary does not love cats.

8-5. Construct a truth table analysis of the following propositions: John is good in either science or history, but not both. Moreover, either he is good at logic or bad at history. If he is not good in science, he is bad at history. If he is bad at history, he is good at logic.

Figure 8-5. Zooming in on Figure 3-2 to create a blow up of the filled in picture by a factor 32.

INTERLUDE #8: MACHINES AND RULES

Mary and John remained seated in the auditorium following the lecture. As other students filed out, Mary turned to John and asked, "What makes you special?"

John said, "All humans are special, we are self-aware. We can think."

Mary said, "Hmm. Some better than others."

John said with amusement, "I suppose. What rules can we use to decide?"

Mary said, "Oh that reminds me, I wanted to discuss that second approach for a 'thought language'. I think it's obvious that there is more to the meaning conveyed through the combinations of words than through the individual words examined alone. Much of the meaning comes from the relationships between the words or concepts. In other words, rule-based systems should be considered."

John said, "Ok. Let's consider what constitutes a rule. If you push buttons for 2×4 on a calculator and get 8, you would be following a simple rule, but how did you get the right answer? Getting the right answer is not the same as calculating it yourself. Where was the thinking?"

Mary said, "But that's all it takes. It is only the behavior that is important, not how the behavior is arrived at."

John said, "Just knowing that a rule can be mechanical like the calculator doesn't mean the rule the brain processes for 2×4 is mechanical. The crux is whether a set of rules alone can serve to generate human cognitive behavior."

Mary said, "Yes, we require rules as opposed to instinct."

"Oh, but sometimes instinct can produce the right results." John quickly interjected.

Mary continued. "Nevertheless, central to the behaviorist view of language acquisition is learning language as a conditioned response."

John said, "In genuine rule following, there must be a difference between actually following a rule and appearing to follow a rule."

Mary nodded, "How can we be certain to follow the same rules as everyone else?"

John said, "There is an acceptance of the rules by the general public."

Mary said, "If making judgments requires language and if language is a rule-governed action requiring general agreement of the rules, then I can only make judgments or carry out thinking if there are additional intelligences?"

John said, "Yes. Then rule-following in one person necessitates rule-following by others. But this means that a computer cannot know that it is following a rule or program and therefore can never be thinking like a human."

Mary said, "Well, regardless of whether language is a picturing relationship between words and objects, or a rule-based system, I still believe thinking can be done by a kind of thought language based upon meaningful universal symbols."

John said, "The idea of a language of thought has problems, while words can be interpreted by reference to what we think, my interpretation of my own thoughts may make no sense."

Mary said, "I think in pictures sometimes. So if thoughts do not give meaning to sentences, they still contain symbolic meaning. But this leads to a regression problem. For example, if I hold a letter and make a statement regarding the contents of the letter, the sentence plus the letter is capable of fewer interpretations than the letter alone."

John said, "In my opinion, there are links betweens thoughts and language. For example, the question 'What are you thinking?' does not elicit the thought process, but rather the train of thought in words."

Mary said, "Then the very process of having a thought requires the capacity to manipulate language symbols."

John said, "Let me summarize; thinking must be equivalent to making judgments, but to make judgments we require language. As a result, some type of language is mandatory for thought. And while thinking requires some symbolic representation of real-world objects, it is not a direct manipulation of symbols in the brain as per a set of linguistic rules. Consequently, I would suggest that there is no explicit universal grammar of thought."

Mary said, "I hold that pure syntax is the essence of language for encoding the universal grammar in the brain. If this is so, then there is no distinction that matters between this and using a computer programming language involving 0s and 1s to replace a human language like English. The more interesting question becomes what kind of formal system can achieve that."

John said, "But what is the meaning of a statement in your scheme. How about 'What color is 4?' The grammar is correct, but its content is nonsense. The syntax is right, but it has zero semantics."

Mary said, "I admit I can't answer that, just yet."

John said, "We agree that a machine needs language as a prerequisite to think, but we disagree on how a machine could acquire language capability."

Mary said, "A language organ in the brain must have a universal syntax structure."

John says, "On the other hand, meaning is the essence of language and that can only be acquired in social context, namely, semantics."

Mary said, "Well, how would you tell whether another human was thinking? We can't assess each others mental states. We must judge on the basis of that person's behavior. I say something, you respond. After a while I decide that you are a thinking being."

John said, "Thanks. From my perspective thinking requires mental states and human life. And meaning comes from the participation in life's experience."

Mary said, "A computer changing symbols on a tape into new symbols is exactly the same kind of process that the human brain goes through in the process of thinking when it causes changes in synaptic patterns of the brain."

John said, "So you argue, but what distinguishes humans is our ability to use language to express new thoughts and communicate."

Mary said, "Do you conclude that to duplicate human thought it will be necessary for a machine to duplicate human language?"

John said, "Now there's a thought. To pass the Turing Test, a computer must acquire language capability."

9

SEMANTIC WEB RULE LANGUAGE

OVERVIEW

The goal of incorporating logic, inference, and rules processing onto the Semantic Web is to enable the automated use of classical perspectives on rules, and thereby extend the reasoning capabilities of the Semantic Web. There are several rule languages available for use on the Semantic Web including Rule Markup Language (RuleML), Web Service Modeling Language (WSML), Semantic Web Service Language (SWSL), and Semantic Web Rule Language (SWRL). The SWRL specification has strong support, but this language is likely to undergo further development, extension, and merger with features of competing technologies.

Semantic Web Rule Language is based on a combination of the OWL DL and OWL Lite sublanguages with the sublanguages of the Rule Markup Language. It includes a high-level abstract syntax for Horn-like rules.

Chapter 8 discussed how inference engines apply rule systems in general. This chapter briefly describes rule languages and introduces SWRL as the likely rule system for the Semantic Web.

RULE SYSTEMS

Prolog, which stands for PROgramming in LOGic, was introduced in the early 1970s and marked the beginning of rule language development. Prolog became the most commonly used language for logic programming. Logic programming is based on the mathematical concepts of relations and logical inference. Prolog consists of a database of facts and logical relationships (rules) that describe the relationships that hold for the given application. When a user queries the system, it searches through the database of facts and rules to determine (by logical deduction) the answer. In cases where there is more than one solution, the system may backtrack to generate alternative solutions. Prolog is used in Artificial Intelligence (AI) applications, such as natural language, automated reasoning, and expert systems.

Rules allow the expression of certain logical relationships in a form suitable for machine processing. They include declarations like: "IF A is true, then B must also be true."

Software designed to interpret rules, known as "rule engines," have become an increasingly popular tool for implementing business rule applications for dynamic business logic. Migration of business applications onto Web rule engines empowers new business rule applications. These applications enable users to personalize their preferences while empowering providers to customize their products to meet customer needs.

There have been several efforts by industry groups to develop rule engine capabilities to facilitate automated business practices. To date, rule engines have been based on the use of XML, which embeds data in a formal structure with mutually agreed upon semantic definitions. Industry initiatives using XML have included the development of the following standards: ebXML (Electronic Business XML Initiative), OTP (Open Trading Protocol), OBI (Open Business on the Internet), CBL (Common Business Language), RosettaNet, eBis-XML, BizTalk, and xCBL.

Rules may be explicitly stated or implicitly inferred. While explicit rules are readily expressed and acted upon by rule engines, rules implicitly embedded on the Web may not be processed even with XML. Implicit rules need to be implemented in such a way as to allow software agents to process them.

The formal foundations of the Semantic Web allow us to infer additional (implicit) statements that are not explicitly made. Unambiguous semantics allow question answerers to infer that objects are the same; objects are related; or that objects have certain restrictions. Ontologies for the Semantic Web can use rules to define axioms operating on taxonomy. An important feature of SWRL is that it allows us to make additional inferences beyond those provided by the ontology.

First-Order Logic (FOL) provides significant flexibility in writing down the required axioms for a Semantic Web rule system. However, FOL sublanguages Descriptive Logic (DL) and Horn Logic (HL) are both interesting as a rule system because they have the properties of decidability and tractability.

RULE LANGUAGES

Rules have classically been used in formal languages, compiler technology, databases, logic programming, knowledge representation, and object-oriented modeling. Rule markup techniques for the Semantic Web, however, incorporate rule systems (e.g., extended HL) suitable for the Web. Both derivation rules and reaction rules are considered.

Examples of Rule languages for the Semantic Web include the Rule Markup Language, Web Service Modeling Language, Semantic Web Service Language, and Semantic Web Rule Language.

Rule Markup Language is based on XML, although it includes an RDF syntax. A FOL version of RuleML is available.

Web Service Modeling Language provides an overall framework for different logic languages. The main language paradigms supported in WSML are Description Logics and Logic Programming.

Semantic Web Service Language is a language for describing Semantic Web services. It has two parts: a process ontology (Semantic Web Services Ontology) and a rules language. The rule language consists of two parts: SWSL–FOL is a formal specification of the ontology and provides interoperability with other first-order based process models and service ontologies. SWSL-Rules is the actual language for service specification. Semantic Web Rule Language is a Semantic Web language based on combining features of OWL and RuleML.

SEMANTIC WEB RULE LANGUAGE

The Semantic Web Rule Language was developed in 2003 by the Joint US/EU ad hoc Agent Markup Language Committee in collaboration with RuleML Initiative, in order to extend the expressiveness of OWL. The SWRL provides a high-level abstract syntax that extends the abstract syntax of OWL and uses URIs to identify things, making it compatible with RDF and OWL. For example, in RDF, an organization can express the fact that a particular person is an employee who is granted access to certain information. We can use SWRL to generalize this relationship. In SWRL, one can express the rule that being an employee implies authorization for access to this information. Given this rule and the fact that someone is an employee, a SWRL reasoner can conclude that the particular person is granted information access.

Semantic Web Rule Language is an extension of OWL DL. Applications of OWL DL can add rules to their ontologies thereby maintaining clear semantics. Some rule systems offer meta-processing (rules about rules). The SWRL has high expressive power, but raises questions about computational complexity for implementation. There may be a need for selecting suitable subsets for efficient ways to balance expressive power against execution speed and termination of the computation.

An OWL ontology contains a sequence of axioms and facts. These axioms may include a variety of kinds (e.g., subClass axioms and equivalentClass axioms). However, rule axioms can be extended.

The rules form an implication between antecedent (body) and consequent (head). The intended meaning implies whenever the conditions specified in the antecedent hold, then the conditions in the consequent must also hold (see Chapter 8).

Both the antecedent and consequent consist of atoms or elementary statements. An empty antecedent is treated as trivially true; an empty consequent is treated as trivially false. Multiple atoms are treated as a conjunction. The rules with conjunctive consequents can be transformed into multiple rules each with an atomic consequent.

Atoms in rules can be of the form $C(x)$, $P(x,y)$, sameAs(x,y) or differentFrom(x,y), where C is an OWL description, P is an OWL property, and x,y are either variables, OWL individuals or OWL data values. However, OWL DL becomes undecidable when extended in this way.

An XML syntax is also given for these rules based on RuleML. Atoms may refer to individuals, data literals, individual variables, or data variables. Variables are treated as universally quantified, with their scope limited to a given rule. Using this syntax, a rule asserting that the composition of parent and brother properties implies the uncle property would be written as:

```
<ruleml:imp>
  <ruleml:_body>
   <swrlx:individualPropertyAtom swrlx:property="hasParent">
     <ruleml:var>x1</ruleml:var>
     <ruleml:var>x2</ruleml:var>
   </swrlx:individualPropertyAtom>
   <swrlx:individualPropertyAtom swrlx:property="hasBrother">
     <ruleml:var>x2</ruleml:var>
     <ruleml:var>x3</ruleml:var>
   </swrlx:individualPropertyAtom>
  </ruleml:_body>
  <ruleml:_head>
   <swrlx:individualPropertyAtom swrlx:property="hasUncle">
     <ruleml:var>x1</ruleml:var>
     <ruleml:var>x3</ruleml:var>
   </swrlx:individualPropertyAtom>
  </ruleml:_head>
</ruleml:imp>
```

A simple use of these rules would be to assert that the combination of the hasParent and hasBrother properties implies the hasUncle property. From this rule, if John has Mary as a parent, and Mary has Bill as a brother, then John has Bill as an uncle.

CONCLUSION

This chapter introduced Semantic Web Rule Language (SWRL). The SWRL is based on a combination of the OWL DL and OWL Lite sublanguages with the sublanguages of the Rule Markup Language. It includes a high-level abstract syntax for Horn-like rules. Semantic Web Rule Language has some problems, such as limits on some properties of rule languages and the fact that it is as undecidable and untractable as a first-order logic.

EXERCISE

9-1. Create a rule to distinguish a family with first cousins.

INTERLUDE #9: MACHINES AND LANGUAGE

John and Mary were preparing to play a game of scrabble in the recreation room. John chose an "e" to Mary's "g" and won the right to go first. He studied his letters for a moment before placing the word "apple" vertically with the "e" landing on the center square. "Twenty points," he murmured as he reached into the bag to replace his letters. "You know looking at the characters arranged on that board reminds me of characters listed on a tape feeding into a Turing machine. I would venture to say that the letters are mere symbols without meaning themselves until we associate the word 'apple' with our own experiences."

"Hmm," said Mary. "Well, to restate what I believe our positions are, I would say that we have already agreed that thinking is equivalent to making judgments and that to make judgments requires language. As a result, some type of language is mandatory for thought. However, we still disagreed about whether thinking is a direct manipulation of symbols in the brain as per a set of linguistic rules and about how important social interactions are to learning. But to duplicate human thought we agree it will be necessary for a machine to duplicate human language. So getting back to the symbolic meaning for 'apple,' I still am satisfied with the 0s and 1s representation." Mary placed "dge" to the right of the letter "e" and said "six points."

John shuffled his letters and stared at the board before placing "knowl" in front of 'edge.' "Knowledge, 19 points," John said. "Yes, for a Turing machine to pass the Turing test, it must display human-like language capabilities. But we are held back by the language we think in and the assumptions we make, and a Turing machine would also be limited by the language it uses to process its programs and the assumptions used to build those programs. So how can you give natural language capability to a machine?"

Mary said, "Consider how language is acquired by humans. We learn languages best as children. Understanding how children acquire language skills would help to understand language and thoughts." Mary placed "earn" vertically down from the letter "l" and claimed six more points.

"Yes!" John said triumphantly. He placed "lan" and "uage" around the "g" on the board. "Fourteen points plus an extra 50 points for using all seven letters," said John. "And you've got a problem, because a child can create statements that he never heard before. This is in contrast to rote memorization learning and would be difficult to duplicate in a computer."

Mary placed "zer" vertically above the "o" in the word knowledge and claimed, "26 points for double word score. Nevertheless, I believe that direct manipulation of symbols in the brain learned in childhood according to a strict set of rules, produces language that in turn permits judgments and thinking."

John added an "o" and an "e" around the "n" in the word "learn" and said, "Four points. Let me interject another issue. Certain translations are difficult, even for people. To begin with, you have to know two languages intimately. Even if you speak two or more languages fluently, it is not a trivial matter to produce a good translation. When people start talking about the possibility of a computer replacing a human translator, someone will often bring up a sentence similar to the following: 'Time flies like an arrow.' I assert that this sentence is an example that a computer could not translate."

"False," said Mary as she placed "f" and "lse" around the second "a" in language and said, "As a matter of fact, a computer could handle this sentence if it were programmed to handle just this sentence. The problem is getting a computer to deal adequately with sentences it has not been specifically programmed to handle. That's eight points for me by the way."

"True," said John.

"You're agreeing with me?" asked Mary looking up.

"No," said John placing "tru" vertically above the "e" in "false." "Six points. This sentence about time flying is a figure of speech that combines a metaphor and a simile. Time does not really fly in the literal sense of a bird flying, but here we metaphorically say it does. Another example of a metaphor would be when we say that a ship ploughs the water, since there is no real plough and no dirt involved. The simile in this expression is the comparison between the metaphorical flight of time with the flight path of an arrow. The point of this sentence for human versus computer translation is that a human translator would know to handle the variation."

"John," Mary said, "nothing you have said precluded a future computer programmer from overcoming these issues. You should think of an argument that would be conclusive or else amend your position." Mary placed "thin" and "ing" horizontally around the "k" in knowledge. She used a blank to substitute for the letter "t" in thinking. "I'm thinking," she said grinning, "That's good for 17 points, plus 50 for using all 7 letters. Oh look, the score is even, 113 to 113."

10

SEMANTIC WEB APPLICATIONS

OVERVIEW

Today, computers and small devices are being used to access, from any location, an ever-increasing flood of Web information. As the size of the Web expands, and with it its information content, it is becoming more and more difficult to search, access, maintain, and manage network resources. Creating machine-processable semantics could alleviate some of these difficulties. The resulting Semantic Web applications could provide intelligent access to heterogeneous, distributed information, enabling software products (and agents) to mediate between user needs and the information sources available.

This chapter, describes some of the application areas for semantic technology. We focus on ongoing work in the fields of knowledge management and electronic commerce. Some opportunities for Semantic Web applications include Semantic Web Services, Semantic Search, e-Learning, Semantic Web and Bio-Informatics, Semantics-based Enterprise application and data integration, and Knowledge Base.

SEMANTIC WEB APPLICATIONS

Semantic Web applications are those web-based applications that take advantage of semantic content: content that includes not only information, but also metadata, or information about information. The Semantic Web can be used for more effective discovery, automation, integration, and reuse across various applications.

The Semantic Web will provide an infrastructure not just for Web pages, but databases, services, programs, sensors, and personal devices. Software agents can use this information to search, filter, and repackage information. The ontology and logic languages will make information machine readable and power a new generation of tools.

Web technologies can link information easily and seamlessly. The majority of network systems now have Web servers, and the Web interfaces make them seem part of the same world of information. Despite this, transferring content between Web applications is still difficult.

The Semantic Web can address and improve the linking of databases, sharing content between applications, and discovery and combination of Web Services.

Under the current Web architecture, linkages between dissimilar systems are provided by costly, tailored software. Again and again, special purpose interfaces must be written to bring data from one systems into another. Applications that run in a given company involve a huge number of ways they can be linked together. That linking requires a lot of custom code. Use of XML can help, but the problem of effectively exchanging data remains. For every pair of applications someone has to create an "XML to XML bridge."

The problem is that different databases are built using different database schemas, but these schemas are not made explicit. Just as older database systems suddenly became compatible by adopting a consistent relational model, so unstructured Web data, or XML schema definitions, can adopt a relational model.

The use of Resource Description Framework (RDF) in addition to XML can be appropriate when information from two sources need to be merged or interchanged. It is possible to concatenate the files joining on defined terms to correspond to the same Universal Resource Indicators (URIs). When you want to extend a query on one RDF file to include constraints from another, you just add in the constraints as part of the merging. Where XML is made up of elements and attributes, RDF data is made up of statements where each statement expresses the value of one property.

The Semantic Web is bringing to the Web a number of capabilities, such as allowing applications to work together in a decentralized system without a human having to custom handcraft every connection. The business market for this integration of data and programs is huge, and we believe the companies who choose to start exploiting Semantic Web technologies will be the first to reap the rewards.

Some opportunities for Semantic Web applications include Semantic Web Services, Semantic Search, e-Learning, Semantic Web and Bio-Informatics, Semantics-based Enterprise Application and Data Integration, and Knowledge Base.

We will discuss these in the following sections.

SEMANTIC WEB SERVICES

Semantic Web Services can bring programs and data together. Just as databases cannot be easily integrated on the current Web without RDF, the same applies to programs. Unfortunately, many e-business applications particularly in business-to-business (B2B) interactions have difficulty loading someone else's program to run locally.

Consider the case of a company that wishes to purchase parts from a vendor, arrange shipping from a large freight company, and have those parts delivered to one of several manufacturing locations based on which plant has the most capacity at the time of the delivery. Further, they would like this deal to be brokered on the Web with the minimum amount of human interaction. These programs that execute this brokering may be running on special purpose machines and/or behind security and firewall protections. How can all these programs interoperate on the Web to provide protocols and descriptions of the "services" that these various programs offer?

Web Services are self-contained, self-described, component applications invoked across the Web to perform complex business processes. Once a Web Service is deployed, other applications can discover and invoke the service. At present, Web Services require human interaction in order to identify and implement.

Tim Berners-Lee has suggested that the integration of Web Services and the Semantic Web could be done in such a way as to combine the business logic of Web Services with the Semantic Web's meaningful content. There are several areas where the current technologies for discovery (UDDI or Universal Description, Discovery, and Integration), binding (WSDL or Web Services Description Language), and messaging (SOAP or Simple Object Access Protocol) could use OWL to provide an ontology for automatic Semantic Web Services thereby allowing greater interaction with Web business rules' engines.

The vision for Semantic Web Services is to automate the discovery, invocation, composition, and monitoring of Web Services through the use of machine processing. Web sites will be able to use a set of classes and properties by declaring and describing an ontology of services. Web Ontology Language for Services (called OWL-S) has been designed to meet this goal. Semantic Web Services and OWL-S will be described, in greater detail in Chapter 11.

SEMANTIC SEARCH

Semantic search methods can augment and improve traditional search results by using, not just words, but concepts and logical relationships. There are two approaches to improving search results through semantic methods: (*1*) the direct use of Semantic Web metadata and (*2*) Latent Semantic Indexing (LSI).

The Semantic Web will provide more meaningful metadata about content, through the use of RDF and OWL documents that will help to form the Web into a semantic network. In a semantic network, the meaning of content is better represented and logical connections are formed between related information.

However, most semantic-based search engines suffer increasingly difficult performance problems because of the large and rapidly growing scale of the Web. In order for semantic search to be effective in finding responsive results, the network must contain a great deal of relevant information. At the same time, a large network creates difficulties in processing the many possible paths to a relevant solution. We once again find ourselves facing a basic trade-off between finding the minimum necessary expressive power and the maximum possible reasoning capability for the Semantic Web. Semantic Search technology will be described in greater detail in Chapter 12.

e-LEARNING

The big question in the area of educational systems is what is the next step in the evolution of e-learning? Are we finally moving from scattered applications to a coherent collaborative environment? How close we are to the vision of the Educational Semantic Web and what do we need to do in order to realize it?

On the one hand, we wish to achieve interoperability among educational systems and on the other hand, to have automated, structured, and unified authoring. The Semantic Web is the key to enabling the interoperability by capitalizing on (*1*) semantic conceptualization and ontologies, (*2*) common standardized communication syntax, and (*3*) large-scale integration of educational content and usage.

The RDF describes objects and their relationships. It allows easy reuse of information for different devices, such as mobile phones and PDAs, and for presentation to people with different capabilities, such as those with cognitive or visual impairments.

It is possible that in the near future students will be able to extract far more data from a networked computer or wireless device, far more efficiently. Based on a few specific search terms, library catalogues could be scanned automatically and nearest library shelf marks delivered immediately to students, alongside multimedia and textual resources culled from the Web itself. Students could also be directed to relevant discussion lists and research groups.

By tailored restructuring of information, future systems will be able to deliver content to the end-user in a form applicable to them, taking into account users' needs, preferences, and prior knowledge. Much of this work relies on vast online databases and thesauri, such as wordnet, which categorize synonyms into distinct lexical concepts. Developing large multimedia database systems makes materials as useful as possible for distinct user groups, from schoolchildren to university lecturers. Students might, therefore, search databases using a simple term, while a lecturer might use a more scientific term thus reflecting scaling in complexity.

The educational sector can also use the Internet Relay Chat (IRC) (http://www.irc.org/) a tool that can be used by the Semantic Web. The IRC is a chat protocol where people can meet on channels and talk to each other. The Semantic Web community is enhancing this capability by writing robots that can help to log the chat when members are away. It can also assist with meetings, discussions, and recording of results.

The IRC and related tools could work well within education, for project discussion, remote working, and collaborative document creation. Video-conferencing at schools is increasingly becoming useful in widening the boundaries for students. The incorporation of Semantic Web technologies could create the ability to work across distributed locations in communities of learning and enable content creation outside of the classroom.

SEMANTIC BIOINFORMATICS

The Semantic Web could unlock a great deal of scientific data contained within disparate applications' formats otherwise limited by institutional factors. Life scientists, in particular, could find the Semantic Web a useful tool. The World Wide Web Consortium recently announced the formation of the Semantic Web Health Care and Life Sciences Interest Group (HCLSIG) aimed to help life scientists tap the potential benefits of using Semantic Web technology by developing use cases and applying standard Semantic Web specifications to healthcare and life sciences problems.

The initial foundation and early growth of theWeb was based in great part on its adoption by the high-energy physics community when six high-energy physics Web sites collaborated allowing their participating physicists to interact on this new network of networks. A similar critical mass in life sciences could occur if a half dozen ontologies for drug discovery were to become available on the Semantic Web.

Life science is a particularly suitable field for pioneering the Semantic Web. For example, in the area of drug discovery, many databases and information systems are used by drug researchers on a global scale. In this regard, the Biological Pathways Exchange (http://www.biopax.org/) is developing a standard data exchange format for metabolic, signaling, genetic regulatory, and genetic pathway information as an example.

ENTERPRISE APPLICATION INTEGRATION

The Semantic Web can impact industry as a tool for enterprise application integration. Just as the Web today integrates human-oriented information systems, the Semantic Web could integrate applications in which data has well-defined meaning.

As an example, consider the British Telecom Call Center (http://www.bt.com/). Call centers are platforms for companies to communicate with their customers and the market. Current call center technology lacks the support of the operator in solving incoming requests. The investment in call center technology could offer better customer service, lower overheads, and lower operational costs. For British Telecom, a system for supporting intranet-based virtual communities is being developed. It allows the automatic sharing of information. The system, OntoShare, allows the storage of best practice information in an ontology and the automatic dissemination of information to relevant call center agents. The ontology provides a sharable structure for the knowledge base and a common language for communication between call center agents.

The business integration technology uses XML documents that might first be "lifted up" to an RDF data model. Then different private RDF data models are mapped to the shared mediating data model enriched with different constraints and formal specification of shared semantics of the concepts.

Middleware could facilitate the interaction between applications across heterogeneous computing platforms. The increasing use of the Web as a channel to access information systems force middleware platforms to provide support for Web application development. This support is typically provided in the form of application servers and Web Services.

The complexity of managing a distributed application remains a challenge for developers and administrators. For example, managing component dependencies, versions, and licenses is a typical problem in an ever-growing repository of programming libraries. Both types of middleware try to counter increasing complexity by managing various issues (transactions, session management, user rights, etc.) in an application independent way. An ontology could harmonize conceptual models covering aspects from the heterogeneous areas of component and service descriptions. The ontology could be leveraged to support developers and administrators in their complex tasks during development, deployment, and runtime.

An ontology covers aspects from the heterogeneous areas of component and service descriptions, policies, quality of service, service level agreements, and privacy. Ontologies formalize concepts and concept relationships (associations) very similar to conceptual database schemas or Unified Modeling Language (UML) class diagrams However, ontologies are expressed in logic-based representation languages. Inference engines are allowed to query and reason with ontologies at runtime. The UML is a standard language for specifying, visualizing, constructing, and documenting software systems, as well as for business modeling, and other nonsoftware systems. It represents a collection of engineering practices that have proven successful in the modeling of large and complex systems.

Semantics-based management of middleware comprises two layers. First, one formally specifies a conceptual model of middleware in several aligned ontologies. Thereby, the conceptual model for the middleware proper needs to be built only once, while the conceptual model for the application domain, for example, Web shopping for books may vary. Second, a formal specification of a concrete set of services and the properties they have by providing semantic metadata that are aligned to the ontologies from the first layer. The semantic metadata formalizes a particular instantiation of a distributed application.

While some of the semantic metadata can be generated automatically, a full specification will always require manual provision. This is usually a rather cumbersome and error-prone work for the developer. Hence, the goal is to decrease the costs.

The idea behind foundational ontologies has arisen from experience in ontology and software engineering. The experience has shown that ad hoc conceptual models may adequately reflect a given state of requirements at a certain point in time, however, the extension of requirements has easily led nowhere, because a given ontology proved to be unextendable for new requirements. The problem could often be attributed to a design of the ontology. Foundational ontologies capture insights from philosophy, logics, and software engineering in order to prescribe good ontology engineering practice at an upper level of the ontology.

Ontologies can provide more complex definitions for information retrieval. They are a key asset in automating query answering, maintenance, and automatic document generation.

KNOWLEDGE BASE

In a number of parallel efforts, knowledge systems are being developed to provide semantic-based and context-aware systems for the acquisition, organization, processing, sharing and use of the knowledge embedded in multimedia content. Ongoing research aims to maximize automation of the complete knowledge lifecycle and to achieve semantic interoperability between Web resources and services.

In one particularly interesting application, Cycorp (http://www.cyc.com/) intends to sell products and services using its inference engine, which has been designed to work with the Cyc Knowledge. Cycorp provides a reference Cyc Server executable for Intel-based Linux and for Windows 2000.

OpenCyc is the open source version of the Cyc technology, the world's largest and most complete general knowledge base and common sense reasoning engine. Cycorp, the builders of Cyc, have set up an independent organization Open-Cyc.org, to disseminate and administer OpenCyc. OpenCyc can be used as the basis for a wide variety of intelligent applications, such as speech understanding (using the KB to prune implausible choices via common sense, discourse context, and prosodics), database integration and consistency-checking, rapid development of an ontology, and email prioritizing, routing, summarizing, and annotating.

CONCLUSION

This chapter described some of the application areas for semantic technology. We focused on ongoing work in the fields of knowledge management and electronic commerce. Some opportunities for Semantic Web applications include

Semantic Web Services, Semantic Search, e-Learning, Semantic Web and Bio-Informatics, Semantics-based Enterprise Application and Data Integration, and Knowledge Base.

EXERCISE

10-1. List three potential applications that would benefit from the Semantic Web environment.

INTERLUDE #10: DISTRIBUTED INTELLIGENCE

John said, "Boy, am I tired of math and computer science after this week's midterm exams. Our debate on machine intelligence has proven to be a welcome distraction."

Mary said, "Actually, I found that our discussions over the past few weeks were helpful with some of the essay questions. It's a funny sort of problem and I don't mind admitting that I'm puzzled by many aspects."

John said, "Well, we have covered a lot of material. Based on our earlier discussions, however, I doubt if we will ever come to agreement on the precise meaning of intelligence, either for humans or for machines; but surely we can agree on some of its attributes."

Mary said, "I'd like nothing more than to find agreement, but given our earlier chats, that may prove elusive."

John said, "How about this? We seem to agree that human intelligence is related to synaptic brain patterns, and learning requires social behavior in humans. Can we agree on that?"

Mary said, "Yes. But I'm a little suspicious when you try to characterize the basis of something we can't really define. Nevertheless, I can accept that intelligent actions are not some out-of-body phenomenon, but are based on well-defined biological processes."

John said, "In that case, it seems clear to me that human intelligence, whatever it is and however it works, must be distributed across the multiple regions of the brain. Consciousness, memory recall, problem solving, and sensory perception involve different parts of our physiology and therefore must be considered to be distributed, at least in some sense."

Mary said, "I guess I can agree with that. Maybe we agree in more ways than I thought. Computers have some similarities to that, when we consider their functions in emulating human intelligence. For example, memory may be stored in one place, while an act of logical inference is taking place in the CPU. Information may be "perceived" from sensor inputs that could also be remote from the computer itself."

John said, "I think you are underestimating the process of human thought, but I can't disagree with your point that artificial intelligence may also be composed of activities that are spread out in space result from the accumulation of individual components."

Mary said, "I'm glad you agree up to a point, but now let me take a giant leap and propose that intelligent behavior in machines may be conductive to even greater decentralization. What if the various components of what we consider intelligent behavior: perception, analysis, memory and recall, problem solving, inference, and so on, were to take place at different nodes on a vast network of interconnected machines. Could we then consider the collective behavior of such a system to be intelligent? Could intelligence be an emergent property of a complex system of interconnected machines? Or in fact distributed intelligence over a global network?"

John said, "Now you've gone too far. You've given me a headache. It's time for our next class."

11

WEB ONTOLOGY LANGUAGE FOR SERVICES

OVERVIEW

Web Services are self-contained, self-described, component applications that can be published, located, and invoked across the Web. They perform functions that can be anything from simple requests to complex business processes involving multiple simple services. Once a Web Service is deployed, other applications can discover and invoke the service. At present, Web Services require human interaction for identification and implementation.

Tim Berners-Lee has suggested that the integration of Web Services and the Semantic Web could offer significant performance improvement for Web applications. Integration could combine the business logic of Web Services with the Semantic Web's meaningful content. There are several areas where the two could work well together. For example, the current technologies for discovery (Universal Description, Discovery and Integration, UDDI), binding (Web Services Description Language, WSDL), and messaging (Simple Object Access Protocol, SOAP) technologies could use OWL to provide an ontology for automatic Semantic Web Services thereby allowing interaction with Web business rules' engines.

This chapter presents the building blocks for the next generation of Web Services: Semantic Web Services. Web Ontology Language and OWL for Services (OWL-S) create logic statements for inference engines utilizing Semantic Web Rule Language (SWRL) that allow manipulation of application logic directly through Web markup languages.

Thinking on the Web: Berners-Lee, Gödel, and Turing, by H. Peter Alesso and Craig F. Smith
Copyright © 2006 John Wiley & Sons, Inc.

Currently, OWL-S and SWRL are not yet W3C recommendations and each has several competing submittals. However, any future Semantic Web Service W3C recommendation is likely to grow out of OWL-S and SWRL components, so their presentation is included to illustrate the basic ingredients needed.

XML-BASED WEB SERVICES

Web Services provide a standard means of interoperating between different software applications running on a variety of platforms. The XML provides the extensibility and language neutrality that is the key for standard-based interoperability of Web Services.

Web Service discovery and composition is led by Universal Description Discovery and Integration (UDDI) developed by IBM and Microsoft. Well accepted standards like Web Services Description Language (WSDL) for binding and Simple Object Access Protocol (SOAP) for messaging make it possible to dynamically invoke Web services.

Web Service Architecture requires discrete software agents that must work together to implement functionality. Furthermore, the agents do not all operate in the same processing environment so they must communicate by protocol stacks that are less reliable than direct code invocation. This requires developers to consider the unpredictable latency of remote access, and take into account issues of partial failure and concurrency.

In XML-based Web Services, an agent sends and receives messages based upon their architectural roles. If a requester wishes to make use of a provider's Web Service, he uses a requester agent to exchange messages with the provider agent. In order for this message exchange to be successful, the requester and the provider must first agree on both the semantics and the mechanics of the message exchange.

The message exchange mechanics are documented using WSDL. The service description is a specification that can be processed by a machine using message formats, data types, and protocols that are exchanged between the requester and provider. It also specifies the network location of the provider.

NEXT GENERATION WEB SERVICES

The vision for Semantic Web Services is to automate the discovery, invocation, composition, and monitoring of Web Services through the use of machine processing. Web sites will be able to use a set of classes and properties by declaring and describing a ontology of services. Web Ontology Language for Services has been designed to meet this goal.

When the semantics of the service is known, its WSDL description can be accessed by a program using the WSDL description for the interface, binding, and operations. If Web sites publish their metadata, then software agents can extract the information. In this way software agents can automatically exploit Web Services from semantic descriptions that are machine processable.

To use a Web Service, a software agent requires a computer-interpretable description of the service and access. Making and sharing these descriptions is an important goal for Semantic Web markup languages. The ontology structuring mechanisms of OWL provide the appropriate framework for Web sites to be able to employ a set of basic classes and properties for declaring and describing services.

For any piece of data to be automatically processable, first it has to have a well-defined format. A well-defined metadata description language allows automatic processing of the description to obtain the metadata. However, to interpret the metadata automatically, the meaning (or semantics) must also be known. The meaning of data is given through domain specific ontologies.

The OWL-S is a high-level ontology meant to answer the "what" and "why" questions about a Web Service for the application level. An ontology for Web Services makes Web Services machine understandable and supports automated Web Service composition and interoperability.

OWL-S provides an ontology for Web Services that automates four functions:

1. Discovery: A program must be able to automatically find, or discover, an appropriate Web service.

2. Invocation: Software must automatically determine how to invoke or execute the service. For example, if executing the service is a multistep procedure, the software needs to know how to interact with the service to complete the necessary sequence. A Semantic Web service provides a descriptive list of what an agent needs to execute the service including the inputs and outputs.

3. Composition: Software must be able to select and combine a number of Web services to complete a given objective. The services have to interoperate with each other seamlessly so that the combined results produce a valid solution.

4. Monitoring: Agent software must verify and monitor the service properties during operation.

Program agents must locate Web Services that satisfy a given set of constraints. This requires equally smart execution monitoring to go along with discovery and invocation.

Developers will want to build up complex Web Services from simpler ones using the inputs, outputs, preconditions, and effects of the simpler services. Intelligent composition of services will provide interoperation and automatic translations between clients and services.

The ontology of services provides three essential types of knowledge about a service: service profile, service model, and service grounding. The class Service provides an organizational point of reference for a declared Web Service.

1. The class Service "presents" a `ServiceProfile`: "What does the service provide for and require of agents?"
2. The class Service is "`describedBy`" a `ServiceModel`: "How does it work?"
3. The class Service "supports" a `ServiceGrounding`: "How to access the service?"

The `ServiceProfile` provides information about a service offered by a Web site, as well as services needed by a requestor. An agent determines if the service meets its needs while satisfying constraints, such as security, locality, and quality requirements.

The `ServiceModel` enables an agent to (1) determine whether the service meets its needs, (2) compose a service description from multiple services, (3) coordinate the activities of different agents, and (4) monitor the execution of the service.

The `ServiceGrounding` specifies the details of how to access the service, such as protocol and message formats, serialization, transport, and addressing. The grounding is basically, the inputs and outputs of atomic processes.

The current specification OWL-S 1.1 is available at: http://www.daml.org/services/owl-s/1.1/.

In general, the `ServiceProfile` provides the information needed for an agent to discover the service while the `ServiceModel` and `ServiceGrounding` objects provide information for an agent to use the service (see Fig. 11-1). The properties "presents" "describedBy," and "supports" are properties of Service. The classes `ServiceProfile`, `ServiceModel`, and `ServiceGrounding` are the respective ranges of those properties. Each instance of Service will present a `ServiceProfile` description, describedBy a `ServiceModel` description, and support a `Service-Grounding` description. The details of profiles, models, and groundings may vary widely from one type of service to another.

We will describe each of these three classes (`ServiceProfile`, `ServiceModel`, `ServiceGrounding`) in the following sections.

ServiceProfile

A transaction in the Web service marketplace involves three parties: the service requester, the service provider, and the infrastructure components. The service

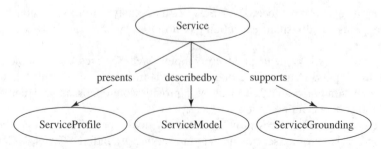

Figure 11-1. Upper ontology of services.

requester (buyer) seeks a service to perform work and the service provider (seller) offers a service. The infrastructure components are available to facilitate the process, and include items, such as registries to match the request with the available offers. Within the OWL-S framework, the `ServiceProfile` provides a way to describe the services being offered, and the services required.

By using OWL subclassing it is possible to create specialized service profiles of services. The OWL-S provides one possible representation through the class "Profile." A `ServiceProfile` describes a service as a function of three basic pieces of information: what organization provides the service, what functions the service computes, and what features characterize the service.

There is a two-way relationship between a service and a profile that is expressed by the properties "presents" (relates an instance of service and an instance of profile) and "presentedBy" (specifies the inverse of presents).

`ServiceProfile` expresses two functions: first, the information transformation and second, the state change produced by the execution of the service. The information transformation includes the input and output properties of the profile. For example, a book-selling service could require the buyer's credit card number and information on the book. The state change produced by the execution of the service results from the "precondition and effect properties" of the profile. Precondition presents logical conditions that should be satisfied prior to the service being requested. Effects are the result of the successful execution of a service.

For example, to complete the sale, a book-selling service requires a credit card number and expiration date, but also requires the precondition that the credit card account actually exists and is in good standing. The result of the sale is the transfer of the book from the warehouse to the address of the buyer with the corresponding accounting transfer.

In addition, the `ServiceProfile` provides a description of the service to a registry. Although the `ServiceProfile` and the `ProcessModel` play different roles during the transaction, they reflect the same service, and so the IOPEs (inputs, outputs, parameters, and effects) are related.

The information is encoded in modeling primitives of OWL-S classes and properties, such as:

```
<rdfs:Class rdf:ID="OfferedSevices">
  <rdf:label>OfferedService</rdf:label>
  <rdfs:subClassOf rdf:resource=
        "http://daml.semanticweb.org/services/owl-s/1.1/">
</rdfs:Class>
```

Table 11-1 lists the Profile properties used to provide a description of the service on this class, such as, `serviceName`, `textDescription`, and `contactInformation`.

The Profile of a service provides a concise description of the service to a registry, but once the service has selected the Profile, the client will use the Process Model to control the interaction with the service. Although the Profile and the

TABLE 11-1. `ServiceProfile` **Property Description**

Property	Description
serviceName	Name of the service
textDescription	Provides a brief description of the service including what the service requires to work
contactInformation	Referring to individuals responsible for the service

Process Model play different roles, they use the same input, output, precondition, and effects (IOPEs). Table 11-2 lists the functional description parameters.

Additional information is provided by functional attributes, such as guarantees of response time or accuracy, the cost of the service, or the classification of the service in a registry.

ServiceModel

Service models are based on the concept of processes that describe inputs, outputs, preconditions, effects, and subprocesses. A detailed perspective of a service can be viewed as a process. A subclass of the `ServiceModel` is defined as the `ProcessModel` that draws upon Artificial Intelligence (AI), planning, and workflow automation to support a wide array of services on the Web. Figure 11-2 presents the relationships of `ServiceModel` and includes the `Process` and `ProcessControl`, IOPEs, and constructs.

ProcessModel

The process model comprises subclasses and properties of the `ProcessModel` class.

TABLE 11-2. Service Profile Functional Description

Function Description: The Profile ontology defines the following properties of the Profile class for pointing to IOPEs:

hasParameter	Ranges over a Parameter instance of the Process ontology. Parameter class models intuition that Inputs and Outputs (which are kinds of Parameters) are both involved in information transformation and therefore they are different from Preconditions and Effects.
hasInput	Ranges over instances of Inputs as defined in the Process Ontology.
hasOutput	Ranges over instances of type Output, as defined in the Process ontology.
hasPrecondition	Specifies one of the preconditions of the service and ranges over a Precondition instance defined according to the schema in the Process ontology.
hasResult	Specifies one of the results of the service, as defined by the Result class in the Process ontology. It specifies under what conditions the outputs are generated.

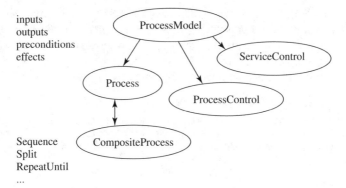

Figure 11-2. `ServiceModel`.

The chief components of the process model are the Process Ontology that describes a service in terms of its inputs, outputs, preconditions, effects, and component subprocesses, and Process Control Ontology, which describes each process in terms of its state, including initial activation, execution, and completion. The process control model allows agents to monitor the progression of a service request as part of the Process Control Ontology.

Process Ontology

Process Ontology can have any number of inputs and outputs representing the information required for execution. Besides inputs and outputs, parameters for physical devices, such things as rates, forces, and control settings can be included. The Process Ontology serves as the basis for specifying a wide array of services on standardizations.

The OWL-S defines three types of processes (see Fig. 11-3): Atomic (directly invokable), Simple (single-step, but not directly invokable), and Composite (decomposable into other processes).

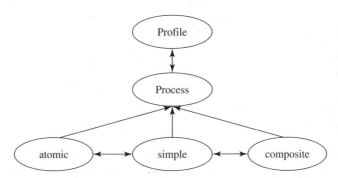

Figure 11-3. Process ontology.

In Figure 11-3, the three types of processes are related: atomic, simple, and composite. They are represented in the following serializations. Process encompasses the three disjoint subprocesses: atomic, simple, and composite, where a simple process can include atomic processes and a composite process can include more than one simple process, such as

```
<owl:Class rdf:ID="Process">
 <rdfs:comment> The most general class of processes </rdfs:comment>
 <owl:disjointUnionOf rdf:parseType="owl:collection">
  <owl:Class rdf:about="#AtomicProcess"/>
  <owl:Class rdf:about="#SimpleProcess"/>
  <owl:Class rdf:about="#CompositeProcess"/>
 </owl:disjointUnionOf>
```

AtomicProcess

The atomic processes can be invoked directly and are executed in a single step. For each atomic process, there is a grounding that enables a service requester to construct messages. An AtomicProcess is a subclass of a Process, such as

```
<owl:Class rdf:ID="AtomicProcess">
 <owl:subClassOf rdf:resource="#Process"/>
</owl:Class>
```

SimpleProcess

Simple processes are not associated with a grounding. They are single-step executions. Simple processes are used as elements of abstraction; a simple process may be used either to provide a view of some atomic process, or a simplified representation of some composite process. A SimpleProcess is

```
<owl:Class rdf:ID="SimpleProcess">
 <owl:subClassOf rdf:resource="#Process"/>
</owl:Class>

<rdf:Property rdf:ID="realizedBy">
 <rdfs:domain rdf:resource="#SimpleProcess"/>
 <rdfs:range rdf:resource="#AtomicProcess"/>
 <owl:inverseOf rdf:resource="#realizes"/>
</rdf:Property>
<rdf:Property rdf:ID="expandsTo">
 <rdfs:domain rdf:resource="#SimpleProcess"/>
 <rdfs:range rdf:resource="#CompositeProcess"/>
 <owl:inverseOf rdf:resource="#collapsesTo"/>
</rdf:Property>
```

This listing identified a SimpleProcess as a subclass of the Process and says that a simple process can realize an atomic process, and may be the result of collapsing a composite process.

CompositeProcess

Composite processes are decomposable into other processes. The decomposition shows how the various inputs and outputs are accepted, such as

```
<owl:Class rdf:ID="CompositeProcess">
 <owl:intersectionOf rdf:parseType=" owl:collection">
  <owl:Class rdf:about="#Process"/>
  <owl:Restriction owl:cardinality="1">
   <owl:onProperty rdf:resource="#composedOf"/>
  </owl:Restriction>
 </owl:intersectionOf>
</owl:Class>
```

A CompositeProcess must have a composedOf property by which is indicated the control structure of the composite, using a ControlConstruct.

```
<rdf:Property rdf:ID="composedOf">
 <rdfs:domain rdf:resource="#CompositeProcess"/>
 <rdfs:range rdf:resource="#ControlConstruct"/>
</rdf:Property>
<owl:Class rdf:ID="ControlConstruct">
</owl:Class>
```

Building upon SOAP and WSDL technologies, the OWL-S ontology-based Web services can be dynamically invoked by other services on the Web.

The following illustrates a Process:

```
<owl:Class rdf:ID="Process">
 <rdfs:comment> The most general class of processes </rdfs:comment>
 <owl:disjointUnionOf rdf:parseType="owl:collection">
  <owl:Class rdf:about="#AtomicProcess"/>
  <owl:Class rdf:about="#SimpleProcess"/>
  <owl:Class rdf:about="#CompositeProcess"/>
 </owl:disjointUnionOf>
</owl:Class>
```

The atomic processes can be invoked directly and are executed in a single step. For each atomic process, there is a grounding that enables a service requester to construct messages. The OWL-S atomic processes specify the basic actions for larger processes and can also communicate the primitives of a process specification. The following listing illustrates the AtomicProcess.

```
<owl:Class rdf:ID="AtomicProcess">
 <owl:subClassOf rdf:resource="#Process"/>
</owl:Class>
```

Simple processes are not associated with a grounding. They are single-step executions. Simple processes are used as elements of abstraction; a simple process may be used either to provide a view of some atomic process, or a simplified representation of some composite process.

Constructs

A `CompositeProcess` must have a `composedOf` property to indicate the control structure using a `ControlConstruct`. Each control construct, in turn, is associated with an additional property called components to indicate the ordering and conditional execution of the subprocesses. For example, the control construct, Sequence, has a components property that ranges over a `ProcessComponent` List (see Table 11-3).

Process Control Ontology

To monitor and control the execution of a process, an agent uses a model with three characteristics that provide: mapping rules for the input state properties and preconditions to the corresponding output state properties; a model of the temporal or state dependencies described by constructs, such as sequence, split, and split + joi; and representation for messages about the execution state of atomic and composite processes sufficient to do execution monitoring. This allows an agent to keep track of the status of executions, including successful, failed, and interrupted processes.

Process Ontology Control is still an area under significant development (see Fig. 11-4).

ServiceGrounding

In OWL-S, both the `ServiceProfile` and the `ServiceModel` are thought of as abstract representations; only the `ServiceGrounding` deals with the

TABLE 11-3. Process Constructs

Construct	Description
Sequence	A list of Processes to be done in order.
Split	A bag of process components to be executed concurrently. Similar to other ontologies' use of Fork, Concurrent, or Parallel.
Split + Join	Invoke elements of a bag of processes and synchronize.
Concurrent	Execute elements of a bag of processes concurrently.
Unordered	Allows the process components (specified as a bag) to be executed in some unspecified order, or concurrently.
Choice	Choose between alternatives and execute one.
If-Then-Else	If specified condition holds, execute "Then," else execute "Else."
Repeat-Until	Iterate execution of a bag of processes until a condition holds.
Repeat-While	Iterate execution of a bag of processes while a condition holds.

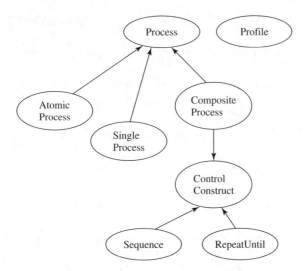

Figure 11-4. Top level process ontology.

concrete level of specification. The grounding of a service specifies the details of how to access the service, including protocol and message formats, serialization, transport, and addressing.

Relationship between OWL-S and WSDL and SOAP

An OWL-S/WSDL grounding involves complementary use of the two languages. Both languages are required for the full specification of grounding even though there is some overlap. Web Services Description Language specifies abstract types using XML Schema, but OWL-S allows for the definition of logic-based OWL classes.

An OWL-S/WSDL grounding uses OWL classes as the abstract types of message parts declared in WSDL. The job of an OWL-S/WSDL grounding is to define the messages and operations for the atomic processes that are accessed, and then specify correspondences.

Because OWL-S is an XML-based language, and its atomic process declarations and input–output types already fit with WSDL, it is useful to extend existing WSDL bindings for OWL-S, such as the SOAP binding.

The OWL-S concept of grounding is generally consistent with the WSDL concept of binding. The WSDL is used as the ground of an OWL-S atomic process. Grounding OWL-S with WSDL and SOAP involves the construction of a WSDL service description with the message, operation, port type, binding, and service constructs. The OWL-S grounding shows how the inputs and outputs of an atomic process are realized as messages in transmittable format.

CREATING AN OWL-S ONTOLOGY FOR WEB SERVICES

Creating an OWL-S based Ontology for a Web Service requires five steps:

1. Describe individual programs: describe the individual programs that comprise the service. The process model provides a declarative description of a program's properties.
2. Describe the grounding for each atomic process: relate each atomic process to its grounding.
3. Describe compositions of the atomic processes: describe the composite process that is a composition of its atomic processes.
4. Describe a simple process: describe a simple process for the service (optional).
5. Profile description: provide a declarative advertisement for the service. It is partially populated by the process model.

CONCLUSION

This chapter discussed the markup language standards that form the building blocks for the next generation of Web Services: Semantic Web Services. We presented the state of development of Web Ontology Language for Services (OWL-S). In addition, related Web architectures and grounding OWL-S services with WSDL and SOAP were discussed.

EXERCISES

11-1. How could .NET and J2EE Web Services evolve toward automated discovery and delivery?

11-2. Can Semantic Web Services be implemented immediately without waiting for the full development of the Semantic Web?

11-3. Why would Semantic Web Services promote open Web standards and a distributed Web?

INTERLUDE #11: THE SEMANTIC WEB

Mary said, "Hi John; I hope you're headache is better."

John said, "I'm feeling much better; and I have to admit that your comments on distributed thinking—in machines—got me thinking as well. When we talk about artificial intelligence, it seems that we're focused on how or to what extent an individual computer could emulate the human behaviors that we call "thinking." But machine intelligence of that form is really old fashioned. Computers have been around for many decades, and while their capabilities continue to improve, they're not fundamentally different than they used to be, general purpose Turing machines with ever-improving software. The real advances seem to be in networks of computers."

Mary said, "You're right there. The advent of the Internet caught many by surprise, and when the basic ideas for the World Wide Web were laid out by Tim Berners-Lee in the 1980s, the power of a global network of interconnected networks really took off. The evolution of an increasingly powerful global network continues to be amazing; the Internet now touches people's lives in ways we couldn't have imagined only a few years ago. Still, the main value of the Internet is in connectivity and access to ever increasing amounts of information. One of these days, we will begin to see a shift from human-to-machine information access to a new paradigm where the vast information content of the Web will be machine processable. That's when the door will open for more intelligent behavior to emerge from the Web."

John said, "I don't know about the emergence of a human-like intelligence from the Web, but clearly the reforming of Web information to be machine processable could represent a major advance in the evolution of the Web. It would enable much more automated processing of information and would open the door for software agents to perform many automated functions that can now only be done by humans."

Mary said, "That's exactly my point. The conversion of the Web from a repository of static information to a place where software agents could begin to take on more of the actions now considered the realm of the human being could have profound impact. Berners-Lee calls this vision "The Semantic Web." I think this is where we'll begin to see more "intelligent" applications become commonplace. And as this develops, at some point we'll have to say that the Web has become at least more useful."

John said, "As usual, you have now pushed the point too far. The emergence of intelligent behavior in a network of interconnected machines is too big a leap for me. I think you've been reading too much science fiction. Let's be content that, if the obstacles of complexity and scaling can be overcome, the Semantic Web will offer new paths for the growth and evolution of the Web."

Mary said, "Do you think so?"

12

SEMANTIC SEARCH TECHNOLOGY

OVERVIEW

Today, searching the Web is an essential capability whether you are sitting at your desktop PC or wandering the corporate halls with your wireless PDA. As a result, the business of commercial search engines has become a vital and lucrative part of the Web. As search engines have become commonplace tools for virtually every user of the Web, companies, such as Google and Yahoo!, have become household names.

Recently, efforts have been made to implement limited semantic search by Google and other innovators. However, even with Google, it is common that searches return substantial unwanted results and may well miss the important information that you need.

Semantic search methods could augment and improve traditional search results by using not just words, but concepts and logical relationships. There are two basic approaches to improving search results through semantic methods: (*1*) using Semantic Web documents and (*2*) Latent Semantic Indexing (LSI).

This chapter explores semantic search engines and semantic search agents, including their current development and progress. Google's Page Rank algorithm, a Latent Semantic Indexing algorithms and the Semantic Web search applications TAP and Swoogle will also be discussed.

SEARCH ENGINES

Commercial search engines are based upon one of two forms of Web search technologies: human directed search and automated search.

Thinking on the Web: Berners-Lee, Gödel, and Turing, by H. Peter Alesso and Craig F. Smith
Copyright © 2006 John Wiley & Sons, Inc.

The human directed search engine technology utilizes a database of keywords, concepts, and references. The keyword searches are used to rank pages, but this simplistic method often leads to voluminous irrelevant and spurious results. In its simplest form, a content-based search engine will count the number of the query words (keywords) that occur in each of the pages that are contained in its index. The search engine will then rank the pages accordingly. More sophisticated approaches take into account the location of the keywords. For example, keywords occurring in the title tags of the Web page are more important than those in the body. Other types of human-directed search engines, like Yahoo! use topic hierarchies to help to narrow the search and make search results more relevant. These topic hierarchies are human created. Because of this, they are costly to produce and maintain in terms of time, and are subsequently not updated as often as the fully automated systems.

The fully automated form of Web search technology is based upon the Web crawler, spider, robot (bot), or agent, which follows HyperText Transfer Protocol (HTTP) links from site to site and accumulate information about Web pages to create a complex indexing system for storage. This agent-based search technology accumulates data automatically and is continuously updating information. (Note that the information is automatically collected as links to words, not as meaningful concepts as would be expected from a Semantic Web application.)

Current search engines are based upon huge databases of Web page references. There are two implementations of search engines: individual search engines and Metasearchers. Individual search engines (e.g., Google) compile their own searchable databases on the Web, while Metasearchers do not compile databases, but instead search the databases of multiple sets of individual engines simultaneously.

Ranking and Relevancy

In ranking Web pages, search engines follow a certain set of rules. Their goal, of course, is to return the most relevant pages at the top of their lists. To do this, they look for the location and frequency of keywords and phrases in the Web page document and, sometimes, in the Hypertext Markup Language (HTML) Meta tags. They check out the title field and scan the headers and text near the top of the document. Some of them assess popularity by the number of links that are pointing to a given site: the more links, the greater the popularity of the page.

Because Web search engines use keywords, they are subject to the two well-known linguistic phenomena that strongly degrade a query's precision and recall: Polysemy (one word might have several meanings) and Synonymy (several words or phrases might designate the same concept).

There are several characteristics required to improve a search engine's performance. It is important to consider useful searches as distinct from fruitless ones. To be useful, there are three necessary criteria: (*1*) maximum relevant information; (*2*) minimum irrelevant information; and (*3*) meaningful ranking, with the most relevant results first.

The first of these criteria, getting all of the relevant information available, is called recall. Without good recall, we have no guarantee that valid, interesting results will not be left out of our result set. We want the rate of false negatives, relevant results that we never see, to be as low as possible.

The second criterion, minimizing irrelevant information so that the proportion of relevant documents in our result set is very high, is called precision. With too little precision, our useful results get diluted by irrelevancies, and we are left with the task of sifting through a large set of documents to find what we want. High precision means the lowest possible rate of false positives.

There is an inevitable trade-off between precision and recall. Search results generally lie on a continuum of relevancy, so there is no distinct place where relevant results stop and extraneous ones begin.

This is why the third criterion, ranking, is so important. Ranking has to do with whether the result set is ordered in a way that matches our intuitive understanding of what is more and what is less relevant. Of course, the concept of "relevance" depends heavily on our own immediate needs, our interests, and the context of our search. In an ideal world, search engines would learn our individual preferences, so that they could fine-tune any search based on our past interests.

Google Search Algorithm

The heart of Google search software is PageRank, a system for ranking Web pages developed by the founders Larry Page and Sergey Brin at Stanford University. PageRank relies on the vast link structure as an indicator of an individual page's value. Essentially, Google interprets a link from page A to page B as a vote, by page A, for page B. Important sites receive a higher PageRank. Votes cast by pages that are themselves "important," weigh more heavily and help to make other pages "important."

Google combines PageRank with sophisticated text-matching techniques to find pages that are both important and relevant to the search. Google goes far beyond the number of times a term appears on a page and examines all aspects of the page's content (and the content of the pages linking to it) to determine if it is a good match for the query (see Google's PageRank Algorithm section).

Google's PageRank Algorithm. The PageRank algorithm is calculated as follows:

$$PR(A) = (1 - d) + d[PR(T1)/C(T1) + \cdots + PR(Tn)/C(Tn)]$$

where,

PR(A) is the PageRank of a page A

PR(T1) is the PageRank of a page T1

C(T1) is the number of outgoing links from the page T1

d is a damping factor in the range $0 < d < 1$, usually set to 0.85

The PageRank of a Web page is therefore calculated as a sum of the PageRanks of all pages linking to it (its incoming links), divided by the number of links on each of those pages (its outgoing links).

Traditional search engines are based almost purely on the occurrence of words in documents. Search engines like Google, however, augment this with information about the hyperlink structure of the Web. Nevertheless their shortcomings are still significant, including, there is a semantic gap between what a user wants and what they get, users cannot provide feedback regarding the relevance of returned pages, users cannot personalize the ranking mechanism that the search engine uses, and the search engine cannot learn from past user preferences.

SEMANTIC SEARCH

Google, with its 800 million hits per day, and >8 billion indexed Web pages, is undeniably the most popular commercial search engine used today, but even with Google, there are problems. For example, how can you find just the right bit of data that you need out of the ocean of irrelevant results provided?

As Web ontologies become widely available, it is reasonable to ask for better search capabilities that can truly respond to detailed content requests. This is the intent of semantic-based search engines and search agents. Semantic search seeks to find documents that have similar concepts, not just similar words.

There are two approaches to improving search results through semantic methods: Latent Semantic Indexing and Semantic Web Documents.

One short-term approach to garner semantic information from existing Web pages is to use LSI, which is an information retrieval method that organizes existing HTML information into a semantic structure that takes advantage of some of the implicit higher order associations of words with text objects. The resulting structure reflects the major associative patterns in the data. This permits retrieval based on the "latent" semantic content of the existing Web documents, rather than just on keyword matches. The LSI offers an application method that can be implemented immediately with existing Web documentation.

The Semantic Web will provide more meaningful metadata about content, through the use of Resource Description Framework (RDF) and Web Ontology Language (OWL) documents that will help to form the Web into a semantic network. In a semantic network, the meaning of content is better represented and logical connections are formed between related information.

However, most semantic network-based search engines would suffer performance problems because of the scale of the very large semantic network. In order for the semantic search to be effective in finding responsive results, the network must contain a great deal of relevant information. At the same time, a large network creates difficulties in processing the many possible paths to a relevant solution.

Once again, we are faced with the Semantic Web's basic trade-off between finding the maximum expressive power and the minimum computational complexity. Most of the early efforts on semantic-based search engines were highly dependent on natural language processing techniques to parse and understand the query sentence. One of the first and the most popular of these search engines is Cycorp (http://www.cyc.com). Cyc combines the world's largest knowledge base with the Web. Cyc (which takes it name from en-**cyc**-lopedia) is an immense, multi-contextual knowledge based. With Cyc Knowledge Server it is possible for Web sites to add common-sense intelligence and distinguish different meanings of ambiguous concepts.

SEMANTIC SEARCH TECHNOLOGY

As Web ontology becomes more advanced, using RDF and OWL tags will offer semantic opportunities for search.

Searching Techniques

Semantic search deals with concepts and logical relationships. If we examine the practical problems of semantic search, we will find that the search tree faces an incompleteness of logic resulting in the Incompleteness Problem, or the Halting Problem.

Inference can be viewed as a sequence of logical deductions chained together. At each point along the way, there might be different ways to reach a new deduction. So, in effect, there is a branching set of possibilities for how to reach a correct solution. This branching set can spread out in novel ways. For example, you might want to try to determine "Whom does Kevin Bacon know?" based on information about his family relationships, his movies, or his business contacts. So, there is more than one path to some conclusions. This results in a branching set of possibilities. Therefore, the inference in our system is a kind of search problem, displayed as a search tree.

It is possible to start at the top of the tree, the root, or with the branches. Taking the top of the tree, the query can be asked, Whom does Kevin Bacon know? Each step down from parent-to-child nodes in this tree can be viewed as one potential logical deduction that moves toward trying to assess the original query using this logical deductive step. The fan out of possibilities can be viewed as a branching tree, getting bushier and deeper. Each of the successful steps we take ends up becoming a parent node from which we seek additional child nodes. Eventually, a list of people "whom Kevin Bacon actually knows?" will be accumulated.

Imagine that each node in this tree represents a statement or fact to prove. Each link from a parent node to a child node represents one logical statement. Now the problem is that we have a big tree of possibilities and this could result in any search being limited to incomplete results.

In a complex logical system, there is an arbitrarily large number of potential proofs. Some of the potentially factual nodes may be arbitrarily long, and it may be uncertain if a determination of whether or not it is factual can be made (i.e., it may be uncertain if there is a proof). Gödel proved in the 1930s that any sufficiently complicated logical system is inherently incomplete (Undecidable). In other words, there are statements that cannot be logically proven. His argument in proving undecidability is also related to the Halting Problem.

The Halting Problem is a decision problem that can be informally stated as follows: Given a description of an algorithm and a description of its initial arguments, determine whether the algorithm, when executed with these arguments, ever halts (the alternative is that it runs forever without halting). Alan Turing proved in 1936 that there is no general method or algorithm that can solve the halting problem for all possible inputs.

The importance of the Halting Problem lies in the fact that it was the first problem to be proved undecidable. Subsequently, many other such problems have been described; the typical method of proving a problem to be undecidable is to reduce it to the Halting Problem.

The Halting Problem implies that certain algorithms will never end in a definite answer. When you consider the Web, you referring to millions of facts and tens of thousands of rules that can chain together in arbitrarily complicated and interesting ways; so the space of potential proofs is infinite and the tree becomes logically infinite. Due to this, you will run into some inherent incompleteness issues; for example, in a complex network, you cannot simply look at every possible factual statement, determine its truthfulness, and collect a complete set of all such results.

You run into incompleteness because the search tree is too large. So our approach must be to search only portions of the tree. There are well-known strategies for how one addresses search problems like this. One strategy is to search the tree in a depth-first fashion.

A depth-first search would start at the top of the tree and go as deeply as possible down some path, expanding nodes as you go, until you find a dead end. A dead end is either a goal (success) or a node where you are unable to produce new children. So the system cannot prove anything beyond that point.

Let us walk through a depth-first search and traverse the tree. Start at the top node and go as deeply as possible:

1. Start at the highest node.
2. Go as deeply as possible down one path.
3. When you run into a dead-end (i.e., a false statement), back-up to the last node that you turned away from. If there is a path there that you have not tried, go down it. Follow this option until you reach a dead-end or a goal (a true statement with no child nodes).
4. If this path leads to another dead-end, go back up a node and try the other branches.
5. This path leads to a goal. In other words, this final node is a positive result to the query. So you have one answer. Keep searching for other answers by going up a couple more nodes and then down a path you have not tried.
6. Continue until you reach more dead-ends and have exhausted search possibilities.

The advantage of depth-first search is that it is a very algorithmically efficient way to search trees in one format. It limits the amount of space that you have to keep for remembering the things you have not looked at yet. All you have to remember is the path back up. The disadvantage with depth-first search is that once you get started down some path, you have to trace it all the way to the end.

Another strategy for searching is a breadth-first search. Here you search layer by layer. First, you try to do all of the zero-step proofs, then you try to do all of the one-step proofs, and so on. The advantage of breadth-first search is that you are guaranteed to get the simplest proofs before you get anything that is strictly more complicated. This is referred to as the Ockham's Razor benefit. If there is an n-step proof, you will find it before you look at any $n + 1$-step proofs. The disadvantage of breadth-first search becomes apparent when you encounter huge deep trees. We also have huge bushy trees where you could have thousands, or tens of thousands, of child nodes. Another disadvantage of breadth-first searching is the amount of space you have to use to store what you have not examined as yet. So, if the third layer is explosively large, you would have to store all of the third level results before you could even look at them. With a breadth-first search, the deeper you go into the tree, the more space you will need. So, you find that each of the two traditional algorithms for search, depth-first and breadth-first, are going to run into problems with large systems.

There are two basic classes of search algorithms used to attempt to overcome the incompleteness and halting limitations: uninformed and informed. Uninformed, or blind, searches are those that have no information about the number of steps or the path cost from the current state to the goal. These searches include: depth-first, breadth-first, uniform-cost, depth-limiting, and iterative deepening search. Informed, or heuristic, searches are those that have information about the goal; this information is usually either an estimated path cost to it or estimated number of steps away from it. This information is known as the search agent heuristic. It allows informed searches to perform better than the blind searches and makes them behave in an almost "rational" manner. These searches include best-first, hill-climbing, beam, A*, and IDA* (iterative deepening A*) searches. These methods can provide significant improve in search.

WEB SEARCH AGENTS

While Web search engines are powerful and important to the future of the Web, there is another form of search that is also critical: Web search agents. A Web search agent will not perform like a commercial search engine. Search engines use database lookups from a knowledge base.

In the case of the Web search agent, the Web itself is searched and the computer provides the interface with the user. The agent's percepts are documents connected through the Web utilizing HTTP. The agent's actions are to determine if its goal of seeking a Web site containing a specified target (e.g., keyword or phrase), has been met and if not, find other locations to visit. It acts on the environment using output methods to update the user on the status of the search or the end results.

What makes the agent intelligent is its ability to make a rational decision when given a choice. In other words, given a goal, it will make decisions to follow the course of actions that would lead it to that goal in a timely manner.

An agent can usually generate all of the possible outcomes of an event, but then it will need to search through those outcomes to find the desired goal and execute the path (sequence of steps) starting at the initial or current state, to get to the desired goal state. In the case of the intelligent Web search agent, it will need to utilize a search to navigate through the Web to reach its goal.

Building an intelligent Web search agent requires mechanisms for multiple and combinational keyword searches, exclusion handling, and the ability to self-seed when it exhausts a search space. Given a target, the Web search agent should proceed to look for it through as many paths as are necessary. This agent will be keyword based. The method advocated is to start from a seed location (user provided) and find all other locations linked in a tree fashion to the root (seed location) that contains the target.

The search agent needs to know the target (i.e., keyword or phrase), where to start, how many iterations of the target to find how long to look (time constraint), and what methods should determine criteria for choosing paths (search methods). These issues are addressed in the software.

Implementation requires some knowledge of general programming, working with sockets, the HTTP, HTML, sorting, and searches. There are many languages with Web-based utilities, advanced application programming interfaces (APIs), and superior text parsing capabilities that can be used to write a Web search agent. Using a more advanced, efficient sorting algorithm will help improve the performance of the Web search agent.

The Web search agent design consists of four main phases: initialization, perception, action, and effect. In the initialization phase, the Web search agent should set up all variables, structures, and arrays. It should also get the base information it will need to conduct the hunt for the target, the goal, a place to start, and the method of searching. The perception phase is centered on using the knowledge provided to contact a site and retrieve the information from that location. It should identify if the target is present and should identify paths to other Universal Resource Locator (URL) locations. The action phase takes all of the information that the system knows and determines if the goal has been met (the target has been found and the hunt is over).

If the hunt is still active it must make the decision on where to go next. This is the intelligence of the agent, and the method of search dictates how "smart" the Web agent will be. If a match is found, the hunt is complete, and it provides output to the user. The Web search agent moves from the initialize phase to a loop consisting of the perception, action, and effect phases until the goal is achieved or cannot be achieved.

SEMANTIC METHODS

Semantic search methods augment and improve traditional search results by using not just words, but meaningful concepts. Several major companies are seriously addressing the issue of semantic search. There are two approaches to improving search results through semantic methods: (*1*) LSI and (*2*) Semantic Web documents.

LATENT SEMANTIC INDEX SEARCH

So far, we have reviewed search technology in general, and identified today's search limitations. Now, future technologies based upon the semantics will be explored. First, we will discuss implementing LSI, which may improve today's search capabilities without the extreme limitations of searching large semantic networks.

Building on the criteria of precision, ranking, and recall requires more than brute force. Assigning descriptors and classifiers to a text provides an important advantage, by returning relevant documents that do not necessarily contain a verbatim match to our search query. Fully described data sets can also provide an image of the scope and distribution of the document collection as a whole. This can be accomplished by examining the structure of categories and subcategories called taxonomy.

A serious drawback to this approach to categorizing data is the problem inherent in any kind of taxonomy: The world sometimes resists categorization. For example, is a tomato a fruit or a vegetable? What happens when we combine two document collections indexed in different ways? Solutions are called ontology taxonomies.

Regular keyword searches approach a document collection where either a document contains a given word or it does not. Latent semantic indexing adds an important step to the document indexing process. In addition to recording which keywords a document contains, the method examines the document collection as a whole, to see which other documents contain some of those same words.

Latent semantic indexing was first developed at Bellcore in the late 1980s and considers documents that have many words in common to be semantically close, and ones with few words in common to be semantically distant. Although the LSI algorithm does not understand anything about what the words mean, it notices the patterns.

When you search an LSI-indexed database, the search engine looks at similarity values it has calculated for every content word, and returns the documents that it thinks best fit the query. Because two documents may be semantically very close even if they do not share a particular keyword, LSI does not require an exact match to return useful results. Where a plain keyword search will fail if there is no exact match, LSI will often return relevant documents that do not contain the keyword at all.

Searching for Content

A semantic search engine is a remarkably useful solution. It can discover if two documents are similar even if they do not have any specific words in common and it can reject documents that share only uninteresting words in common.

Latent semantic indexing looks at patterns of words within a set of documents. Natural language is full of redundancies, and not every word that appears in a document carries semantic meaning. Frequently used words in English often do not carry content: examples include functional words, conjunctions, prepositions, and auxiliary verbs. The first step in doing LSI, therefore, is culling these extraneous words from a document. This is called stemming.

Stemming

Some of the preparatory work needed to get documents ready for indexing (e.g., stemming) is very language specific. For English documents, an algorithm called the Porter stemmer is used to remove common endings from words, leaving behind an invariant root form.

To obtain semantic content from a document, first make a complete list of all the words that appear in the collection and then stem them as follows: discard articles, prepositions, and conjunctions; discard common verbs (know, see, do, be); discard pronouns; discard common adjectives (big, late, high); discard frilly words (therefore, thus, however, albeit, etc.); discard any words that appear in every document; and discard any words that appear in only one document.

After stemming is complete, the results are modified according to algorithmic insights. The first of these insights applies to individual documents, and it is referred to as local weighting. Words that appear multiple times in a document are given a greater local weight than words that appear once.

In broad strokes, we present an algorithm that forms a web of documents and words: connecting all documents to all words. Given such a model of words and documents one can then establish values based on the distance of documents from each other. The "value" of any document to any other document might be designated as a function of the number of connections that must be traversed to establish a connection between documents. If two documents are connected by multiple routes, then those documents might have a high degree of correlation.

Term weighting is a formalization of two common-sense insights: content words that appear several times in a document are probably more meaningful than content words that appear just once; and infrequently used words are likely to be more interesting than common words. The implementation algorithm follows:

For each document: (1) Stem all of the words and throw away any common 'noise' words; (2) For each of the remaining words, visit and remember each document that has a direct relationship to this word. Score each document based on a distance function from the original document and the relative scarcity of the word in common; (3) For each of the as-of-yet-unvisited new related documents now being tracked. Recursively perform the same operation as above.

The particular weighting algorithm that was used is this: (*1*) For each increase in distance, divide a baseline score by two; (*2*) The score of each document is equal to the baseline divided by the square root of the popularity of the word. Overall this algorithm delivers a cheap semantic lookup based on walking through a document and creating a word graph.

The specification shown here is the simplest case and it could be improved in a variety of ways. There are many other scoring algorithms that could be used. Additionally, a thesaurus could be applied to help bridge semantic issues.

One interesting challenge would be to make the algorithm work "on the fly" so that as new documents were added they would self-score. Another challenge would be to find a way to distribute the algorithm over multiple machines for scalability.

The word stemming process gets rid of common words, such as "the" and "etc." This feeds input into the semantic algorithm that first stems the words appropriately, scores them according to the semantic algorithm, and sorts the results into the new rank order reflecting the semantic analysis.

Semantic Search Engine Application

We have developed a Semantic Search Engine as a Windows application, that uses Google APIs for an initial search that serves as input into our LSI stemming and ranking methods. The following is the completed application for download.

```
Download Demo: http://www.web-iq.com/downloadSSE.htm
```

TAP

An example of semantic search technology is TAP, where TAP (http://tap.stanford.edu/) is a distributed project involving researchers from the Stanford, IBM, and Worldwide Web Consortium (W3C). TAP leverages automated and semiautomated techniques to extract knowledge bases from unstructured and semistructured bodies of text. The system is able to use previously learned information to learn new information, and can be used for information retrieval.

Ontology describes concepts and relationships with a set of representational vocabulary. The aim of building ontologies is to share and reuse knowledge. Since the Semantic Web is a distributed network, there are different ontologies that describe semantically equivalent things. As a result, it is necessary to map elements of these ontologies if we want to process information on the scale of the Web. An approach for semantic search can be based on text categorization. In text categorization ontology, maps compare each element of an ontology with each element of the other ontology, then it determines a similarity metric on a per pair basis. Matched items are those whose similarity values are greater than a certain threshold.

In TAP, existing documents are analyzed using semantic techniques and converted into Semantic Web documents using automated techniques or manually by the document author using standard word processing packages. Both automated and guided analyses are used for intelligent reasoning systems and agents. As a result, traditional information retrieval techniques are enhanced with more deeply structured knowledge to provide more accurate results.

The solutions are built on a core technology called Semantic Web Templates. Utilizing knowledge representation, the creation, consumption, and maintenance of knowledge becomes transparent to the user, where TAP utilizes RDF, RDF Schema, and OWL.

SWOOGLE

"Swoogle" is a crawler-based indexing and retrieval system for Semantic Web documents using RDF and OWL. It is being developed by the University of Maryland Baltimore County (http://pear.cs.umbc.edu/swoogle/). It extracts metadata and computes relations between documents. Discovered documents are also indexed by an information retrieval system to compute the similarity among a set of documents and to compute rank as a measure of the importance of a Semantic Web document (SWD).

Semantic Web RDF and OWL documents are essentially a parallel universe to the Web of online HTML documents. A SWD is known for its semantic content. Since no conventional search engines can take advantage of semantic features, a search engine customized for SWDs, especially for ontologies, is necessary to access, explore, and query the Web's RDF and OWL documents.

A prototype Semantic Web search engine, Swoogle facilitates the finding of appropriate ontologies, and helping users specify terms and qualify type (class or property). In addition, the Swoogle ranking mechanism sorts ontologies by their importance.

Swoogle helps users integrate Semantic Web data distributed on the Web. It enables querying SWDs with constraints on the classes and properties. By collecting metadata about the Semantic Web, Swoogle reveals interesting structural properties, such as how the Semantic Web is connected, how ontologies are referenced, and how an ontology is modified externally.

Swoogle is designed to scale up to handle millions of documents and enables rich query constraints on semantic relations. The Swoogle architecture consists of a database that stores metadata about the SWDs. Two distinct Web crawlers discover SWDs and compute semantic relationships among the SWDs.

Semantic Web Documents

A Semantic Web Document is a document in RDF or OWL that is accessible to software agents. Two kinds of SWDs create Semantic Web ontologies (SWOs) and Semantic Web databases (SWDBs). A document is an SWO when its statements define new classes and properties or by adding new properties. A document is considered as a SWDB when it does not define or extend terms. An SWDB can introduce individuals and make assertions about them.

Swoogle Architecture

Swoogle architecture can be broken into four major components: SWD discovery, metadata creation, data analysis, and interface. These components work independently and interact with one another through a database.

The SWD discovery component discovers potential SWDs on the Web. The metadata creation component caches a snapshot of an SWD and generates objective metadata about SWDs at both the syntax and the semantic level. The data analysis component uses the cached SWDs and the created metadata to derive analytical reports, such as classification of SWOs and SWDBs, rank of SWDs, and the Information Retrieval (IR) index for the SWDs. The interface component focuses on providing data service.

Finding SWDs

It is not possible for Swoogle to parse all the documents on the Web to see if they are SWDs, however, the crawlers employ a number of heuristics for finding SWDs starting with a Google crawler that searches URLs using the Google Web service.

By looking at the entire Semantic Web, it is hard to capture and analyze relations at the RDF node level. Therefore, Swoogle focuses on SWD level relations that generalize RDF node level relations.

Ranking SWDs

The Swoogle algorithm, Ontology Rank, was inspired by Google's Page Rank algorithm and is used to rank search results. Ontology Rank takes advantage of the fact that the graph formed by SWDs has a richer set of relations and the edges represent explicit semantics derivable from the RDF and OWL.

Given SWDs A and B, Swoogle classifies inter-SWD links into four categories:

1. Imports (A,B): A imports all content of B.
2. Uses-term (A,B): A uses some of terms defined by B without importing B.
3. Extends (A,B): A extends the definitions of terms defined by B.
4. Asserts (A,B): A makes assertions about the individuals defined by B.

These relations should be treated as follows: if a surfer observes the imports (A,B) relation while visiting A, it will follow this link because B is semantically part of A. Similarly, the surfer may follow the extends (A,B) relation because it can understand the defined term completely only when it browses both A and B. Therefore, the assigned weight is different, which shows the probability of following that kind of link, to the four categories of inter-SWD relations.

The RDF node level relations to SWD level relations counts the number of references. The more terms in B referenced by A, the more likely a surfer will follow the link from A to B.

Indexing and Retrieving SWDs

Central to a Semantic Web search engine is the problem of indexing and searching SWDs. It is useful to apply IR techniques to documents not entirely subject to markup. To apply search to both the structured and unstructured components of a document it is conceivable that there will be some text documents that contain embedded markup.

Information retrieval techniques have some value characteristics, such as researched methods for ranking matches, computing similarity between documents, and employing relevance feedback. These complement and extend the retrieval functions inherent in Swoogle.

Currently, the most popular kinds of documents are Friend of a friend (FOAF) files and RSS files (RSS, an acronym for Really Simple Syndication, is a Web content syndication format). Swoogle is intended to support services needed by software agents and programs via web service interfaces. Using Swoogle, one can find all of the Semantic Web documents that use a set of properties or classes.

CONCLUSION

Today, searching the Web is an essential capability whether you are sitting at your desktop PC or wandering the corporate halls with your wireless PDA. However, even with Google, it may be difficult to find the right bit of data that you need and interface with the search results efficiently. However, semantic search methods augment and improve traditional search results by using not just words, but concepts and logical relationships.

This chapter explored semantic search engines and semantic search agents, including their current development and progress. Google's Page algorithm, Latent Semantic Indexing algorithm, and Semantic Web search applications TAP and Swoogle were discussed.

EXERCISES

12-1. Compare page ranking for traditional search engines with Google's Page Ranking method.

12-2. How do semantic networks improve relevancy?

INTERLUDE #12: THE HALTING PROBLEM

Mary returned to the corner fireplace and handed John his Latte. She was smirking as she took a sip from her cup and asked, "John, let me pose a question. Given the average Ph.D. student, will he ever complete his dissertation?"

John responded with a self-conscious grin, "Were you thinking of anyone in particular? Or were you merely posing an amusing form of the 'Halting Problem'?"

Mary said, "Well, the 'Halting Problem' is a decision problem where a given algorithm may never reach a conclusion. That may not be completely irrelevant to your case."

John said, "Don't go there." Then he added, "But consider a real 'Halting Problem'. The Web may be the largest graph ever created. It is really the market place of buyers and sellers: supply and demand. It's no coincidence that Google and Yahoo! are the fastest growing internet companies. In a perfect market, demand is simply a computer bit of information and supply is another; matching the two is very profitable. As a result, search must be one of the most important technologies of the future. Search will eventually mediate supply and demand globally. But all collected data has yet to be completely correlated and put together in useful relationships. What will happen when Google indexes the world?"

Mary said, "My issue with the 'Halting Problem' is not simply finding something. My problem is understanding something. The future of search is more about understanding than merely finding. Search will cross into the realm of intelligence when it understands a request, the way you and I understand this sentence. The perfect search must equal the perfect answer to any question. In short, search must build upon finding and understanding to develop inference and intelligence. Search is the obvious place for intelligence to happen and that leads to the Semantic Web."

John said, "The problem with trying to automatically derive truthful statements from known facts is a difficult one. Isn't that related to our earlier debate about 'truth and beauty'? Anyway, the search for true solutions by computer algorithm runs head on into the issue that some truths may not be provable at all, and we might not know whether or not this is the case in a particular situation. Our proving algorithm could continue forever without completing its task. So, we cannot simply say 'let's just look at every possible proof and gather up all the answers'."

Mary said, "However, there are practical methods to finding solutions to interesting decision problems."

John responded, "That's true enough, but it's an even more difficult problem when we consider search on a knowledge base such as the Semantic Web. In that case, we have to deal with millions of facts and thousands of rules that can be chained together in arbitrarily complicated and interesting ways. The number of truths that can be derived from known facts and accepted rules is immense, and the tree that represents these connections is effectively infinite. As a result, trying to follow a sequence of logical steps that can halt at some inherently practical solution still implies limitations on completeness."

Mary answered, "It seems to me that you're seeking to find nothing but insurmountable difficulty."

John came back: "Based on Gödel's Incompleteness Theorem, Turing found that the 'Halting Problem' was undecidable."

Mary answered, "Nevertheless, we still do have functioning search technology. Even though we run into incompleteness because the search tree that we're describing for the Web is too large, the approach has to be to search only portions of the tree. There are well-known strategies for how one addresses search problems like this. One strategy is to search the tree in a "depth-first" fashion. Another strategy for searching is the breadth-first search. The advantage of breadth-first search is that we're guaranteed to get the simplest and most immediate search results before we get anything that's more complicated. This is referred to as the Ockham's Razor benefit. If there is an n-step result, we'll find it before we look at any $n + 1$-step nodes."

John responded, "Well there are many useful strategies for the search in general. But I find it hard to believe that any search technology will produce practical results in dealing with the 'Halting Problem' for the Semantic Web."

Mary shrugged, "Try thinking positive for a change and maybe you will be the one to find a way."

13

SEMANTIC PATTERNS
AND ADAPTIVE SOFTWARE

OVERVIEW

Someone may have already solved your problem and a pattern might exist that you can mimic. Semantic patterns along with adaptive software is an area of innovation that could offer significant efficiency gains for the highly structured Semantic Web through the process of automatically implementing performance improvements. Semantic patterns may prove useful to bridge the different representations and different ways of modeling knowledge. Because patterns are often found in highly structured, repetitive environments, they offer an important methodology for improving the efficiency of agents on the Semantic Web. By creating agents that can self-organize, respond to feedback, and adapt, the agents may be able to find efficiencies that make finding logic solutions on the Semantic Web practical. This chapter, presents some basic concepts of semantic patterns followed by a brief discussion of adaptive software.

PATTERNS IN SOFTWARE DESIGN

What does it take to become a software design master? To some extent, becoming a master of software design is like becoming a master chess player. The process of becoming a chess master consists of several steps. First, learn the rules including the names of pieces, legal movements, chess board geometry and orientation. Second, learn the basic principles including the relative value of the pieces, the

Thinking on the Web: Berners-Lee, Gödel, and Turing, by H. Peter Alesso and Craig F. Smith
Copyright © 2006 John Wiley & Sons, Inc.

strategic value of the center squares, and the power of a threat. Then, third, study the games of the masters including those games containing patterns that must be understood and applied.

Similarly, becoming a software design master requires the following analogous steps: (*1*) Learn the rules: algorithms, data structures, and languages of software. (*2*) Learn the principles: structured programming, modular programming, object oriented programming, and generic programming. (*3*) Study the designs of masters: Find patterns to be understood and applied. By taking this approach, it is abundantly clear how patterns play a vital role in developing deep programming expertise. But understanding recognized patterns is just the beginning of the process of thinking in terms of using patterns and creating new programs.

PATTERN FRAME

The pattern frame delineates the problem space and shows the relationships between patterns. The pattern frame represents progressive levels of abstraction: architecture, design, and implementation. It represents perspectives of the solution including database, application, deployment, and infrastructure.

Design Pattern History

The origin of design patterns lies in work of architect Christopher Alexander during the late 1970s. He began by writing two books, "A Pattern Language" and "A Timeless Way of Building" which, in addition to giving examples, described his rationale for documenting design patterns.

The pattern movement remained quiet until 1987 when the topic of patterns and their application to software design reappeared at an Object Oriented Programming Systems Languages and Applications (OOPSLA) conference. Since then, many papers and presentations have emerged. In 1995, Erich Gamma, Richard Helm, Ralph Johnson, and John Vlissides published "Design Patterns: Elements of Reusable Object-Oriented Software," which stimulated other similar articles.

Patterns Defined

Software reuse provides a basis for drastic improvement in software quality and developer productivity. Patterns support reuse of software architecture, ontologies, and design. There are many successful solutions to various areas of human endeavor, all of which are deeply rooted in patterns. Patterns are devices that allow programs to share knowledge about their design.

In daily programming, many problems that have occurred will occur again. The question is how will we solve them this time. Documenting patterns is one way to reuse and possibly share the information that is learned, about how it is best to solve a specific program design problem.

A pattern describes a recurring problem that occurs in a given context and based upon a set of guiding forces recommends a solution. The solution is usually a simple mechanism, a collaboration between two or more classes, objects, services, processes, threads, components, or nodes that work together to resolve the problem identified in the pattern.

Because patterns can readily be found in highly structured, repetitious environments, they offer a very attractive methodology for improving the efficiency of agents on the Semantic Web.

SEMANTIC PATTERNS

One area where semantic patterns may be useful is as a communication tool between Semantic Web developers and designers who are mapping different target languages with different representations and different ways of modeling knowledge. While seeking to reuse semantics across boundaries that include different representation languages and different formal models, we may recognize characteristics of the semantic models that remain constant.

The goal is for semantic interchangeability through the capturing of these characteristics. However, this is difficult because different language definitions come with different formal models. In general, the models of two different languages may not be comparable. Or there may be several semantically equivalent statements within one language. Their equivalence may be, in general (e.g., for first-order predicate logic), undecidable. Thus, a translation may not exist.

Software design patterns may prove helpful where they are able to describe successful solutions to common software problems. Design patterns are a valuable technique in software engineering because they capture experts' successful experience, make implicit design knowledge explicit, and explain the deep structure and rationale of a design.

A design pattern is an abstract solution for how a problem can be solved without prescribing how the concrete implementation should be done. Consequently, the reuse of successful design patterns may be easier to achieve.

Design patterns include several varieties. Creational patterns deal with initializing and configuring classes and objects. Structural patterns deal with decoupling interface and implementation of classes and objects. Behavioral patterns deal with dynamic interactions among societies of classes and objects.

Useful patterns for semantics could include upper ontologies and domain ontologies, closure axioms and open world reasoning, n-ary relations, and classes as values.

Some choices for representation are not semantically motivated, but are made in order to generate some particular behavior of the system.

Direct translation from one representation language into another does not seem a viable approach. Alternatively, one can construct a particular representation according to an explicit model and then compile the final representation into the other target language. Semantic characteristics (e.g., inheritance conditions) show up in common representation languages (e.g., `rdfs:subclass` and `rdf:type` in RDFS). Other semantic characteristics can be modeled independently from a particular target language to be mapped into a wide range of languages.

However, there exists no comprehensive concept for engineering semantics in a way that is fully reusable across several languages. The problem of describing formal model characteristics for all representation languages cannot be solved by producing a closed list of modeling primitives. Therefore, there is a need for a technique of describing new semantic primitives at a higher level of abstraction.

Semantic Patterns for the Semantic Web

Patterns are used to solve a problem. They capture solutions, not just abstract principles or strategies. As a result, patterns prove concepts and capture solutions with a track record, and they describe relationships.

A semantic pattern may be implemented by translating its primitives into the target language. Thus, if one gives an instantiation of a semantic pattern together with some example facts related to the pattern, the implementation may yield semantic consequences.

Semantic patterns can be used for communicating some information to developers and computer systems. Resource Description Framework (RDF) may be the ideal format for the representation of the semantic pattern itself.

Semantic Pattern Libraries

Eventually, the need for particular semantic patterns will be driven by Semantic Web developers. With the engineering of ontologies on the Web, new ideas will come up about what type of inferencing should be supported and what type of representation systems should be used. Building the basic idea of semantic patterns on the Web requires technical representation and the establishment of semantic pattern libraries.

Semantic Patterns Language

The problem of computational semantics is central for making computer systems intelligent. The ability to code and process semantics efficiently will be essential to the Semantic Web. New trends in computing (e.g., pervasive computing) with the emphasis on intelligence of content processing and intellectual interfaces will lead to the development of new methods like the Semantic Patterns Language (SEMPL) (see http://sempl.net/) and increase the importance of computational semantics problem solving.

Semantic Patterns Language is a model for efficient coding of semantics. It has supported the results of the Universal Semantic Code (USC), which has already demonstrated applicability to multitude of problems.

SELF-ORGANIZING AND ADAPTIVE SOFTWARE

Self-organizing network software refers to a network's ability to organize and configure itself according to environmental conditions. Adaptation software refers to the ability of applications to learn and adapt to the changing conditions in the network. As a result self-organizing and adaptive software may use information from the environment to improve its performance and function over time.

These new approaches to software function are in the research stages compared to more traditional programming. In the 1970s, Structured Programming made it feasible to build larger scale software systems based on existing specifications. A typical application was a database program that read an input file and produced an output file. In the 1980s, Object-Oriented Programming made it easier to reorganize for changes because functionality was split up into separate classes. A typical application was a desktop publishing system using user-initiated events (mouse clicks or menus).

Hundreds of programming languages have been developed since 1952, but some of the more significant languages include FORTRAN, ALGOL, LISP, COBOL, APL, SIMULA, BASIC, PL/I, Prolog, C, Pascal, Scheme, Ada, Parlog, C++, Eiffel, Mathematica, Oberon, Haskell, and Java. Yet, despite this diversity of language types, traditional software development with these tools has always been based on principles requiring exact specification, complex maintenance, and high levels of abstraction.

Adaptive Programming is aimed at the problem of producing applications that can readily adapt in the face of changing user needs and environments. Adaptive software explicitly represents the goals that the user is trying to achieve. This makes it possible for the user to change goals without a need to rewrite the program. A typical application is an information filter.

Adaptive software may offer functionality based upon a feedback loop that updates information based on successful performance. The design criterion itself becomes a part of the program and the program reconfigures itself as its successful performance changes. The highly structured architecture of the Semantic Web should offer a significant number of semantic patterns that could produce optimized performance through adaptive software processing.

Genetic Algorithms

A genetic algorithm is a model for machine learning in which a population of randomly created units goes through a selection process of evolution: A digital "survival of the fittest" in which each unit represents a point in a problem's solution search space.

Individual units are referred to as chromosomes and consist of genes or parameters of the problem being optimized. A collection of chromosomes on which a genetic algorithm operates is called a population. Through fitness functions, chromosomes are evaluated and ranked according to their relative strength within the population. The fitter are chosen to reproduce while the remaining fails to survive succeeding generations. After a number of generations, the algorithm should converge on the chromosomes representing an optimal solution. It is worth noting the implicit parallelism of genetic algorithms.

While genetic algorithms exist mostly as research activities at academic institutions and commercial applications are still largely in developmental stages, they do offer Web applications the potential ability to adapt to their environment.

In the digital world, genetic algorithms, capable of adapting to their environment faster than their competition, can obtain a significant advantage for survival. Already, software engineers are introducing Genetic Algorithms for the Web using Java, but progress in this area would most likely benefit from the development of a language with specific qualifications for these types of applications.

Learning Algorithm

We can define a learning algorithm as a process that takes a data set from a database as input and after performing an algorithmic operation returns an output statement representing learning. As the Semantic Web increases the percentage of applications and protocols with learning algorithms, we can expect improvements in performance both in quality and type. The Web may become a learning network through a composition of the Semantic Web architecture plus the addition of components of AI agents built with adaptive software languages.

CONCLUSION

Semantic patterns on the Web will make it easier to reuse software modules in representation systems and easier to communicate between different Semantic Web developers. Semantic patterns may be useful to communicate between Semantic Web developers and designers that produce mappings for reuse into different target languages, thus bridging between different representations and different ways of modeling knowledge.

This chapter presented the basic concepts of Patterns and adaptive software and their application to semantics.

EXERCISE

13-1. Suggest innovative technologies that have the potential to compete for the next generation Web architecture.

INTERLUDE #13: THE SEMANTIC WEB AND RULES

Apparently lost in thought, John was sitting in the study hall, when Mary walked up to him. Seeing that he was studying Web architecture she said, "Well, have you done enough thinking to reach a conclusion?"

"How much is enough thinking?" John asked looking up.

"I don't exactly know," said Mary, "but it seems to be always a little more than anyone ever does." Mary put her books on the table and took a seat across from John.

John said, "Nevertheless, I have been thinking about the Semantic Web language pyramid and the amount of effort it will require to design automated applications: never mind producing a 'thinking' Web."

Mary said, "The addition of logic to Web architecture is a complex process, but could yield great dividends. Google is already preparing to put millions of library books on-line. Consider what would happen if that information could eventually be access as part of a semantic network with a semantic search engine."

John said, "Perhaps, but wouldn't it be easier to use proprietary server AI applications to express and manipulate semantic information. The current method of proprietary frameworks on servers for Web service applications could merely be extended."

Mary frowned, "At the cost of incompatibility between proprietary framework applications. Not to mention the loss of global machine processing of all that Web information. No, adding logic and rule systems to the Web will permit a scheme for constructing valid Web inferences. Related proof systems can be formed from a set of rules, which can be chained together to form proofs, or derivations. Through the Semantic Web, logic can be used by software agents to make decisions and search terabytes of data. It is a *beautiful* possibility."

John said, "But the ugly *truth* is it can lead to undecidability, paradox, and recursion. Under completely open standards, the Web could remain a distributed network. However, proprietary server standards with critical portal and hub access could focus Web traffic to produce a decentralized network with dominating sites (e.g., AOL, Google, Yahoo!, and MSN). These hubs may just be the best places to develop and access AI applications."

Mary said, "Currently, vendors support different frameworks on their specialized Web servers. The J2EE framework works to optimize UNIX/LINUX flavor servers for applications provided by one group of vendors and .NET framework works to optimize Windows servers for applications provided by Microsoft and its supporters. So long as the business logic is controlled by vender-specific frameworks, interoperability, overall efficiency, trust, security, and unbiased growth will remain problematic. I think that moving toward an open markup language standard will level the playing field worldwide and allow business logic, inference and other intelligent applications to be more fully utilized."

John said, "I think I can safely say that you are thinking too much."

14

SEMANTIC TOOLS

OVERVIEW

The unique needs of the Semantic Web require tools for ontology development, content generation, and content analysis. Tools for ontology development include ontology editing, visualization, and analysis. Content generation requires static and dynamic mark-up generation. Needed content analysis and validation tools include APIs, inference engines, query, persistence, and translation. Semantic tools are already being developed; these include Resource Description Framework (RDF) and Web Ontology Language (OWL) editors, parsers, servers, databases, and inference engines. Some of the more widely used tools include Jena, SMORE, and Drive.

This chapter identifies and examines some of the latest Semantic Web tools. In addition, the early development tools in the area of Semantic Web Services are discussed, which include WSDL2DAML-S Converter, Web Service Composer, DL Mapping, and DAML-S Matchmaker.

SEMANTIC TOOLS

A layered approach to ontology creation and annotation has been adopted by the Worldwide Web Consortium (W3C) in order to support the Semantic Web. Tools to support these efforts are making significant progress. However, the tools themselves are partly dependent on the ontology language they are intended to support.

Thinking on the Web: Berners-Lee, Gödel, and Turing, by H. Peter Alesso and Craig F. Smith
Copyright © 2006 John Wiley & Sons, Inc.

Semantic Web languages will depend on distributed computing principles. Software agents must move as mobile code from host-to-host carrying their state with them. They will be built for moving data between different applications. The ability to act autonomously through true mobility of the code comes from the execution of computational tasks and not from the data.

Table 14-1 displays a list of some of the Semantic Web software tool developers and their products.

In the following sections, several of the more prominent tools are presented and evaluated.

Ontology Tools

Software tools are available to accomplish most aspects of ontology development. While ontology editors are useful during each step of the development process, other types of ontology building tools are also needed. Development projects often involve solutions using numerous ontologies from external sources as well as existing and newly developed in-house ontologies. Ontologies from any source may progress through a series of versions. In the end, careful management of heterogeneous ontologies will become necessary.

Ontologies may be derived from or transformed into forms, such as W3C extensible Markup Language (XML) Schemas, database schemas, and Unified Modeling Language (UML) to achieve integration with associated enterprise applications. Tools can help to map and link between ontologies, compare them, reconcile and validate them, merge them, and convert them into other forms.

Some editors are intended for building ontologies in a specific domain, but still are capable of general-purpose ontology building regardless. These ontology editors may have enhanced support for information standards unique to their target domain. An example in medicine is the OpenKnoMe editor's support of the GALEN reference medical terminology.

Editors may also support a broad upper level ontology, as in the case of the editing environment that has grown up around the unique Cyc ontology. Ontolingua and OpenCyc offer development environments affording highly expressive and complete ontology specifications. OpenCyc also provides native access to the most complete upper level ontology available (Cyc).

The enterprise-oriented products have often started out as data integration tools like Unicorn Solutions and Modulant. Or as content management tools like Applied Semantics. These products include linguistic classification and stochastic analysis capabilities to aid in information extraction from unstructured content. This information can potentially become instance data or extend the ontology itself.

A few ontology editors like Microsoft's Visio for Enterprise Architects, use an object-oriented specification language to model an information domain. When ontology technologies emerged in the 1990s, the focus on knowledge acquisition influenced new capabilities. Early ontology editors adopted the popular "KADS" (Knowledge Analysis and Documentation System) method for developing knowledge bases.

TABLE 14-1. Semantic Software Developers and Tools

Company	Product	Category
AIdministrator www.aidministrator.nl/	Sesame Spectacle	RDF(S) storage and retrieval Ontology-based information presentation
Applied Semantics www.appliedsemantics.com/	Circa	Ontology-based automatic categorization
Cycorp www.cyc.com/	Cyc Knowledge Server	Multicontextual knowledge base/inference engine
DigitalOwl www.digitalowl.com/	KineticEdge	Content management/ publishing
Empolis www.empolis.co.uk/	K42	Topic map server
Eprise www.eprise.com/	Participant Server	Content management
Epigraph www.epigraph.com/	Xcellerant	Content management/ontology management
Forward look inc www.forwardlook.com/	ContextStreams	Data asset management
GlobalWisdom www.globalwisdom.org/	Bravo engine	Facilitated ontology construction/dynamic knowledge engine
Intellidimension www.intellidimension.com/	RDF Gateway	RDF data management system
Inxight www.inxight.com/	ThingFinder Server Star Tree Viewer	Content extraction Web content navigation
Mohomine www.mohomine.com/	Several	Information extraction and classification
Network Inference www.networkinference.com/	Cerebra	Inference engine and tools
Ontoprise www.ontoprise.de/	Ontobroker	Inference middleware
Stanford Univ. protege.stanford.edu/	Protégé	Ontology Editor
Persist www.persistag.com	Semantic Base	Knowledge management system
Profium www.profium.com/	Smart Information Router (SIR)	Semantic content management based on RDF
R-Objects www.r-objects.com/	Pepper	Personal knowledge management
SC4 Solution Clustering www.sc4.org/	SemTalk	RDFS editor based on Visio
Semio www.semio.com/	SemioMap	Content categorization and indexing
SMORE—Semantic Markup, Ontology and RDF Editor www.mindswap.org	MindSwap	SMORE is a application that incorporates four applications in one.

(*continued overleaf*)

TABLE 14-1 (*continued*)

Company	Product	Category
Tarragon Consulting Corporation www.tgncorp.com/	High-performance knowledge and content management systems	Custom systems design and development
TheBrain.com http://www.thebrain.com/	TheBrain	Information organizer
Unicorn Solutions www.unicorn.com/	Unicorn Coherence	Ontology modeling and data integration
Verity www.verity.com/	K2	Business portal infrastructure
Voquette www.taalee.com/	Semantic Engine WorldModel	Knowledge-based rich media content management

Some editors incorporate the ability to add additional axioms and deductive rules to the ontology. Rule extensions are mostly proprietary. Protégé from Stanford offers an editing environment with several third-party plug-ins. Protégé is a free, open source ontology editor and knowledge-base framework. It is based on Java, is extensible, and provides a foundation for customized knowledge-based applications. Protégé supports Frames, XML Schema, RDF(S), and OWL. It is a tool that allows users to construct domain ontologies, customize data entry forms, and enter data.

Cerebra

Cerebra is an OWL DL tool development software company. By leveraging inference driven technology, Cerebra provides solutions to business problems in innovative ways. Cerebra develops ontologies and external source. Cerebra developed a commercial-grade inference platform, providing industry-standard query, high-performance inference, and management capabilities with emphasis on scalability, availability, robustness, and 100% correctness. The CEREBRA repository for metadata, vocabulary, security, and policy management is available at: www.cerebra.com.

Visual Ontology Modeler

The Visual Ontology Modeler by Sandpiper Software www.sandsoft.com develops business semantics infrastructure solutions for context-driven search, collaborative applications, and cross-organizational content interoperability. This includes semantically aware, knowledge-based products and provides context development services that facilitate business information interoperability, terminology normalization, and context resolution across web-based and enterprise information systems. The Visual Ontology Modeler includes UML-based modeling, add-in to Rational Rose, and produces RDF, OWL, DAML, and UML.

Jena: Java API for RDF

Researchers at Hewlett Packard Labs have been developing a Java-based open source Semantic Web toolkit called Jena. Jena is compliant with the current decisions made by the RDF-core and WebOnt Working Groups of W3C. Jena can be downloaded from SourceForge and includes the ARP RDF parser; an RDF API including RDF datatyping; an ontology API; ontology readers; storage mechanisms; plug-in reasoner API; reasoners for RDFS and for the rules-based subset of OWL; and Query language and implementation: RDQL. Jena is in widespread use within the semantic community. Such toolkits enable the development of myriad example applications, helping to embody the Semantic Web vision.

SMORE: Semantic Markup, Ontology, and RDF Editor

Semantic Markup, Ontology, and RDF Editor (SMORE) is a tool that allows users to markup their documents in RDF using Web ontologies in association with user-specific terms and elements.

This software provides the user with a flexible environment to create a Semantic Web page. It allows the user to markup a document with minimal knowledge of RDF terms and syntax. However, the user should be able to semantically classify thus data set for annotation, that is, breakup sentences into the basic subject–predicate–object model. It also provides a reference to existing ontologies in order to use more precise references in Web pages/text. The user can also create their own ontology from scratch and borrow terms from existing ontologies.

Drive

A C# parser named "Drive" is a relatively uncomplicated API. The Drive RDF browser is a tool for parsing and validating RDF documents using the Drive RDF Parser. It works like a standard Web browser. The browser displays any document just like a regular Web browser with one exception: If you type in a URL and hit enter or click the Parse RDF button, the browser will attempt to parse and validate the RDF document at that URL. If it do not find any RDF, it switches back to standard browser mode. Drive parses RDF/XML documents and builds an abstract graph that can be recursively traversed. Drive is fully compliant with the RDF Syntax Specification.

SEMANTIC WEB SERVICES TOOLS

There are a number of new development tools and toolmakers for the Semantic Web Services already available and more are coming. The currently available

TABLE 14-2. Semantic Web Services Software Tools

Author and Affiliation	Product	Visit
Massimo Paolucci, Carnegie-Mellon University	WSDL2DAML-S Converter	www.daml.ri.cmu.edu/wsdl2damls
Ervin Sirin, Mindswap.org	Web Service Composer	www.daml.ri.cmu.edu/wsdl2damls
Joachin Peer, University of St. Gallen	DL Mapping Tool	sws.mcm.unisg.ch/xmldl/mapper-win32.zip for win32 systems.
Katia Sycara, Carnegie-Mellon University	DAML-S Matchmaker	www.damlsmm.ri.cmu.edu/

Semantic Web Services tools under development include: profile, process, and profile tools for services, as well as composition, conversion, and parsing tools.

Table 14-2 displays a list of some of the leading Semantic Web Services software tool developers.

Each of these software tools is discussed in further detail in the following sections.

WSDL2DAML-S Converter

Massimo Paolucci of Carnegie-Mellon University has developed a tool for converting WSDL into DAML-S called "WSDL2DAML-S Converter." It provides a partial conversion from WSDL Web-services descriptions to DAML-S descriptions. The tool provides a complete specification of the grounding and the atomic processes of the DAML-S Process Model. In addition, it provides a partial specification of the DAML-S Profile. After the transformation, the specification of the complex processes in the Process Model requires providing the XSLT transformation from the data types used by WSDL and the DAML ontologies used by the DAML-S description. Finally, it is necessary to complete the description of the DAML-S Profile.

Web Service Composer

Ervin Sirin of Mindswap.org has developed a tool called the Web Service composer (see http://www.mindswap.org/~evren/composer/). The Web Service composer is a prototype tool that guides a user in the dynamic composition of Web Services. The semiautomatic process includes presenting matching services to the user of a composition, and filtering the possibilities by using semantic descriptions of the services. The generated composition is then directly executable through the WSDL grounding of the services.

The basic functionality of the composer is to let the users invoke Web Services annotated with DAML-S. The user is presented a list of services registered to the system and can execute an individual Web service by entering input parameters. The DAML-S services are executed using the WSDL grounding information.

By using the composer, it is possible to create a workflow of Web Services. The composition is done in a semiautomatic fashion where composer presents the available choices. Composer provides a filtering mechanism to limit the services shown and let the user locate the most relevant service for the current task. The ontology of DAML-S ServiceProfiles are used to dynamically build up a filtering panel, where constraints on various properties of the service may be entered.

DL Mapping Tool

Joachin Peer University of St. Gallen has created a Semantic Web Services description of (using DAML-S) for XML Web Services, that tells agents how to transform an XML element into a Description Logics (DAML/OWL) construct and vice versa. In DAML-S, there exists an attribute "xsltTransformation" that carries this kind of "mapping information" using XSL. The XSL document specifies how the mapping between XML grammars and Description Logic concept descriptions is carried out. Since the construction of such mapping documents is an error, this tool is aimed to support developers during this process; the tool allows mapping documents via mouse clicks and the tool allows verification of the mappings created "on the fly." The mapping tool was developed using Java2 and the Eclipse SWT library.

DAML-S Matchmaker

Katia Sycara of Carnegie Mellon University has developed the DAML-S Matchmaker. The Matchmaker is a Web Services tool that helps make connections between service requesters and service providers. The Matchmaker serves as a "yellow pages" of service capabilities. It allows users and/or software agents to find each other by providing a mechanism for registering service capabilities. Registration information is stored as advertisements. When the Matchmaker agent receives a query from a user or another software agent, it searches its dynamic database of advertisements for agents that can fulfill the incoming request. The Matchmaker serves as a liaison between a service requester and a service provider.

The DAML-S Matchmaker employs techniques from information retrieval, AI, and software engineering to compute the syntactical and semantic similarity among service capability descriptions. The matching engine of the matchmaking system contains five different filters for namespace comparison, word frequency comparison, ontology similarity matching, ontology matching, and constraint matching. The user configures these filters to achieve a trade-off between performance and matching quality.

CONCLUSION

This chapter introduced some of the rapidly developing tools and toolmakers for the Semantic Web Services. The currently available Semantic Web tools under development include editors, parsers, servers, databases, and inference engines. The early Semantic Web Services development tools included WSDL2DAML-S, DAML-S Converter, Web Service Composer, DL Mapping, and DAML-S Matchmaker.

EXERCISE

14-1. Download, install, and create a Semantic Web page using one of the Semantic Editors (e.g., Protégé). Provide comments.

INTERLUDE #14: THE SEMANTIC WEB AND LANGUAGE

John walked up the steps at the library and sat down next to Mary who was typing away on her laptop responding to an email she had received over the campus wireless broadband.

Mary interrupted her correspondence to comment, "I really look forward to the next few years as ubiquitous computing and smart applications really take-off."

John replied, "Does that include the Semantic Web as well?"

Mary said, "Of course, in some form. The Semantic Web could bring not just order, but "meaning" to the vast amount of information on the Web. Scalability will undoubtedly be the finally determining factor on whether the Semantic Web is a practical."

John said, "Frankly, given the difficulty in producing AI in small closed environments, I find it hard to believe that the Semantic Web isn't a mirage."

Mary said, "Everyone agrees that bringing more intelligence and order to the Web is the right thing to do. The RDF, RDF Schema, and OWL standards allow programmers to embed information in Web content that, theoretically, tells a computer everything it needs to know about the meaning, the ontology, of the information and how one word relates to another."

John said, "Display languages, and data languages, and relationship languages, and schema, and ontology languages, and rule languages, and security, and trust. It seems to me that you've forgotten what made the Web a success. It was the simple, easy to use tools, like HTTP, HTML, and URL. A high school student could easily publish their own Web pages. The Semantic Web has become so burdensome that at a minimum it will require computer science graduate students to develop ontologies and applications."

Mary said, "It is possible that the Semantic Web is somewhat overdesigned to be the future Web architecture and it is possible that an elegant alternative may offer a startling solution. After all, in the late 1980s when AOL, CompuServe, and Microsoft were investing fortunes in proprietary networks that offered mostly duplicated and limited amounts of information to the public for a fee, Berners-Lee was designing a cheap, efficient, easy, and simple way for universal access to great stores of information for free. It shouldn't be a surprise if history repeated itself. But for now the Semantic Web is the best game in town."

John said, "My best guess for the future of the Semantic Web is that it is too overly structured with its many layers of languages for logic and machine processing, and that the computational complexity and trust issues will ultimately prove unsolvable."

Mary concluded, "Nevertheless, one must still travel the path to the journey's end, if only to learn the way, grasshopper."

15

CHALLENGES AND OPPORTUNITIES

OVERVIEW

Today, computers and small devices are creating ubiquitous access to a flood of Web information that is becoming more and more difficult to search, access, and maintain. Creating machine-processable semantics could alleviate these difficulties and open the way for a new burst of growth and utility for the Web. The question is, At what cost?

Kurt Gödel, Alan Turing, and Tim Berners-Lee have all made important contributions to the development of the Information Revolution we are immersed in today, and as a result, the Web is evolving into a resource with intelligent features and capabilities. The Semantic Web promises to make Web content machine understandable, allowing agents and applications to access a variety of heterogeneous resources and to carry out more automated functions without the need for human interaction or interpretation. The languages of the Semantic Web are much richer than Hypertext Mark-up Language (HTML) and eXtensible Markup Language (XML). They represent the meaning, logic, and structure of content.

On the other hand, significant ontology and logic limitations that challenge the development of the Semantic Web have been identified. These limitations touch some of the most difficult problems in logic, such as paradox, recursion, trust, undecidability, computational complexity, and machine intelligence.

This chapter discusses the challenges and opportunities facing the development of the Semantic Web.

Thinking on the Web: Berners-Lee, Gödel, and Turing, by H. Peter Alesso and Craig F. Smith
Copyright © 2006 John Wiley & Sons, Inc.

SEMANTIC DOUBTS

Berners-Lee intended the Semantic Web to bring not just order, but "meaning" to the vast amount of information on the Web. His dream is to make it possible for computers to understand the Web and perform complex tasks. Agents would attempt to find available information and automatically solve problems. However, computer scientists have had considerable trouble trying to impart artificial intelligence even under highly controlled laboratory environments. Developing an intelligent agent that could operate across the World Wide Web is proving to be an extremely demanding endeavor.

Everyone agrees that bringing more intelligence and order to the Web is the right thing to do; however, the question is how best to do it. The World Wide Web Consortium (W3C) is pushing forward with a highly structured approach to the problem by supporting the development of complex new languages for posting meaningful Web content.

Resource Description Framework (RDF), RDF Schema (RDFS), and Web Ontology Language (OWL) standards allow programmers to embed information in Web content that, theoretically, tells a computer everything it needs to know about the meaning of the information: how one word relates to another word, for example, or the classes and subclasses of objects. But introducing a completely effective system of Web-based metadata may be too bold a structured vision.

Larry Page and Sergey Brin, as Stanford students, looked at how to impart meaning to all the content. For example, they used information about which Web sites link into a target site to infer value and relevance of the target site. They founded Google as a result. What differentiates Google's approach from Berners-Lee's is that Google does not require changes in the method of posting content. They seek to place the burden on what computers already understand, rather than what humans have to describe.

Many businesses are now using XML metadata to tag content so that computers can readily find, identify, and manipulate the data, much as an intelligent agent would. The RSS feeds, based on XML, allow individuals to have specific content sent directly to them. The net result is that Berners-Lee's dream for the next stage of the Web is slowly unfolding, just not the way he envisioned. In the end, we may not end up with a highly structured Semantic Web. Instead, it may be more of a patchwork quilt of special case option solutions and standards. But isn't that what the Web has always been?

What is the best guess for the future of the Semantic Web? The highly structured layering of many languages to deliver logic and machine processing is probably an overdesign of the future Web architecture. It is more likely that, as the layers of the Semantic Web evolve, a surprisingly simple, but elegant alternative using adaptive software or patterns or something totally unexpected may offer a startling solution.

After all, in the late 1980s when AOL, CompuServe, and Microsoft were investing fortunes in proprietary networks that offered mostly duplicated and limited amounts of information to the public for a fee, Berners-Lee was designing a cheap, efficient, easy, and simple way for universal access to great stores of information for free. It should not be surprised if history repeated itself and we find that an exploitive, yet simplified technology produces much of Semantic Web's vision without the tremendously burdensome structural demands of a complete FOL Web. Nevertheless, one must still travel the path to the journey's end, if only to learn the way.

SEMANTIC OPPORTUNITIES

There are several areas were semantics could offer significant technical and financial opportunities including the following:

- Semantic Web Enterprise Applications: The Semantic Web can impact industry as a tool for Enterprise Application Integration. Just as the Web integrates human-oriented information systems, so the Semantic Web could integrate applications in which data has well-defined meaning (see Chapter 10).
- Semantic Web Services: Semantic Web Services can bring programs and data together. Just as databases cannot be easily integrated on the current Web without RDF, the same applies to programs. Unfortunately, many e-business applications particularly in business-to-business (B2B) applications, have difficulty loading someone else's program to run locally (see Chapter 11).
- Semantic Search: The Semantic Web will provide more meaningful metadata about content through the use of RDF and OWL documents that will help to form the Web into a semantic network. In a semantic network, the meaning of content is better represented and searched due to the logical connections that are formed between related information (see Chapter 12).

THE CHALLENGES

The Semantic Web may play a vital role in transforming the Information Age into the Information Revolution, however, there are specific challenges ahead including: (*1*) balancing expressive power verses efficient reasoning; (*2*) ontology availability, development and evolution; (*3*) scalability of Semantic Web content; (*4*) multilingualism; (*5*) proof and trust of the Semantic Web content; (*6*) Semantic Web Services implementation; and (*7*) ease of development and deployment verses payoff.

Challenge 1: Balancing Expressive Power Verses Useful Reasoning

Currently, there exist Web languages that extend facilities for content description. The RDFS is recognizable as an ontology language that provides classes and properties. It is too weak, however, to describe resources in sufficient detail. As a result, RDFS is unable to provide reasoning support.

Three "species" of OWL have been developed to overcome the limitations of RDF and RDFS. Web Ontology Language Full is the union of OWL syntax and RDF, however, OWL Full is undecidable, and therefore cannot provide complete reasoning support. The OWL DL is a sublanguage of OWL Full that has efficient reasoning support, but is not fully compatible with RDF, and OWL Lite is an "easier to implement" subset of OWL Descriptive Logic (DL). These choices between ontology languages have important implications for the expressive abilities that will be implemented on the Semantic Web.

In addition, DL and rule systems (Horn logic) are orthogonal, which means that they overlap, but one does not subsume the other. In other words, there are capabilities in Horn logic that are different than those available for descriptive logic. In effect, OWL DL is unable to provide full expressive power without the additional capabilities available in a rule system. Therefore, to provide the additional capabilities, OWL DL must be used in conjunction with a rules system language. The W3C specification, the Semantic Web Rule Language (SWRL), is likely to be the rule system that will prevail. The choice of OWL implementation and supporting rule system will decide the balancing of expressive power verses efficient reasoning,

Challenge 2: Ontology Availability, Development, and Evolution

Ontology development is key to the Semantic Web because ontologies are the carriers of the meaning contained in the Semantic Web; that is, they provide the vocabulary and semantics of the annotations. As they are developed for the many areas of knowledge that must be codified, there will be maintenance and reuse issues. More importantly, the developers of ontologies must be highly trained and skilled. This means that the general public will be unable to participate in its development. This translates into higher costs and longer development times as with the original Web.

Challenge 3: Scalability of Semantic Web Content

As Semantic Web content grows, we will have to manage it in a scalable manner. It will be necessary to organize and search it. The Semantic Web consists of ontology-based annotated pages whose linking structure reflects the structure. But hyperlinked configuration does not fully exploit the underlying semantics of Semantic Web pages. The use of semantic indexes to group Semantic Web content based on particular topics may be useful. This is a necessary step to aggregate content for easy application development. Aggregation on a global scale will be difficult.

Challenge 4: Multilingual

Even if English is the predominant language for Web documents, there are important resources written in other languages. Multilingual access plays an increasing role at the level of ontologies, of annotations, and of user interface.

At the ontology level, ontology builders may want to use their native language for the development of the ontologies in which annotations will be based.

Challenge 5: Proof and Trust of the Semantic Web Languages

In order to advance the state of the Semantic Web, it is important that such standards appear that lead to consumer confidence in the accuracy of information. This promotion of proof and trust of Semantic Web content will take time and must constantly be updated to be valid.

Challenge 6: Semantic Web Services Implementation

Semantic Web Services can bring programs and data together using automatic components: discovery, implementation, and maintenance.

Building upon SOAP and WSDL technologies, Semantic Web Services can be dynamically invoked by other services in the network. In addition, Semantic Web Services can be marked up with the OWL-S ontology using WSDL as the service grounding. The challenge will be developing a standard that venders will uniformly accept.

Challenge 7: Ease of Development and Deployment Verses Payoff

The approach of using highly structured layering of many languages to deliver logic and machine processing is tremendously demanding. In the late 1980s when AOL, CompuServe, and Microsoft were investing fortunes in proprietary networks that offered mostly duplicated and limited amounts of information to the public for a fee, Berners-Lee was designing a cheap, efficient, easy, and simple way for universal access to great stores of information for free. It is necessary to find a cheap simple and convenient way to produce onotologies and maintain logics for the Semantic Web to succeed. In effect, the Semantic Web cannot succeed if it solves the automation of Web information by creating an impossibly demanding labor-intensive requirement for ontology and logic processing and/or content generation.

BALANCING PROPRIETARY AND OPEN STANDARDS

As the Web adds layers of open markup languages, proprietary forces will continue to compete. Under completely open Web standards and access, the Web should grow into a straightforward distributed network. However, proprietary server standards with critical portal and hub access could dominate Web traffic to produce a decentralized network with dominating sites (e.g., AOL, Google, Yahoo!, and MSN). Finally, a monopoly on standards by one vendor could ultimately produce a centralized network around the owner of the standards. The latter two cases will face security, trust, and reliability difficulties.

How will the standards of new Web languages be resolved? We can conclude that future search and Web Services will need metadata and logic constructs available globally.

Global Web standards (open vs. proprietary) are truly a key element for the future of the Web. But how can we assure that the Web remains primarily based upon compatible standards despite fierce vender competition for various standards' control?

Traditionally, standards have evolved through three methods:

1. A vendor dominates a market and sets a *de facto* standard (e.g., telephony by AT&T, or PC operating systems by Microsoft). This would lead to a Web monopoly and a centralized network.

2. Vendors and markets collaborate in ways that may not be clearly attributed to any one organization, but over time emerge as the leader (e.g., TCP/IP). This would lead to the Web as a decentralized network.

3. Standards organizations establish standards that are so useful that they are rapidly universally adopted (e.g., HTML, by W3C). This would lead to a Web as a distributed network.

Currently, vendors support different frameworks on their specialized Web servers. The J2EE framework works to optimize UNIX flavor servers for Web Service applications provided by one group of vendors and .NET framework works to optimize Windows servers for Web Service applications provided by Microsoft and its supporters. So long as the business logic is controlled by vender-specific frameworks, interoperability, overall efficiency, inference, and smooth growth will remain problematic. Moving toward an open markup language standard will level the playing field worldwide and allow business logic, inference, and other intelligent applications to be more fully utilized.

Ultimately, there will be a competition between proprietary developers working toward focusing data flow through their portals and over their specialized framework servers and open standards that allow business logic to be implemented directly on the Web.

CONCLUSION

Tim Berners-Lee, Kurt Gödel, and Alan Turing played a pivotal role as pioneers who have opened the door to the Information Revolution. Through their contributions, we bare witness to the remarkable conversion of the Information Age into the Information Revolution as the Web acquires intelligent features and capabilities.

This book explored the contributions of Gödel (what is decidable?), Turing (what is machine intelligence?), and Berners-Lee (what is solvable on the Web?) and evaluated how "intelligence" can be projected onto the Web.

The Semantic Web will probably not unleash an Artificial Intelligence (AI) revolution of new capabilities. However, the Semantic Web will add ontology and logic to produce a more useful Web. The goal of this book was to explore many of the facets for achieving powerful reasoning with reasonable complexity.

Part I of this book, "What us Web Intelligence," discussed the development of the Information Age. Then reviewed the contributions of Gödel, Turing, and Berners-Lee.

Part II presented Web Ontology and Logic: The solution of the World Wide Web Consortium (W3C) to deliver machine processing and services automation on a global scale through Semantic Web architecture built upon layers of open markup languages.

Throughout the book we struggled with both abstract and practical questions in order to delineate both the opportunities and challenges of a "smarter" Web. In addition, some of the philosophical issues that underpin the information revolution with a threaded series of vignettes between the chapters were highlighted. We found that the Semantic Web is still a vision. While the Web will grow toward this vision, the Semantic Web communities must work to overcome the challenges they face.

INTERLUDE #15: THE SEMANTIC WEB AND ZENO'S PARADOX

Mary and John were in the endgame of a chess match when Mary asked, "What is that strange flag at the end of the university track? It reminds me is some ways of my favorite artist, M. C. Escher."

John looked up from the chess board where his two remaining pieces, his king at a5 and a pawn at c6, threatened to reach a promotion position against Mary's lone king at b8. "It's called Zeno's flag and the ring in the middle represents a Möbius strip that Escher once drew," John answered.

Mary said, "The endless trip around the Möbius strip reminds me of the endless problems in implementing the Semantic Web. How can any Web architecture cope?" Then she moved Kc8.

John said, "Well, let me respond with a little slight of hand." He moved Kb5, and continued, "Do you recall Zeno's Paradox of the motionless runner?"

Mary replied, "Certainly, Zeno's paradox is where in each step a mathematician runs exactly half the remaining distance toward an end point where Zeno's flag is planted: 100 m from the starting point. In the first step he covers 50 m, in the second step he covers 25 m, in the third step he covers 12.5 m, and so on. At each step, the mathematician approaches closer to Zeno's flag; however, in each subsequent step he covers a smaller distance until the steps become infinitesimal." Mary moved Kb8 and continued, "As a result the mathematician can never actually reach Zeno's flag."

John moved Ka6 and said, "Yes. But suppose, instead of a mathematician we use an engineer and at the end point we have a beautiful girl holding Zeno's flag."

Mary grimaced as she moved Kc8 and said, "How could that make a difference? The engineer would still go half the distance in the first step, then half the remaining distance in each step, and so on. The engineer would still never reach Zeno's flag or the girl."

John: said, "That's true," moving his pawn to c7. "Check. But remember my brother is an engineer, and he would say that after a reasonable effort he might be convinced that he got close enough!"

"Kb8, stalemate!" exclaimed Mary, ending the match.

BIBLIOGRAPHY

Alesso, H. P. and Smith, C. F., *The Intelligent Wireless Web*, Addison-Wesley, Boston, MA, 2001.

Alesso, H. P. and Smith, C. F., *Developing Semantic Web Services*, A.K. Peters, Ltd., Wellesley, MA, 2004.

Antoniou, G. and van Harmelen, F., *A Semantic Web Primer*, The MIT Press, Cambridge, MA, 2004.

Barland, I. et al. "First-Order Logic: Inference rules," The Connexions Project and Connexions module: m10774, 2005.

Battle, S. et al. *Semantic Web Services Language (SWSL)*, W3C Member Submission, September 2005.

Bechhofer, S., "OWL and Inference: Practical examples," PowerPoint presentation 2002.

Bechhofer, S. et al. "Tutorial on OWL," ISWC, Sanibel Island, Florida, 20th October, 2003.

Benjamins, R., Contreras, J., Corcho, O., and Gómez-Pérez, A., "Six Challenges for the Semantic Web," Technical University Madrid, Spain, 2003.

Berners-Lee, T., "Semantic Web Primer." Available at www.w3.org/2000/10/swap/ Primer.html. Accessed 2002.

Berners-Lee, T., Biography. Available at www.w3.org/People/Berners-Lee/#Bio. Accessed 2005.

Berners-L. T., Hendler, J., and Ora, L., "The Semantic Web," *Sci. Am.* 35–43 (May 2001).

Boley, H., "The Open RuleML Standard for Semantic Web Rule Interchange," NRC IIT e-Business, MOST Workshop—Maritimes Open Source Technologies Université de Moncton, Nov. 10, 2004, Revised: April 14, 2005.

Bonino, D., Corno, F., Farinetti, L. and Bosca, A., "Ontology Driven Semantic Search," Torino, ITALY, 2005.

Brin, S. and Page, L., *The Anatomy of a Large-Scale Hypertextual Web Search Engine*, Computer Science Department, Stanford University, Stanford, CA, 1996.

Broder, A. et al. *Graph structure in the Web*, IBM Report, Oct. 1999.

Casti, J. L., *The Cambridge Quintet*, Perseus Books, Reading, MA, 1998.

Cawsey, A., *The Essence of Artificial Intelligence*, Prentice Hall, Boston, MA, 1998.

Ceglowski, M., Coburn, A., and Cuadrado, J., "Semantic Search of Unstructured Data using Contextual Network Graphs," National Institute for Technology and Liberal Education, Middlebury College, Middlebury, Vermont, 2005.

Cerf, Vinton, "PARRY meets THE DOCTOR," DATAMATION, pp. 62–64, July 1973.

Choi, Namyoun, Song, I. and Han, H., "A Survey on Ontology Mapping," SIGMOD, 2006.

Cohen, S. et al. "XSEarch: A Semantic Search Engine for XML," School of Computer Science and Engineering, The Hebrew University of Jerusalem, Israel, 2005.

"Mapping Tools," Drexel University, 2006.

Costello, R. L. and Jacobs, D. B., "Inferring and Discovering Relationships using RDF Schemas," The MITRE Corporation, 2003.

Costello, R. L. and Jacobs, D. B., "Examples Using the OWL Camera Ontology," The MITRE Corporation, 2003.

Crawford, J. M. and Kuipers, B. J., *Negation and proof by Contradiction in Access Limited Logic*, in Proceedings of the Ninth National Conference on Artificial Intelligence (AAA1-91), Cambridge, MA, 1991.

Crawford, J. M. and Kuipers, B. J., "Access-Limited Logic—A Language for Knowledge representation;" Ph.D. dissertation, University of Texas at Austin Available as Technical Report number AI90-141; Artificial Intelligence Laboratory, The University of Texas at Austin. 1990.

The DAML Services Coalition: Ankolenkar A. et al. "DAML-S: Web Service Description for the Semantic Web." Available at http://www.daml.org/services. Accessed 2002.

Dean, M. et al. "OWL Web Ontology Language 1.0," Available at http://www.w3.org/TR/owl-ref/. Accessed July 2002.

Doan, A., Madhavan, J., Domingos, P., and Halevy, A., "Learning to Map Between Ontologies on the Semantic Web," Available at http://www2002.org/CDROM/refereed/232/, 2002.

Dogac, A. et al. "Review of the State-of-the-Art—Semantic Web and Web Service Semantics," Aug 20, 2005.

Dou, D., McDermott, D., and Qi, P., "Ontology Translation on the Semantic Web," Yale Computer Science Department, New Haven, CT.

Fensel, D., "The Semantic Web and Its Languages," *IEEE Intelligent Systems*, 15(6), 67–73 (Nov./Dec. 2000).

Fensel, D., "A Rule Language for the Semantic Web," PowerPoint Presentation, SDK cluster meeting on WSMO, June 14, 2004.

Fensel, D. and Bussler, C., "Semantic Web enabled Semantic Web enabled Web Services," PowerPoint Presentation, 2004.

Fensel, D. et al. "Semantic Web Application Areas," Free University Amsterdam, Amsterdam, The Netherlands and Oracle Corporation, 2005.

Fensel, D. and Musen, Mark A., "The Semantic Web: A Brain for Humankind," *IEEE Intelligent Systems*, 1094-7167/01/2001 IEEE.

Ferrara, A. and MacDonald, M., *Programming .NET Web Services*, ISBN: 0596002505, September 2002.

Fernandex, E. B. and Yuan, X., *Semantic Analysis Patterns* Department of Computer Science and Engineering, Florida Atlantic University, Boca Rotan, Fl, 2004.

Ferrara, A., "Methods and Techniques for Ontology Matching and Evolution in Open Distributed Systems," Ph.D. dissertation, Universit'a degli Studi di Milano, Italy, 2004.

Filkorn, Roman, "Feature-based filtering in Semantic Web," Powerpoint Presentation, Department of Computer Science and Engineering, Faculty of Electrical Engineering and Information Technology, Slovak University of Technology, 2003.

Finin, T. et al. "Information Retrieval and the Semantic Web," University of Maryland, 2005.

Forums: Discussion groups public-sws-ig@w3.org, www-ws@w3c.org, and seweb-list@www1-c703.uibk.ac, 2006.

Gandon, F., "Experience in Ontology Engineering for a Multi-Agents Corporate Memory System," ACACIA project—INRIA, 2004, route des Lucioles, Sophia Antipolis, France, 2003.

Gil, R., García, R., and Delgado, J., "Are We able to Characterize Semantic Web Behavior," Universitat Pompeu Fabra (UPF), Departament de Tecnologia, Pg. Circumval·lació 8, E-08003 Barcelona, Spain, 2003.

Gil, Y. and Ratnakar, V., "Markup Languages: Comparisons and Examples," Trellis Project. Available at trellis.semanticweb.org/. Accessed 2002.

Godel, K., biography. Available at www.groups.dcs.stand.ac.uk/~history/Mathematicians/Godel.html.

Greer, K. et al. "Ontology Based Access to Web Services Through Agents," 2003.

Griffin, N. L. and Lewis, F. D., "A Rule-Based Inference Engine which is Optimal and VLSI Implementable," University of Kentucky, Lexington, KY, 2003.

Grosof, B. N. et al. SweetRules: Tools for Semantic Web Rules and Ontologies, including Translation, Inferencing, Analysis, and Authoring. B.N. Available at sweetrules.projects.semwebcentral.org. Software toolkit and documentation. Version 2.0. Accessed Dec. 2004.

Harold, E. R. and Means, W. S., *XML in a Nutshell*, 2nd ed., ISBN: 0-596002920, June 2002.

Harmelen, F. and Horrocks, I., "FAQs on OIL: The Ontology Inference Layer," *IEEE Intelligent Systems*, 15(6), 69-72. (Nov./Dec. 2000).

Hendler, J., Berners-Lee, T., and Miller, E., "Integrating Applications on the Semantic Web," *J. Ins. Elect. Eng. Jpn.*, 122(10), 676-680 (Oct. 2002).

Hendler, J. and McGuinness, D., "DARPA Agent Markup Language." *IEEE Intelligent Systems*, 15(6): 72-73 (2001).

Highsmith, JA. III, Adaptive Software Development: A Collaborative Approach to Managing Complex Systems, Dorset House, 2000.

Hau, J., Lee, W., and Newhouse, S., "The ICENI Semantic Service Adaptation Framework," London e-Science Centre, Imperial College London, Science, Technology and Medicine, August 14, 2003.

Horridge, M. et al. "A Practical Guide To Building OWL Ontologies Using The Protégé-OWL Plugin and CO-ODE Tools," The University Of Manchester, August 27, 2004.

Hook, A., C# Semantic Search Algorithm. Available at http://www.headmap.com. Accessed 2003.

Horrocks, I., "Applications of Description Logics State of the Art and Research Challenges," Powerpoint presentation, University of Manchester, Manchester, UK, 2003.

Horrocks, I. and Patel-Schneider, P., "Reducing OWL entailment to description logic satisfiability," *J. Web Semantics*, 1(4): 345–357 (2004).

Horrocks, I. and Patel-Schneider, P., A proposal for an OWL rules language. In Proceedings of the Thirteenth International World Wide Web Conference (WWW 2004), pp. 723–731, ACM 2004.

Horrocks, I. and Sattler, U., OWL Tutorial. Available at www.cs.man.ac.uk/\ ~horrocks/ESSLI203/, 2005.

Horrocks, I., Parsia, B., Patel-Schneider, P., and Hendler, J., "SemanticWeb Architecture: Stack or Two Towers," School of Computer Science, University of Manchester, UK, 2005.

Jain, L. C., *Knowledge-Based Intelligent Techniques in Industry*, CRC Press, 1998.

Jasper, R. and Uschold, M., "A Framework for Understanding and Classifying Ontology Applications," *Boeing Math and Computing Technology*, Seattle, WA, 2003.

Jiang, G., Chung, W., and Cybenko, G., "Dynamic Integration of Distributed Semantic Services," Dartmouth College, Hanover, NH, 2003.

Joint US/EU ad hoc Agent Markup Language Committee, Reference Description of the DAML+OIL (March 2001) Ontology Markup Language. Available at www.daml.org/2001/03/reference. Accessed March 2001.

Kifer, M. and Martin, D., "Semantics to Web Services," 2004.

K¨ ungas, P., "Logic and AI Planning: Introduction," Norwegian University of Science and Technology. Available at www.idi.ntnu.no/emner/tdt14. Accessed 2003.

Lacy, L. W. and Pawloski, Captain J., "Semantic Web Applications for Modeling and Simulation," DMSO Technical Exchange Meeting, July 11, 2001.

Larson, E., "A Client Side Approach to Building the Semantic Web," Digital Media Collaboratory, IC2 Institute The University of Texas at Austin, TX, 2003.

Lassila, O. and Swick, R., Resource Description Framework (RDF) Model and Syntax Specification, W3C Recommendation, World Wide Web Consortium, Feb. 1999. Available at www.w3.org/TR/REC-rdf-syntax. Accessed 11 Apr. 2001.

Lassila, O., Serendipitous Interoperability. In E. Hyv¨ onen, Ed., The Semantic Web—Proc. the Kick-O_ Seminar in Finland. Accessed 2002.

Lee, J. K. and Sohn, M. M., "Enhanced Knowledge Management with eXtensible Rule Markup Language," Korea Advanced Institute of Science and Technology 207-43 Cheongryang, Seoul 130-012, Korea, 2003.

Lesser, V. et al. "BIG: A Resource-Bounded Information Gathering Agent," Proceedings of the Fifteenth National Conference on Artificial Intelligence (AAAI-98). 1998.

Levesque, H. et al. GOLOG: A Logic programming language for dynamic domains. *J. Logic Programming*, 31(1–3): 59–84, (April–June 1997).

Leymann, F., "Web Services Flow Language," Member IBM Academy of Technology IBM Software Group, May 2001.

Lu, S. Dong, M., and Fotouhi, F., "The Semantic Web: opportunities and challenges for next-generation Web applications," *Information Re.* 7 (4), (July 2002).

Luke, S. and Heflin, J., SHOE 1.01. Proposed Specification. Available at www.cs.umd. edu/projects/plus/SHOE/spec1.01.html. Accessed 2000 (current 20 Mar. 2001).

Madhavan, J., "User-Centric "Active Ontology Matching," PowerPoint Presentation, 2003.

Matthews, B., "Semantic Web Technologies," CCLRC Rutherford Appleton Laboratory, JISC Technology and Standards Watch, 2005.

Martin, D. et al. "Describing Web Services using DAML-S and WSDL." Available at www.daml.org/services/daml-s/0.7/daml-s-wsdl.html, August 2002.

Martin, D. et al. "OWL-S Straw Proposal," Presentation to SWSL Committee, May 23, 2004.

McBride, B., "Jena, An RDF API in Java." Available at http://www-uk.hpl.hp.com/people/ bwm/rdf/jena, 2004.

McCool, R., Fikes, F., and McGuinness, D., "Semantic Web Tools for Enhanced Authoring" Knowledge Systems Laboratory, Computer Science Department, Stanford University, Stanford, CA, 2003.

McCool, R. and Guha, R., "Semantic Search," Stanford University, Stanford, CA, 2003.

McGuinness, D., "Ontologies: What you should know and why you might care," PowerPoint Presentation, Knowledge Systems Laboratory, Stanford University Stanford, Stanford, CA. Available at www.ksl.stanford.edu/people/dlm. Accessed 2003.

McIlraith, S., Son, T. C., and Zeng, H., "Semantic Web Service," *IEEE Intelligent Systems*, 16(2): 46–53 (2001).

McIlraith, S., Son, T. C., and Zeng, H., "Mobilizing the Web with DAML-Enabled Web Service." In Proceedings the Second International Workshop Semantic Web (SemWeb'2001), 2001.

MIT, AI Labs. Available at oxygen.lcs.mit.edu/. Accessed 2001.

Melloul, L. and Fox, A. "Reusable Functional Composition Patterns for Web Services," Computer Science Department, Stanford University, Stanford, CA, 2003.

Mizoguchi, R. and Ikeda, M., "Towards Ontology Engineering," Technical Report AI-TR-96-1, I.S.I.R., Osaka University, Institute of Scientific and Industrial Research, Osaka University, Japan, 2003.

Narayanan, S. and McIraith, S., "Simulation, Verification and Automated Composition of Web Services," WWW2002, May 77–11, 2002, Honolulu, Hawaii.

Naudts, G., An inference engine for RDF. Available at www.agfa.com/w3c/2002/02/thesis/ An_inference_engine_for_RDF.html, 2005.

Noy, N. F. and McGuinness, D. L., "Ontology Development 101: A Guide to Creating Your First Ontology," Stanford University, Stanford, CA. Available at http://protege.stanford.edu/publications/ontology_development/ontology101-noy-mcguinness.html, Accessed 2000.

Oberle, D., Staab, S., and Eberhart, A., "Towards Semantic Middleware for Web Application Development." Institute AIFB, University of Karlsruhe, Germany ISWeb, and University of Koblenz-Landau, Germany. Available at dsonline.computer.org/portal/ site/dsonline/menuitem.9ed3d9924aeb0dcd82ccc6716bbe36ec/index.jsp?&pName=

dso_level1&path=dsonline/topics/was/papers&file=oberle.xml&xsl=article.xsl&. Accessed 2005.

Obrst, L., Nichols, D., Peterson, J., and Johnson, A., "Toward a Standard Rule Language for Semantic Integration of the DoD," Enterprise Suzette Stoutenburg, The MITRE Corporation 1155 Academy Park Loop, Colorado Springs, CO, 2003.

Ogbuji, U., "An introduction to RDF: Exploring the standard for Web-based metadata," IBM Web Site, Dec. 2000.

O'Hara1, K., Hall, W., van Rijsbergen, K., and Shadbolt, N., "Memory, Reasoning and Learning," Foresight Cognitive Systems Project, University of Southampton, 2004.

Pan, D., "The Application of Design Patterns in Knowledge Inference Engine," Ph.D. dissertation, University of Calgary, Calgary, Ontario, Canada, 1998.

Paolucci, M., Kawmura, T., Payne, T., and Sycara, K., Semantic Matching of Web Services Capabilities. In First International Semantic Web Conference, 2002.

Paschke, A., Kiss, C., and Al-Hunaty, S., "A Pattern Language for Decentralized Coordination and Negotiation Protocols," Internet-based Information Systems Technical Conference, University Munich, 2005.

Payne, T., Singh, R., and Sycara, K., Browsing Schedules—An Agent-based approach to navigating the Semantic Web. In First International Semantic Web Conference, 2002.

Peer, J., "Web Service Composition as AI Planning—a Survey," January 25, 2005.

Polleres, A., "Current Efforts towards Semantic Web Services (SWS): OWL-S and WSMO," BIT-Seminar, Bolzano, 16/03/2005.

Powers, S., *Practical RDF*, ISBN: 0–596002637, July 2003.

Rao, J. and Su, X., "Toward the Composition of Semantic Web Services," Department of Computer and Information Science, Norwegian University of Science and Technology, Trondheim, Norway, 2003.

Rector, A. et al. "Ontology Design Patterns and Problems: Practical Ontology Engineering using Protege-OWL," PowerPoint Presentation, 2003.

Riva, A. and Ramoni, M., "LispWeb: a Specialized HTTP Server for Distributed AI Applications," *Computer Networks ISDN Systems*, 28, (7–11), 953. (1999).

Rocha, C., Schwabe, D., and de Aragão, M. P., "A Hybrid Approach for Searching in the Semantic Web," 2005.

Semy, S. K., Hetherington-Young, K. N., and Frey, S. E., "Ontology Engineering: An application Perspective," MITRE Corp. 2004.

Shah, U. et al. "Information Retrieval On The Semantic Web," 2003.

Shvaiko, P. and Euzenat, J., "Tutorial on Schema and Ontology Matching," PowerPoint Presentation ESWC'05—29.05.2005.

Shvaiko, P. and Euzenat, J., "Ontology Matching," Available at www.ontologymatching.org/index.html. Accessed 2005.

Sollazzo, T., "Semantic Web Service Architecture—EvolvingWeb Service Standards toward the Semantic Web," 2005.

Spyns, P., Meersman, R., and Mustafa, V., "Data modelling versus Ontology engineering," JarraUniversiteit Brussel, 2003.

Staab, S., Erdmann, E., and Maedche, A., "Engineering Ontologies using Semantic Patterns," Institute AIFB, University of Karlsruhe, D-76128 Karlsruhe, Germany.

SWRL: A Semantic Web Rule Language Combining OWL and RuleML. By Ian Horrocks (Network Inference), Peter F. Patel-Schneider (Bell Labs Research, Lucent Technologies), Harold Boley (National Research Council of Canada), Said Tabet (Macgregor, Inc.), Benjamin Grosof (Sloan School of Management, MIT), and Mike Dean (BBN Technologies). W3C Member Submission. 21-May-2004. Available at Version URL: www.w3.org/Submission/2004/SUBM-SWRL-20040521/. Latest version URL: www.w3.org/Submission/SWRL/.

"Swoogle: A Semantic Web Search and Metadata Engine," Li Ding Tim Finin Anupam Joshi Yun Peng R. Scott Cost Joel Sachs Rong Pan Pavan Reddivari Vishal Doshi, Department of Computer Science and Electronic Engineering, University of Maryland, 2004.

Sycara, K. and Paolucci, M., "OWL," PowerPoint Presentation, 2003.

Tamma, V., Blacoe, I., Smith, B. L., and Wooldridge, M., "Introducing autonomic behavior in semantic web agents," Department of Computer Science, University of Liverpool, UK, 2003.

The UMR Electromagnetic Compatibility Consortium, Inference Engine, 2005

Thomas, E. et al. "OntoSearch: Retrieval and Reuse of Ontologies," Department of Computing Science, University of Aberdeen, IK, 2004.

Turing, A. M. U.K. 2005. Available at www.groups.dcs.stand.ac.uk/~history/Mathematicians/Turing.html.

Wagner, G., "Seven Golden Rules for a Web Rule Language," Eindhoven University of Technology, Invited contribution to the Trends & Controversies section of *IEEE Intelligent Systems* 18: 5, (Sept/Oct 2003).

Wang, X., "Spot example," available at www.charlestoncore.org, Accessed 2003.

Wang, P., "A Search Engine Based on the Semantic Web," MSc in Machine Learning and Data Mining Project, University of Bristol, May 2003.

Weizenbaum, J., "ELIZA—A computer program for the study of natural language communication between man and machine," *Commun. ACM* 9(1): 36–45, (1966).

Yangarber, R., "NYU Counter Training in Discovery of Semantic Patterns," Courant Institute of Mathematical Sciences, New York University, New York, 2003.

Yang, G. and Kifer, M., "Reasoning about Anonymous Resources and Meta Statements on the Semantic Web." *Journal on Data Semantics, Lecture Notes in Computer Science 2800*, Springer Verlag, September 2003, pp. 69–98.

Zhu, H., Zhong, J., Li, J., and Yu, Y., "An Approach for Semantic Search by Matching RDF Graphs," Department of Computer Science and Engineering Shanghai JiaoTong University, Shanghai, P.R.China, 2004.

GLOSSARY

Adaptive Routing: A form of network routing, whereby the path data packets travel from a source to a destination node depends on the current state of the network.

adjacent: Two vertices are adjacent if they are connected by an edge.

agent: A piece of software that runs without direct human control or constant supervision to accomplish a goal provided by the user. Agents typically collect, filter, and process information found on the Web sometimes in collaboration with other agents.

Amaya: An open source Web browser editor from W3C and friends, used to push leading-edge ideas in Web client design.

analog: Refers to an electronic device that uses a system of unlimited variables to measure or represent flow of data. Radios use variable sound waves to carry data from transmitter to receiver.

arc: A synonym for edge.

Apache: An open source Web server originally formed by taking all the "patches" (fixes) to the NCSA Web server and making a new server out of it.

applet: A small software application or utility that is built to perform one task over the Web.

appliance: Runs applications using a visual interface between user and network.

Application Layer: Establishes communications with other users and provides services by Application Layer of OSI reference model.

Thinking on the Web: Berners-Lee, Gödel, and Turing, by H. Peter Alesso and Craig F. Smith
Copyright © 2006 John Wiley & Sons, Inc.

asynchronous: The ability to send or receive calls independently and in any order.

backbone: The largest communications lines on the Internet that connect cities and major telecommunication centers.

bandwidth: The carrying capacity or size of a communications channel; usually expressed in hertz (cycles per second, cps) for analog circuits and in bits per second (bps) for digital circuits.

binding: A concrete protocol and data format specification for a particular type of port.

bit rate: The rate at which a presentation is streamed, usually expressed in kilobits per second (kbps).

browser: A Web client that allows a human to read information on the Web. Microsoft Internet Explorer and Netscape Navigator are two leading browsers.

Cascade Style Sheets (CSS): Code that ensures important style elements on a Web page appear consistently from page to page.

CERN: Conseil Européen pour la Recherche Nucléaire, European Particle Physics Laboratory of the European Organization for Nuclear Research. The European Particle Physics Laboratory, located on the French-Swiss border near Geneva, Switzerland.

circuit switching: A switching system that establishes a dedicated physical communications connection between end points, through the network, for the duration of the communications session; this is most often contrasted with packet switching in data communications transmissions.

class: A set of things; a one-parameter predicate; a unary relation.

client: Any program that uses the service of another program. On the Web, a Web client is a program, such as a browser, editor, or search robot, that reads or writes information on the Web.

Component Object Model (COM): A group of conventions and specifications that let you create interactions between software components in a structured object-oriented way. COM is the foundation of ActiveX.

Connectivity Software: A wireless system component that provides an interface between the user and the database or application found on the network.

composition: The composition of new services through automatic selection, composition, and interoperation of existing Web services.

connected: A graph is connected if there is a path connecting every pair of vertices. A graph that is not connected can be divided into connected components (disjoint connected subgraphs). For example, this graph is made of three connected components.

CSS (Cascading Style Sheets): A W3C Standard that uses a rule-based declarative syntax that assigns formatting properties to the element either HTML or XML element content.

cwm (Closed world machine): A bit of code for playing with this stuff, as grep is for regular expressions. Sucks in RDF in XML or N3, processes rules, and spits it out again.

Cyc: A knowledge–representation project that expresses real-world facts in a machine-readable fashion.

DAML (DARPA Agent Markup Language): The DAML language is being developed as an extension to XML and the Resource Description Framework (RDF). The latest release of the language (DAML + OIL) provides a rich set of constructs with which to create ontologies and to markup information so that it is machine readable and understandable. http://www.daml.org/

DAML + OIL Web Ontology Language: DAML + OIL is a semantic markup language for Web resources. It builds on earlier W3C standards, such as RDF and RDF Schema, and extends these languages with richer modeling primitives. DAML + OIL provides modeling primitives commonly found in frame-based languages. DAML + OIL (March 2001) extends DAML + OIL (December 2000) with values from XML Schema datatypes.

data model: A data model is what is formally defined in a DTD (Document Type Definition) or XML Schema. A document's "data model" consists of the allowable element and attribute names and optional structural and occurrence constraints for a "type" or "class" of documents.

data typing: Data is said to be "typed" when it takes on additional abstract meaning than what its characters usually represent. "Integers," "dates," "booleans," and "strings" are all examples of "typed" data (data types). A data value that is typed takes on additional meaning, due to the semantic properties known to be associated with specific named "data types."

data rate: the number of bytes per second used to represent a movie. Uncompressed VHS quality video is ~20 megabytes (MB) per second. Single Speed CD-ROM quality is about 100 kilobytes (kB) per second, and Double Speed CD-ROM quality is ~200 kb per second.

Data Link Layer: Transforms the packets of the Network Layer to physical Layer.

DataMining: Intelligent analyzing data to extract hidden trends, patterns, and information. Commonly used by statisticians, data analysts, and Management Information Systems communities.

Decentralized Network: A computer network distributed across many peers rather than centralized around a server.

digital: An electronic devices that uses a predetermined numbering system to measure and represent the flow of data. Modern computers use digital 0's and 1's as binary representations of data.

digraph: A digraph (or a directed graph) is a graph in which the edges are directed. (Formally: A digraph is a (usually finite) set of vertices V and set of ordered pairs (a,b) (where a, b are in V) called edges. The vertex a is the initial vertex of the edge and b the terminal vertex.

Digraph Matrix Analysis (DMA): Is a tool for mathematically representing large complex systems and services in order to evaluate their design structure and reliability.

discovery: Computer-interpretable capability for locating Web Services.

Distributed Artificial Intelligence (DAI): Is concerned with coordinated intelligent behavior, which is intelligent agents coordinating their knowledge, skills, and plans to act or solve problems, working toward a single goal, or toward separate, individual goals that interact.

Document-type declaration (DOCTYPE declaration): A document type declaration is the syntactical "glue" used by an XML document to locate an external DTD (Document Type Definition) so that it can be validated against it.

Document Type Definition (DTD): A formal definition of the data model (the elements and attributes allowed and their allowable content and nesting structure) for a class of documents. The XML DTDs are written using SGML DTD syntax.

DOM (Document Object Model): Within a computer, information is often organized as a set of "objects." When transmitted, it is sent as a "document." The DOM is a W3C specification that gives a common way for programs to access a document as a set of objects.

domain: For a Property, a class of things that any subject of the Property must be in.

Dublin Core: A set of basic metadata properties (e.g., title, etc.) for classifying Web resources.

execution monitoring: Tracking the execution of complex or composite tasks performed by a service or a set of services, thus identifying failure cases, or providing explanations of different execution traces.

extraction pattern: A pattern that represents a predetermined entity or event (corporate names, conferences, and workshops, etc.) in a natural language text.

expert system: A computer program that has a deep understanding of a topic, and can simulate a human expert, asking and answering questions and making decisions.

eXtensible Markup Language (XML): Separates content from format, thus letting the browser decide how and where content gets displayed. The XML is not a language, but a system for defining other languages so that they understand their vocabulary.

fiber: The structure that guides light in a fiber optic system.

fiber optics: The use of light to transmit data, video, and voice. Fiber-optic cable has a better bandwidth and carriers a signal longer than cable wire.

frame: A data packet that consist of a header that identifies it according to network protocols, an address of the recipient's network, a data field, an error-checking field, and an identification trailer.

graph: Informally, a graph is a finite set of dots called vertices (or nodes) connected by links called edges (or arcs). More formally: A simple graph is a (usually finite) set of vertices V and set of unordered pairs of distinct elements of V called edges.

Graphical User Interface (GUI): A GUI is what an end-user sees and interacts with when operating (interacting with) a software application. Sometimes referred to as the "front-end" of an application. HTML is the GUI standard for web-based applications.

grammar: A speech grammar specifies a set of utterances that a user may speak to perform an action or supply information, and provides a corresponding string value to describe the information or action.

header: A chunk of data, delivered from a source to a rendering plug-in when first connecting to a stream, usually used to initialize the stream.

HTML (Hypertext Markup Language): A computer language for representing the contents of a page of hypertext; the language that most Web pages are written in.

HyperLink (see Link hypertext): Nonsequential writing; Ted Nelson's term for a medium that includes links. Nowadays, it includes other media apart from text and is sometimes called hypermedia.

HyperText Transfer Protocol (HTTP): This is the protocol by which web clients (browsers) and web servers communicate. It is stateless, meaning that it does not maintain a conversation between a given client and server, but it can be manipulated using scripting to appear as if state is being maintained. Do not confuse HTML (Markup language for our browser-based front ends), with HTTP (protocol used by clients and servers to send and receive messages over the Web).

Hub: A point where communications lines are brought together to exchange data.

Hyperlink: elements, such as, text, graphics, and other objects embedded in a Web page's HTML code, that establishes connections to related Web pages or elements.

hypernavigation: Occurs when a rendering plug-in directs the client to display a URL at a specified time in a stream. When the plug-in issues a hypernavigation request, the default Web browser opens.

Internet: A global network of networks through which computers communicate by sending information in packets. Each network consists of computers connected by cables or wireless links.

Interoperation: Breaking down interoperability barriers through semantics, and the automatic insertion of message parameter translations between clients and Web services.

Intranet: A part of the Internet or part of the Web used internally within a company or organization.

invocation: Activation and execution of an identified Web Service by an agent or other service.

IP (Internet Protocol): The protocol that governs how computers send packets across the Internet. Designed by Vint Cerf and Bob Khan.

International Standards Organization (ISO): A nontreaty standards organization active in development of Open Systems Interconnections.

Internet Service Provider (ISP): A company that lets users dial into its computers that are connected to the Internet.

InterNIC: Created by several organizations to handle domain name registry.

Internet Protocol (IP): The set of rules that governs the transmission of data from one computer to another over the Internet.

Internet Protocol address (IP address): The numeric address used to locate computers on a TCP/IP network. The numbers include four groups each separated by a period.

Java: A programming language developed (originally as "Oak") by James Gosling of Sun Microsystems. Designed for portability and usability embedded in small devices, Java took-off as a language for small applications (applets) that ran within a Web browser.

kBps: Kilobytes per second.

Knowledge Discovery: The process of complex extraction of implicit, previously unknown, and potentially useful knowledge from large datasets. Coined in 1989 by artificial intelligence and machine learning researchers.

Knowledge Management: The process of creating, capturing, and organizing knowledge objects. A knowledge object might be a research report, a budget for the development of a new product, or a video presentation. Knowledge Management programs seek to capture objects in a repository that is searchable and accessible in electronic form.

kps (kilobytes per second): A measure of the data rate (see kBps).

learning: The process of automatically finding relations between inputs and outputs given examples of that relation.

Lightpath: Analogous to virtual circuits in the ATM world, a lightpath is a virtual circuit in the optical domain that could consist of multiple spans each using a different physical wavelength for transmission of information across an optical network.

link: A link (or hyperlink) is a relationship between two resources. The HTML links usually connect HTML documents together in this fashion (called a "hyperlink"), but links can link to any type of resource (documents, pictures, sound and video files) capable of residing at a Web address.

loop: A loop is an edge that connects a vertex to itself.

markup: Markup is comprised of several "special characters" that are used to structure a document's character data into logical components that can then be labeled (named) so that they can be manipulated more easily by a software application.

markup language: A markup language is used to structure a document's character data into logical components, and "name" them in a manner that is useful. These labels (element names) provide either formatting information about how the character data should be visually presented (for a word processor or a web browser, e.g.) or they can provide "semantic" (meaningful) information about what kind of data the component represents. Markup languages provide a simple format for exchanging text-based character data that can be understood by both humans and machines.

meta: A prefix to indicate something applied to itself; for example, a metameeting is a meeting about meetings.

metadata: Data about data on the Web, including but not limited to, authorship, classification, endorsement, policy, distribution terms, IPR, and so on. A significant use for the Semantic Web.

Meta-markup language: A language used to define markup languages. Both SGML and XML are meta-markup languages. The HTML is a markup language that was defined using the SGML meta-markup language.

Message Authentication Code (MAC): A number computed from the contents of a text message that is used to authenticate the message. A MAC is like a digital signature.

Mean Filter: Replaces a pixel with the average value of its surroundings. Applying a uniform mean filter blurs the image.

Median Filter: Replaces a pixel with the "most typical" value of its surroundings, while ignoring extreme values. Applying a uniform median filter tends to remove small details.

Multimode fiber: One of two forms of optical fiber that has a larger core than single mode fibers. They propagate, or spread, many modes of light through the core simultaneously.

N3: Notation3, a quick notation for jotting down or reading RDF semantic web information, and experimenting with more advanced semantic web features.

Natural Language Processing (NLP): Using software to "understand" the meaning contained within texts. Everyday speech is broken down into patterns. Typically, these systems employ syntactic analysis to infer the semantic meaning embedded in documents. The NLP identifies patterns in sample texts and makes predictions about unseen texts. Also called computational linguistics.

Nanometer: A unit of measurement used to measure a wavelength (1 billionth of a meter).

Network Access Point (NAP): A hub for exchanging information between telecommunication carriers.

Network Services: Services that provide cross-platform methods for managing network communications. Any server-side or client-side RealSystem component can use Network Services to create TCP or UDP connections for reading and writing data. Network Services also provides interfaces that let components resolve DNS host names and listen for TCP connections on specified ports.

object: A unique instance of a data structure defined according to the template provided by its class. Each object has its own values for the variables belonging to its class, and can respond to the methods defined by its class.

Ontologies: Collection of statements written in a language, such as RDF, that defines relationships between concepts and specific logic rules. Semantic data on the Web will be understandable by following the links to specific ontologies.

OIL (Ontology Inference Layer): A proposal for a web-based representation and inference layer for ontologies, which combines the widely used modeling primitives from frame-based languages with the formal semantics and reasoning services provided by description logics. It is compatible with RDF Schema (RDFS), and includes a precise semantics for describing term meanings (and thus also for describing implied information). http://www.ontoknowledge.org/oil/index.shtml

Ontology: From an IT industry perspective, the word ontology was first used by artificial intelligence researchers and then the Web community to describe the linguistic specifications needed to help computers effectively share information and knowledge. In both cases, ontologies are used to define "the things and rules that exist" within a respective domain. In this sense, an ontology is like a rigorous taxonomy that also understands the relationships between the various classified items.

OWL: Web Ontology Language for markup ontology for the Internet.

OWL-S: Web Ontology Language for Services.

Pattern Recognition: The operation and design of systems that recognize patterns in data.

path: A path is a sequence of consecutive edges in a graph and the length of the path is the number of edges traversed.

path-set: Is defined as a set of components whose functioning ensures the functioning of the system. Thus a path vector x yields $\varphi(x) = 1$. A minimum path-set is a path-set that cannot be reduced.

Peer: A conversation participant. An "equal" to whatever person or application it is communicating with across a network (bidirectional communication).

P2P or Peer-to-peer: A blanket term used to describe (*1*) a peer-centric distributed software architecture, (*2*) a flavor of software that encourages collaboration and file sharing between peers, and (*3*) a cultural progression in the way humans and applications interact with each other that emphasizes two way interactive "conversations" in place of the Web's initial television-like communication model (where information only flows in one direction).

predicate: Of the three parts of a statement, the predicate, or verb, is the resource, specifically the Property, which defines what the statement means (see also, subject, object).

property: A sort of relationship between two things; a binary relation. A Property can be used as the predicate in a statement.

protocol: A language and a set of rules that allow computers to interact in a well-defined way. Examples are FTP, HTTP, and NNTP.

Port: A single endpoint defined as a combination of a binding and a network address.

Port Type: An abstract set of operations supported by one or more end points.

Public Encryption Key: An asymmetric scheme that uses two keys from encryption.

Resource Description Framework (RDF): Integrates a variety of web-based metadata activities, including sitemaps, content ratings, stream channel definitions, search engine data collection (web crawling), digital library collections, and distributed authoring, using XML as the interchange syntax.

range: For a Property, its range is a class that any object of that Property must be in.

RDF (Resource Description Framework): A framework for constructing logical languages that can work together in the Semantic Web. A way of using XML for data rather than just documents.

RDF Schema: RDF Vocabulary Description Language 1.0. The Resource Description Framework (RDF) is a general purpose language for representing information in the Web. This describes how to use RDF to describe RDF vocabularies. This is a basic vocabulary for this purpose, as well as conventions that can be used by Semantic Web applications to support more sophisticated RDF vocabulary description. http://www.w3.org/TR/rdf-schema/

Reachability: Is an important characteristic of a directed logic graph that find all paths from every node ni, to any node nj within the graph.

Resource: That identified by a Universal Resource Identifier (without a "#"). If the URI starts "http:," then the resource is some form of generic document.

rule: A loose term for a Statement that an engine has been programmed to process. Different engines have different sets of rules.

Regression prediction: The operation and design of systems that develop models of data useful for the description of the data and for prediction.

Router: A hardware device that receives and transmits data packets from one LAN (or WAN) to another. A router reads the address in a packet and determines the best path for the packet to travel to its destination.

Semantic Web: Communication protocols and standards that would include descriptions of the item on the Web, such as people, documents, events, products, and organizations, as well as, relationship between documents and relationships between people.

Server: A computer that other computers connect to for the purpose of retrieving information. In this manual, generally used to mean the computer that hosts your WWW page.

Semantic: The part of language concerned with meaning. For example, the phrases "my mother's brother" and "my uncle" are two ways of saying the same thing and, therefore, have the same semantic value.

Semantic Web: The Web of data with meaning in the sense that a computer program can learn enough about what the data means to process it. The principle that one should represent separately the essence of a document and the style is presented.

Semantic Web Services: Web Services developed using semantic markup language ontologies.

server: A program that provides a service (typically information) to another program, called the client. A Web server holds Web pages and allows client programs to read and write them.

SGML (Standard Generalized Markup Language): An international standard in markup languages, a basis for HTML and a precursor to XML.

SHOE Simple HTML Ontology Extension: A small extension to HTML that allows web page authors to annotate their web documents with machine readable knowledge. SHOE claims to make real intelligent agent software on the web possible (see http://www.cs.umd.edu/projects/plus/SHOE/).

Spider (crawler): A spider is a program that browses (crawlers) web sites extracting information for search engine database. Spiders can be summoned to a site through search engine registration or they will eventually find your site by following links from other sites (assuming you have links from other sites).

Stemming: The removal of suffixes, and sometimes prefixes from words to arrive at a core that can represent any of a set of related words.

Stemming Algorithm: An algorithm to perform stemming.

Syntactic: The part of language concerned with syntax, sentence structure. For example, the phrases "my mother's brother" and "my brother" express the same relationship, but the way in which the information is expressed differs.

Structured Query Language (SQL): An ISO and ANSI standard language for database access. The SQL is sometimes implemented as an interactive, command line application and sometimes is used within database applications. Typical commands include select, insert, and update.

Standard Generalized Markup Language (SGML): Since 1986, SGML has been the international ISO standard used to define standards-based markup languages. The HTML is a markup language that is defined using SGML. The HTML DTD specifies HTML is written in SGML syntax. The XML is not a markup language written in SGML. There is no predefined DTD for "XML Markup." XML is a subset of the SGML standard itself.

Statement: A subject, predicate, and object that assert meaning defined by the particular predicate used.

Stylesheets: A term extended from print publishing to on-line media. A stylesheet can contain either formatting information (as is the case with CSS,

Cascading Style Sheets, or XSL FOs, XSL Formatting Objects), or it can contain information about how to manipulate the structure of a document, so it can be "transformed" into another type of structure (as is the case with XSLT Transformation "style sheets").

subject: Of the three parts of a statement, the subject is one of the two things related by the predicate. Often, it indicates the thing being described, such as a car whose color and length are being given (see also: object, predicate).

Service Discovery: The process of locating an agent or automatic Web-based service that will perform a required function.

Short Message Entity (SME): Class of devices that can send and receive short messages using SMS.

Short Message Service (SMS): A protocol for sending alphanumeric messages using cell phones and pagers.

Simple Object Access Protocol (SOAP): Is a protocol for exchange of information in a distributed environment. It is an XML-based protocol consisting of three parts: an envelope (a framework for describing what is in a message and how to process it), a set of encoding rules (for expressing instances of application-defined datatypes), and a convention for representing remote procedure calls and responses.

Site: An object that receives rendered data for display. The client core supplies a site, and the rendering plug-in registers as a site user. The plug-in can then send data without providing platform-specific commands for data display.

Taxonomy: This term traditionally refers to the study of the general principles of classification. It is widely used to describe computer-based systems that use hierarchies of topics to help users sift through information. Many companies have developed their own taxonomies, although there are also an increasing number of industry standard offerings. Additionally, a number of suppliers, including Applied Semantics, Autonomy, Verity and Semio, provide taxonomy-building software.

Transmission Control Protocol/Internet Protocol (TCP/IP): Two protocols used together to govern communication between Internet computers. Transmission Control Protocol, HTTP (Hypertext Transfer Protocol) uses TCP as the protocol for reliable document transfer. If packets are delayed or damaged, TCP will effectively stop traffic until either the original packets or backup packets arrive. Among the tools that enabled the development of the Internet and the subsequent explosive growth of the World Wide Web is Transmission Control Protocol/Internet Protocol (TCP/IP), a suite of network communications protocols used to connect hosts on the Internet. TCP/IP is comprised of several protocols, the two main ones being TCP and IP, which has become the *de facto* standard for transmitting data over networks. Even network operating systems that have their own protocols (e.g., Netware) also support TCP/IP.

Topical Maps (TM): Provide a standardized notation for interchangeably representing information about the structure of information resources used to define topics, and the relationships between topics. The structural information conveyed by topic maps includes (*1*) groupings of addressable information objects around topics (occurrences), and (*2*) relationships between topics (associations). A topic map defines a multidimensional topic space.

Thing: In DAML, a generic name for anything abstract, animate, inanimate, whatever. The class that anything is in. (In RDF parlance, confusingly, rdf: Resource.) Identified by a URI with or without a "#" in it.

Transformation: In XSLT, a transformation is the process of a software application applying a style sheet containing template "rules" to a source document containing structured XML markup to create a new document containing a completely altered data structure.

Types: A container for data-type definitions using some type system (e.g., XSD).

Unified Modeling Language (UML): Derived from three separate modeling languages.

Universal Description, Discovery, and Integration (UDDI): Is a specification of Web services' information registries. In this distributed registry, businesses and services are described in common XML format.

Universal Resource Identifier (URI): A URI defines an entity. The URLs are a type of URI.

Universal Resource Locator (URL): The familiar codes (e.g., http://www.sciam.com) that are used as hyperlinks to Web sites.

Valid: An XML document is "valid" if it is both well formed and it conforms to an explicitly defined data model that has been expressed using SGMLs DTD (Document Type Definition) syntax.

W3C (World Wide Web Consortium): A neutral meeting of those to whom the Web is important, with the mission of leading the Web to its full potential. The World Wide Web Consortium (W3C) is an organization that was founded in October 1994 as a forum for information exchange, commerce, communication, and collective education. The W3C is comprised of individuals and organizations located all over the world and involved in many different fields. Members participate in a vendor-neutral forum for the creation of Web standards. The W3C develops interoperable technologies (specifications, guidelines, software, and tools) intended to enable further development of the World Wide Web and lead it to its full potential.

WSDL (Web Service Description Language): This provides a communication level description of the messages and protocols used by a Web Service.

Weblogs: Weblogs (Blogs) are personal publishing Web sites that syndicate their content for inclusion in other sites using XML-based file formats known as RSS. Weblogs frequently include links to contents syndicated from other Weblogs. Organizations use RSS to circulate news about themselves and their business. The RSS version 1.0 supports richly expressive metadata in the form of RDF.

Web Services: Web-accessible programs and devices.

Web server: A Web server is a program that, using the client–server model and the World Wide Web's Hypertext Transfer Protocol (HTTP), serves the files that form Web pages to Web users (whose computers contain HTTP clients that forward their requests).

Well formed: A document is "well formed" if all of its start tags have end tags and are nested properly, with any empty tags properly terminated, and any attribute values properly quoted. An XML document must be well formed by definition.

XML: XML stands for "eXtensible Markup Language." The key feature of XML in comparison with HTML is that it, as it provides the ability to define tags and attributes, is not allowed under HTML. The XML is a subset of the Standard Generalized Markup Language (SGML) designed for use on the Internet. It supports all the features of SGML and valid XML documents are therefore valid SGML documents.

XSDL: XML Schema Description Language is the W3C recommendation that goes beyond DTD with the addition of XML datatypes, namespace support, and inheritance mechanisms.

XML Schema: A formal definition of a "class" or "type" of document that is expressed using XML syntax instead of SGML DTD syntax.

XSL (Extensible Stylesheet Language): XSL has two parts to it. One is a transformation vocabulary (XSL Transformations, XSLT) and the other is a formatting vocabulary (XSL Formatting Objects (XSL FOs).

XSL FOs: (XSL Formatting Objects): The formatting vocabulary part of XSL that applies style properties to the result of an XSLT transformation.

XSLT (XSL Transformations): The transformation vocabulary part of XSL. An XSLT "stylesheet" contains template rules that are applied to selected portions of a source document's "source tree" to produce a "result tree" that can then be rendered for viewing, processed by another application, or further transformed into another data structure.

ACRONYMS

AI	Artificial Intelligence
CBL	Common Business Language
COM	Component Object Model
CSS	Cascade Style Sheets
CWM	Closed World Machine
DAML	DARPA Agent Markup Language
DL	Descriptive Logic
DMA	Digraph Matrix Analysis
DOM	Document Object Model
DTD	Document Type Definition
ebXML	Electronic Business XML
FFOL	Full First Order Logic
FOAF	Friend of a Friend
FOL	First Order Logic
GMP	Generalized Modus Ponens
GUI	Graphical User Interface
HL	Horn Logic
HOL	Higher Order Logic
HTML	Hypertext Markup Language
HTTP	HyperText Transfer Protocol
IP	Internet Protocol
J2EE	Java 2 Enterprise Edition
KB	Knowledge Base

KR	Knowledge Representation
LP	Logic Program
MAC	Message Authentication Code
MP	Modus Ponens
NLP	Natural Language Processing
OBI	Open Business on the Internet
ODM	Ontology Definition Metamodel
OIL	Ontology Inference Layer
OTP	Open Trading Protocol
OWL	Web Ontology Language
P2P	Peer-to-peer
RDF	Resource Description Framework
RDFS	RDF Schema
RSS	Rich Site Summary
Rule ML	Rule Markup Language
SCL	Simple Common Logic
SGML	Standard Generalized Markup Language
SOAP	Simple Object Access Protocol
SQL	Structured Query Language
SWRL	Semantic Web Rule Language
TCP/IP	Transmission Control Protocol/Internet Protocol
TM	Topical Maps
UDDI	Universal Description, Discovery and Integration
UML	Unified Modeling Language
URI	Universal Resource Identifier
URL	Universal Resource Locator
W3C	World Wide Web Consortium
WSDL	Web Service Description Language
WSML	Web Service Modeling Language
XML	eXtensible Markup Language
XSDL	XML Schema Description Language
XSL	Extensible Stylesheet Language
XSLFO	XSL Formatting Objects
XSLT	XSL Transformations

INDEX